Floating
Rate
Instruments

Floating Rate Instruments

Characteristics Valuation and Portfolio Strategies

Frank J. Fabozzi

Walter E. Hanson/Peat, Marwick, Mitchell
Professor of Business and Finance
Lafayette College
and
Managing Editor, *The Journal of Portfolio Management*

Probus Publishing Company
Chicago, Illinois

Library of Congress Cataloging in Publication Data Available

ISBN 0-917253-15-9

Printed in the United States of America

1 2 3 4 5 6 7 8 9 0

To my Lady

PREFACE

Floating Rate Instruments: Characteristics, Valuation and Portfolio Strategies describes the fundamentals of the various instruments currently traded, the investment characteristics that make them attractive to investors, and investment strategies utilizing these instruments. In view of the increasing worldwide market for floating rate instruments and the many forms in which these instruments are issued, the book has been designed to provide valuable information to help professional money managers become proficient and successful participants in the floating rate debt markets.

Given the large number of sectors within the floating rate market—domestic debt, Eurodollar debt, floating rate certificates of deposit, municipal debt, adjustable preferred stock, money market preferred stock and adjustable rate mortgages—the experience of a wide range of market analysts is more informative than that of a single practitioner. Some of the best-known practitioners have contributed to this book.

ACKNOWLEDGMENTS

I wish to thank the contributors individually and collectively for their enthusiastic and knowledgeable participation in this project. In addition to contributing three chapters, Richard S. Wilson was particularly helpful at every stage of this project. He encouraged me to undertake it, and gave freely of his time to help when I encountered a problem. Without his assistance, this book would not have been completed.

Sylvan Feldstein and Dexter Senft also provided valuable assistance in the development of several of the chapters.

My colleagues at Lafayette College provided an atmosphere conducive to my work on this book. My former department chairman, Jerry Heavey, and my current department chairman, Ed Seifreid, provided me with a teaching schedule and resources that facilitated its completion. David Warren assisted at various stages in the book's editing.

Finally, I am grateful to Probus Publishing for its support.

Frank J. Fabozzi

CONTENTS

CHAPTER 1

INTRODUCTION

Frank J. Fabozzi, Ph.D., C.F.A.
Walter E. Hanson/Peat, Marwick, Mitchell
Professor of Business and Finance
Lafayette College
and
Managing Editor
The Journal of Portfolio Management

The market for floating and variable rate securities is broad, with substantial amounts issued in both the U.S. domestic and overseas markets. Hardly a day passes without a new issue being floated in the world's financial markets. These securities come in a variety of currencies including the European Currency Unit (ECU), although the U.S. dollar dominates. Floating rate debt issues have been offered with original maturities as short as under one year to 30 years and longer. While most have the coupon rate adjusted to some financial index, several have been tied to nonfinancial benchmarks such as the price of oil or the volume of trading on the New York Stock Exchange.

Besides floating and variable rate debt (including those convertible into common shares and fixed-rate debt), adjustable rate senior equity securities such as adjustable rate preferred stock, money market preferred stock, and variations of these two types of offerings have been introduced in the last few years. Another instrument in the floating rate market is the adjustable rate mortgage. Originations of adjustable rate mortgages have exceeded that of long-term

1

fixed rate mortgages; moreover, the market for adjustable rate mortgages is almost 20 percent of the long-term corporate debt market.

Floating rate securities made their impact on the financial markets in the 1970s in reaction to high inflation and more volatile interest rates than had existed previously. Borrowers were reluctant to commit to the issuance of fixed-rate long-term issues at relatively high interest rates and lenders were reluctant to invest in them unless they had adequate call protection to ensure that they would have the bonds and the stream of income for a more certain period of time.

WHY FLOATING RATE SECURITIES ARE ATTRACTIVE TO INVESTORS

Why have investors found floating rate instruments attractive? Floating rate instruments are attractive to some institutional investors who participate in the fixed income markets because they allow investors to buy an asset with an income stream that more closely matches the floating rate nature of some of their liabilities. Floating rate instruments reduce the interest-rate risk of their portfolios as the new instruments with their more frequent interest coupon fixings can be less volatile than fixed-rate debt; they are a more defensive holding.

Certain floating rate instruments are viewed by some investors as a passive substitute for short-term holdings, particularly that part of a short-term portfolio that is more or less consistently maintained at certain minimum levels. Thus, floating rate securities save on the costs of constantly rolling over short-term paper as it reaches maturity. Floating rate securities have at times outperformed cash equivalents by a wide margin. For example, for the period January 1, 1980, to December 31, 1984, a floater index, as computed by Ryan Financial Strategy Group, realized a cumulative return (interest and price change) of 110.33 percent. During the same time period, a cash index (consisting of six-month CDs), computed by the same firm, realized a cumulative return of only 82.47 percent. Consequently, a floating rate security may offer an enhanced return in a portfolio strategy calling for the use of a cash equivalent.

Recent innovations in the floating rate market have attracted new investors. For example, in 1984 "mismatched" Eurodollar floating rate notes were first issued. With a mismatched floater, the frequency at which the coupon is reset is generally shorter than the frequency of the coupon payment. The benchmark rate that the coupon rate is tied to is generally equal to the coupon payment frequency. Thus, the coupon payment may be every six months and the benchmark rate may be based on the rate on a six-month instrument. The coupon rate, on the other hand, may be reset every month; the six-month coupon payment thereby being the average of the previous six monthly coupon resets. When the yield curve is steep in the one-month to six-month portion of the yield curve, there is an opportunity for investors to enhance returns by buying mismatched floaters with funds borrowed at the one-month rate and receiving the higher coupon rate offered on the basis of the six-month rates that are determined monthly. This is in fact what occurred in the first quarter of 1985 and explains why the issuance of mismatched Eurodollar floating rate notes exceeded that of other Eurodollar floating rate notes in that period. Recognizing that the risk investors face with such a strategy is that the yield curve may become inverted (that is, short-term money market rates may exceed long-term money market rates), issuers included protection for investors by having the coupon rate reset at the maximum of a short-term and long-term money market rate.[1]

Another recent innovation in the Eurodollar floating rate market that may attract investors is an equity-linked floating rate debt that, instead of offering a coupon payment for a specified number of years, offers a discount on the purchase of the issuer's stock. This allows investors to take advantage of a rising stock market.

WHY BORROWERS HAVE ISSUED FLOATING RATE SECURITIES

As for issuers, the closer matching of their income flows from variable rate assets with their floating rate liabilities is of major impor-

---

[1] Jeffrey Hanna and Gioia M. Parente, *Floating Rate Financing Quarterly*, Bond Research Department, Salomon Brothers Inc (April 22, 1985).

tance, especially with lenders such as banks and finance companies. Issuers can fix or lock in a spread between the cost of borrowed funds and the rate at which they are loaned out. Also, in many cases, issuers are paying short-term rates for what are effectively long-term funds, thereby saving on transaction and other costs associated with the continual rolling over of short-term paper and bank loans. Another reason might be to avoid uncertainties associated with what could be an unreceptive market at some future date. Finally, the issuer can tap a new source for intermediate- to long-term funds at short-term rates, thereby making fewer trips to the marketplace and avoiding related costs.

ORGANIZATION OF THIS BOOK

This book is organized as follows. Chapters 2 through 8 explain the various types of floating rate instruments. Chapters 9 and 10 discuss the various techniques that can be used to evaluate floating rate instruments. The impact of the benchmark index on performance is discussed in Chapter 11. The last five chapters, Chapters 12 through 16, discuss various strategies with these instruments. Chapters 12 and 13 discuss trading strategies and opportunities. Chapter 14 discusses how floating rate securities can be used in portfolio swap strategies instead of a cash equivalent to enhance returns. The role of coupon swaps in floating rate markets is discussed in Chapter 15. Immunization strategies for portfolios of fixed rate securities have been popular in recent years.[2] Chapter 16 explains how to immunize a portfolio of floating rate notes.

[2] For a discussion of immunization strategies, see H. Gifford Fong and Frank J. Fabozzi, *Fixed Income Portfolio Management* (Homewood, IL: Dow Jones-Irwin, 1985), Chapter 6.

CHAPTER 2

DOMESTIC FLOATING RATE AND ADJUSTABLE RATE DEBT SECURITIES

Richard S. Wilson
Vice President
Fixed Income Research Department
Merrill Lynch Capital Markets

This chapter discusses the many varieties of a security called floating rate or adjustable rate debt. It reviews the market for domestic senior securities that have coupons or interest rates that adjust periodically over their stated lifespan, with adjustments occurring as often as once a week to as infrequently as every 11 years.

INTRODUCTION

Floating rate notes originated in Europe and made their appearance in this country in the early 1970s. To the best of our knowledge, the first publicly offered issue was $15 million in Mortgage Investors of Washington Floating Rate (8 percent–12 percent) Senior Subordinated Notes offered on November 1, 1973 and due November 1, 1980. This was quickly followed by $20 million in First Virginia Mortgage and Real Estate Investment Trust Notes with similar terms.

The big impetus to the market was Citicorp's offer of $650 million in Floating Rate Notes, issued July 30, 1974 and due June 1, 1989. The offering was originally structured with the individual investor in mind (Citicorp would be obligated to repurchase any notes every six months after issuance), and Citicorp could probably have sold slightly under $1 billion of the notes. However, opposition from the thrift industry, Congress, and others caused Citicorp to modify the proposed terms so that the date of the first put was June 1, 1976 and semiannually thereafter. (A put provision gives the holder the right to require the issuer to repurchase the security at certain prices, usually 100 percent of face value, at specific dates prior to the stated maturity.) The notes floated 1 percent above the three-month Treasury bill rate, adjusted and payable June 1 and December 1, except that the minimum rate for the first rate was 9.70 percent.

Citicorp's offering was quickly followed by Chase Manhattan Corporation's $200 million issue. Other corporate borrowers flocked to the trough over the next few months, and by year's end 13 issues were outstanding, amounting to $1.36 billion.

Issuance of floaters disappeared as rapidly as it had made its mark on the investment community, and not one issue was offered for the next three years. In mid-1978 Citicorp again tapped the market with a $200 million 20-year note issue. This time it did not give the holder the right to put the notes back to the company, and the interest rate was set at a spread above the six-month Treasury bill rate.

In 1979, 18 issues similar to Citicorp's (except that some could be converted into long-term fixed rate debt) were sold. Over the next two years, only six offerings, totaling $912 million, appeared. However, increased market volatility and high interest rates whetted investors' appetites for variable rate securities, and the market started to mushroom in 1982.

Issues range in quality from triple-A down to single-B. While most are tied in one way or another with various interest rate bases, several have been linked to nonfinancial benchmarks such as the price of West Texas crude oil or the share volume on the New York Stock Exchange. There have also been a few issues convertible into common shares.

SIZE OF THE MARKET

The authors' records show that through June 30, 1985, more than 125 entities had sold 248 issues with a total par value of $40.7 billion. These figures are based on publicly underwritten offerings and exclude certificates of deposit, issues convertible into common stock, and best efforts or continuous offerings, so-called medium-term notes (see Table 2–1). Due to maturity, repurchases and tenders, or redemptions at the request of the holders, some $5.47 billion have been retired, leaving 231 issues with $35.23 billion of par value floating rate debt in the marketplace.

Banks have been the largest issuers of this paper, accounting for 110 issues with a par value of $15.23 billion, or 44.4 percent of total issues and 37.4 percent of the total dollar amount. Industrial companies follow with 23 percent of the issues and 31.5 percent of the total dollar amount. In third place are finance companies with 27 percent of the issues and 21.9 percent of the dollar volume. This is understandable, considering the nature of the floating rate and the turnover of the financial assets of finance companies: in effect, they are trying to provide a matching of floating rate assets with floating rate liabilities.

The most active issuer and largest in terms of amount sold is the highly innovative bank holding company, Citicorp. Lagging far behind are two of its archrivals, BankAmerica Corporation and Chase Manhattan Corporation. Table 2–2 shows those entities that have sold at least $1 billion of floating rate debt in the U.S. markets. It is interesting to note that these 11 names account for only 26.6 percent of the number of issues sold to date but nearly half (52.4 percent) of the dollar volume—or, to be more exact, $21.34 billion.

CLASSIFICATION OF FLOATING RATE DEBT INSTRUMENTS AND SUMMARY OF TERMS

The term "floating rate notes" (FRNs) refers to several types of securities with a similar feature—a coupon or interest rate that is adjusted periodically due to changes in a base or benchmark rate. In the jargon of the investment world, the term will continue to cover all manner of variable rate debt issues (although there are 33

TABLE 2—1
Offerings of Variable Rate Securities by Industry Classification
(Par Value $ Millions—No. of Issues)
(as of 6/30/85)

Year	Banks	Finance	Industrial, Transportation and Not Elsewhere Classified	Utilities (Telephone, Electric, Gas)	International Organizations	Total
1985	$1,975.0 (20)	$2,125 (11)	$6,393.6 (10)	$350 (3)	$ 403.5 (3)	$11,247.1 (47)
1984	5,295.0 (42)	3,315 (26)	4,652.0 (29)	275 (3)	2,500.0 (5)	16,037.0 (105)
1983	3,710.0 (20)	1,025 (9)	300.0 (4)	100 (1)	100.0 (1)	5,235.0 (35)
1982	350.0 (3)	1,890 (13)	775.0 (7)	—	—	3,015.0 (23)
1981	250.0 (1)	25 (1)	85.0 (1)	—	—	360.0 (3)
1980	250.0 (1)	250 (1)	52.0 (1)	—	—	552.0 (3)
1979	2,041.5 (14)	250 (2)	400.0 (2)	—	—	2,691.5 (18)
1978	200.0 (1)	—	—	—	—	200.0 (1)
1974	1,160.0 (8)	10 (1)	157.5 (2)	—	—	1,327.5 (11)
1973	—	35 (2)	—	—	—	35.0 (2)
Total	$15,231.5 (110)	$8,925 (66)	$12,815.1 (56)	$725 (7)	$3,003.5 (9)	$40,700.1 (248)

Note: Excludes those issues convertible into common stock, certificates of deposit, and those offered on a best efforts or continuous offering basis.

TABLE 2–2
Floating Rate Debt Issuers of $500 Million or More

Issuer	No. of Issues	Par Amount ($ Millions)
Citicorp	21	$5,125
Unocal Corp.	2	3,005
Phillips Petroleum	1	2,105
Chase Manhattan Corporation	6	1,800
Merrill Lynch & Co.	8	1,525
Kingdom of Sweden	1	1,500
Ford Motor Credit Company	8	1,425
Student Loan Marketing Assn.	4	1,350
Texaco Capital Inc.	3	1,300
BankAmerica Corporation	6	1,200
Manufacturers Hanover Corp.	6	1,000
	66	$21,335

specific types of debt, ranging from annual adjustable rate notes to variable rate senior subordinated debentures). However, FRNs easily could be divided into two very broad, and at times overlapping, categories:

Floating rate notes.   Those instruments whose coupons are based on a short-term rate index (such as the prime rate or the three-month Treasury bill) and reset more than once a year.

Adjustable rate notes or variable rate notes.   (or debentures, bonds, etc.) Those debt securities that have coupons based on a longer-term index and usually reset no more than once a year, often with longer intervals between the coupon resets (for example, the base rate might be a one-year or two-year Treasury yield).

There is an issue that falls within both categories—Gulf Oil Corporation Variable/Fixed Rate Debentures due June 1, 2009. The coupon is determined twice a year and is equal to the 30-year Treasury constant maturity plus 35 basis points. The bond also has a feature stating that if the 30-year Treasury constant maturity drops to 8.00 percent or less for three consecutive trading days, then the debenture will automatically become a fixed rate debenture 30 days later with an interest coupon of 8.375 percent. This is known as a "drop/lock" feature.

Table 2–3 shows volume details for the 248 issues that have been sold as of June 30, 1985, by the basis for coupon adjustment. The largest amount, $13.476 billion (or 33.1 percent of the total), is based on the one-year and longer Treasury constant maturity. The second largest category, issues based on the one-and-three-month LIBOR rate, amounts to $8.993 billion or 22.1 percent of the total. The smallest segment of the market—$152 million—includes those securities utilizing nonfinancial benchmarks.

The remainder of this section provides a summary of the terms of the presently outstanding issues (those that still have floating or variable rate coupons), including details of the basis for coupon adjustment and interest adjustment and interest payment dates. (The Appendix to this chapter lists the issues outstanding at the time of this writing.) If the issue provides the holder with the option of putting the debt back to the borrower, it is so noted. Generally, in order to exercise the put option, the holder must notify the issuer or its trustee some time prior to the put date (usually 30 to 60 days' notice is required). Often the put, once exercised, is irrevocable, but a few of the note indentures make it possible for one to withdraw the notification of redemption. This is usually found in issues for which a company might wish to forestall early redemptions by increasing the interest rate above that determined by the interest-rate-setting mechanism. Ford Motor Credit Company's Annual Adjustable Rate Notes due August 1994 is an example.

Also, call provisions are not constant among the issues. Some are not optionally redeemable by the issuer for the life of the notes, while others can be called two or three years after sale. In some cases, the call provision applies only part of the time that issue is outstanding. For instance, in the case of Aluminum Company of America's Five-year Extendible notes due July 15, 1997, the notes are redeemable at the option of the company at 101 percent of the principal amount during the one-year periods beginning July 15, 1985, 1990, and 1995; and at 100 percent during the one-year periods beginning July 15, 1986, 1991, and 1996. In other words, the notes are only protected against early call prior to July 15, 1985; from July 15, 1987 to July 14, 1990; and from July 15, 1992 to July 14, 1995—each a period of three years after the setting of the interest rate. This issue was called in July 1985.

TABLE 2-3
Offerings of Variable Rate Securities by Basis of Coupon Adjustment
(Par Value $ Millions—No. of Issues)
(as of 6/30/85)

Year	Prime Rate, Commercial Paper and Other Short-Term Rates	1- and 3-Month LIBOR	12-Month LIBOR	91-Day Treasury Bill Auction Rate	3-Month Treasury Bill Secondary Market Rate	6-Month Treasury Bill Auction Rate	6-Month Treasury Bill Secondary Market Rate	1-Year and Longer Treasury Constant Maturity	Nonfinancial Benchmarks	Total
1985	$ 100.0 (1)	$5,767.6 (18)	$100 (1)	$1,703.5 (10)	$ 100 (1)	—	—	$3,426 (15)	$50 (1)	$11,247.1 (47)
1984	2,000.0 (3)	2,825.0 (25)	125 (1)	1,450.0 (8)	3,562 (26)	—	—	6,050 (41)	25 (1)	16,037.0 (105)
1983	100.0 (1)	400.0 (2)	—	3,010.0 (19)	100 (1)	$475 (3)	—	1,150 (9)	—	5,235.0 (35)
1982	—	—	—	1,000.0 (7)	—	—	—	2,015 (16)	—	3,015.0 (23)
1981	—	—	—	—	—	—	—	335 (2)	25 (1)	360.0 (3)
1980	—	—	—	—	250 (1)	—	—	250 (1)	52 (1)	552.0 (3)
1979	—	—	—	—	—	—	$2,441.5 (17)	250 (1)	—	2,691.5 (18)
1978	—	—	—	—	—	—	200.0 (1)	—	—	200.0 (1)
1974	7.5 (1)	—	—	—	1,320 (10)	—	—	—	—	1,327.5 (11)
1973	35.0 (2)	—	—	—	—	—	—	—	—	35.0 (2)
Total	$2,242.5 (8)	$8,992.6 (45)	$225 (2)	$7,163.5 (44)	$5,332 (39)	$475 (3)	$2,641.5 (18)	$13,476 (85)	$152 (4)	$40,700.1 (248)

Note: Excludes those issues convertible into common stock, certificates of deposit, and those offered on a best efforts or continuous offering basis.

Denominations among the issues vary, ranging from a minimum of $1,000 to $100,000, with increments of $1,000 to $100,000. In cases of large minimum denominations where a put is provided, the put may be exercised in whole or in part. In the latter case, the remaining outstanding holding must be at least equal to the required minimum denomination.

Some of the issues sold in 1979 are convertible at the holder's option, not into common stock but into long-term fixed rate debentures.[1] Two issues may also be converted at the option of the issuer. These underlying debentures carry coupons of 8.375 percent to 9 percent (and in one case it may be higher), with maturities ranging from 1999 to 2009. Because of the low interest rate on the debentures, the conversion feature has had little or no value to date. However, if rates decline substantially, conversion might occur. No known conversions have occurred as of this writing.

The issues include:

- Beneficial Corporation August 1, 1987 into 8 5/8 percent due August 1, 2004.

[1] Bonds convertible into other straight bonds are not all that unusual, but for the most part they have been created out of mergers and acquisitions. *Moody's Bond Record* lists more issues convertible into cash and/or preferred shares than into bonds. In the 1910–1930 period, a number of utility holding companies issued debt convertible into other bonds. For example, Columbus Railway Power & Light Company's Secured Convertible Gold Five and One-Halfs of April 1, 1942 were convertible into a like amount of First and Refunding 5 percent Series "B" of 1962 plus $40 cash per $1,000 bond. Monongahela West Penn Public Service's First and Refunding Convertible Gold Six's Series "A" due February 1, 1928, were convertible into 30-year Series "B" Five and One-Halfs on a 6 percent basis for the first $2 million of Series "A," on a 5.90 percent basis for the next $1.5 million, and on a 5.75 percent basis for the balance of the Series "A" bonds presented for conversion. Also, we should remember the United States Government's Legal Tender Notes issued under the Act of July 17, 1861. The First Series, First Obligation read as follows:

> "This note is legal tender for all debts, public and private . . . , and is exchangeable for U.S. six percent twenty-year bonds, redeemable at the pleasure of the United States after five years."

Finally, the Act of February 26, 1879 provided for circulating refunding certificates that were convertible into 4 percent U.S. bonds upon presentation of the notes "in sums of $50 or multiples thereof."

- Chase Manhattan Corporation May 1, 2009 into 8 1/2 percent due May 1, 2009. (Conversion privilege expires November 1, 2008.)

- Continental Illinois Corporation May 1, 1987 into 8 1/2 percent due May 1, 2004. (Conversion privilege expires May 1, 1986.)

- Georgia Pacific Corporation October 1, 1987 into 8 1/2 percent due October 1, 2009. If the company forces conversion, and that must be done prior to April 1, 1987, the coupon rate may be set higher than 8 1/2 percent. (Holders' conversion privilege expires April 1, 1987.)

- Interfirst Corporation August 1, 1987 into 8 1/2 percent due August 1, 2009. (Conversion privilege expires August 1, 1986.)

- Manufacturers Hanover Corporation May 1, 1987 into 8 3/8 percent due May 1, 2009. (Conversion privilege expires May 1, 1986.)

- Mellon National Corporation May 15, 1987 into 9.00 percent due May 15, 1999. This floater was originally issued by Girard Company. (Conversion privilege expires May 15, 1986.)

- Mellon National Corporation June 15, 1989 into 8 1/2 percent due June 15, 2009. If the company exercises its right to convert the notes (and this must be done prior to June 15, 1988) it will be into debentures with a coupon of 8 1/2 percent or 0.65 percent above the weekly average yields of the 30-year Treasury constant maturity, whichever is higher. (Conversion privilege expires June 15, 1988.)

- Norwest Corporation May 1, 1989 into 8 5/8 percent due May 1, 2009. (Conversion privilege expires May 1, 1988.)

There are also some recent issues which are exchangeable into fixed rate securities, either automatically at a certain date (often five years after issuance) or at the option of the issuer. Most of these issues carry bond ratings below investment grade and must be considered as having speculative elements. Generally, the fixed rate note that is issued upon exchange will mature not later than five years after the exchange, or in some cases, at the maturity date of the variable rate note. The fixed rate notes will bear interest based on a premium to the comparable Treasury constant maturity. For example, Chrysler Financial Corporation's Subordinated Exchangeable Variable Rate Notes due 1994 will be exchanged on August 1, 1989 (unless exchanged earlier) for Subordinated Fixed Rate Notes maturing August 1, 1994. These new notes will bear interest at a rate equal to 124 percent of the base rate, depending upon the exchange date. If the exchange takes place prior to August 1, 1987, the new coupon will be based on the ten-year Treasury constant maturity; if between August 1, 1987 and August 1, 1989, the benchmark rate will be the seven-year Treasury constant maturity; and if issued on August 1, 1989 the new interest rate will be reflective of the five-year Treasury constant maturity.

At the end of May 1981, the investment banking community devised another variety of floaters called "Money Market Notes." The idea never took hold; in fact, none were issued. The interest rate was to be based on the one-month commercial paper rate as reported by the Federal Reserve System (bank discount basis) and paid monthly. As the individual investor was the target market, the minimum denomination was set at $1,000 per note. At that time, investors were looking for interest rates to decline, and thus they were more interested in locking up longer-term rates than having a variable rate piece of paper tied to a short-term instrument. In hindsight, this seems to have been the appropriate posture on the part of investors. The one-month commercial paper rate for the week ending May 29, 1981 was 17.13 percent, and the 30-year Treasury constant maturity yield was 13.16 percent. By the end of the year, the yield curve became positively sloped. If one had purchased the corporate Money Market Notes on June 1, 1981, the total interest income through May 31, 1984 would have been approximately $341 per $1,000 note based on the Federal Reserve report. If, instead, one had purchased a long-term security locked into the 30-year Treasury constant maturity, the total return would have amounted to about $395. These figures do not reflect any compounding of the interest income. Also, these figures probably understate the return from a hypothetical corporate issue at that time since a premium to the 30-year rate would most likely have been added due to the lower quality of the paper.

CONVERTIBLE FLOATING RATE
DEBT SECURITIES

While corporations have issued large amounts of straight floating and variable rate paper, issues convertible into common stock can be literally counted on one hand. Five issues, amounting to $250 million, came to market in the 1982–1984 period, and three are currently outstanding with a par value of $90 million. Two small issues of Sterling Bancorp, a New York City bank holding company, were offering through rights to its common shareholders. The semiannual interest rate is equal to one-half of 1 percent above the daily prime rate of Manufacturers Hanover Trust company. The remaining terms—conversion privilege, redemption provisions, subordination—are essentially the standard boiler plate of regular fixed rate convertible debt.

On the other hand, the adjustable rate convertible notes of three industrial companies (Borg-Warner Corporation, Hercules Incorporated, and MAPCO Inc.[2]) are rather different, as the interest rate feature is partially determined by the dividend paid on the underlying common stock, and the call prices are 55 percent of par (the usual call price is 100 percent of par).[3] The conversion feature is fairly standard, with the notes convertible into a fixed number of shares at any time prior to maturity or call, and they are subject to the

[2] Borg-Warner and MAPCO issues have been called for redemption.

[3] These floating rate notes are similar in some respects to participating bonds (also known as dividend bonds or profit-sharing bonds). They effectively share in the stockholders' earnings above the rate set on the bond when the appropriate earnings tests are met. Few have been issued, but one, the Union Pacific Railroad Company/Oregon Short Line Railroad Company 4 percent and Participating Gold Bonds due August 1, 1927, called for a 4 percent interest payment every calendar year beginning in 1903 and an amount equal to any dividends and interest in excess of 4 percent that may be paid in cash during the year on the deposited collateral. The bonds, dated August 1, 1902, were secured by $82,491,000 of common stock of the Northern Securities Company, and $82,491,000 of the bonds were issued, of which $45,991,000 were held by Union Pacific and $36,500,000 were held by other investors. Due to the 1904 decision by the U.S. Supreme Court in the Northern Securities antitrust case, Northern Securities Company was enjoined from receiving any dividends on railroad shares owned by it and thus was unable to pay any dividends on its own stock. The bonds were called for redemption at $102.50 on February 1, 1905.

usual adjustments in cases of stock dividends, splits, and combinations. The initial conversion prices have been set at the closing prices of the common stock on the day prior to the offering of the notes, thus making the offering price equal to the conversion value of the notes. The conversion value is the number of shares into which the notes are convertible multiplied by the market price of the common stock.

Interest on the notes is payable quarterly and is the higher of a set amount per period or a fixed amount above the cash dividends declared for such interest period on the underlying shares, subject to a maximum amount each quarter. Annualizing the initial dividends shows that the cost to the issuer is lower than selling other bonds that are convertible into fewer shares of stock. The interest translates into a 4.95 percent coupon rate for Borg-Warner; 4.78 percent for Hercules; and 9.01 percent for MAPCO. If these companies had issued regular convertibles, the coupon rates would probably have been several percentage points higher.

Let us examine the Hercules Incorporated issue of subordinated notes due March 25, 2008. On March 9, 1983 the company sold $80 million of notes at $1,000 per note convertible into 29.963 shares or at a conversion price of 33 3/8; the stock closed on March 8 at 33 3/8. Interest is payable quarterly on March 25, June 25, September 25, and December 26, with the first quarterly payment on June 25, 1983 of $11.99 per note, equivalent to $0.40 per underlying share. Thereafter, the interest rate will be the higher of (1) $11.99 per note from September 25, 1983 to March 25, 1988; (2) $16.18 per note ($0.54 a share) to March 25, 1993; (3) $20.52 per note ($0.685 a share) to March 25, 1998; and (4) $27.34 per note ($0.9125 a share) to maturity or $1.87 per note ($0.0625 per share) above the cash dividends declared for the quarter on the 29.963 underlying common shares, subject to a maximum quarterly interest of $60.00 per note. The history of the dividend and the payments on the bonds are shown in the table at the top of page 17.

Thus the bondholder can share in the dividend growth of Hercules and does not fully participate in any dividend reduction due to the minimum interest payments; the interest payments will always exceed the dividend. The dividend rate was boosted from $0.36 a share to $0.40 a share effective with the December 21, 1984 payment. The interest payment equals $0.4626 per share of the underlying stock.

The call feature of these securities contains another gimmick.

Dividend Payable Date	Dividend Per Share	Dividend on Conversion Stock	plus	Adjustment Rate	Quarterly Interest Per Note
9/23/83	$0.36	$10.79		$1.87	$12.66
12/21/83	$0.36	$10.79		$1.87	$12.66
2/23/84	$0.36	$10.79		$1.87	$12.66
6/25/84	$0.36	$10.79		$1.87	$12.66
9/25/84	$0.36	$10.79		$1.87	$12.66
12/21/84	$0.40	$11.99		$1.87	$13.86
3/25/85	$0.40	$11.99		$1.87	$13.86
6/25/85	$0.40	$11.99		$1.87	$13.86
9/25/85	$0.40	$11.99		$1.87	$13.86

Normally, convertibles are callable at the company's option at par or $1,000 per note or debenture. In the case of these convertibles, the call price is 55 or $550 per note. Also, the cash amount payable at maturity is $550. Thus the holder has the risk, in the case of a decline in the market price of the common stock, of receiving less for the bonds than he paid for them (but that is often the case with investments). However, as long as the stock's price is above the conversion parity at the call date (call price divided by the number of shares into which it is convertible) the investor would be better off converting the notes. In the case of Hercules, the conversion parity based on the call price is $18.36 a share.

This is relatively cheap financing for corporations, since they are paying less interest on the notes than is normal. Also, the debt/equity ratio is kept lower than if normal convertibles or other debt are sold. The reason being that of the $1,000 received for each note, $450 is recorded as equity and $550 is recorded as debt.

In light of the attractions of these convertibles from both the investors' and issuers' viewpoints, one might wonder why more have not been sold. A simple reason is a ruling by the Internal Revenue Service in mid-1983 stating that these adjustable convertible notes constitute equity rather than debt, meaning that corporations cannot deduct the interest as a business expense and thus reduce their taxes. They must treat the payments as dividends that are paid from after tax new income. Despite this ruling, there is no reason why another floating rate convertible debt cannot be issued, provided such debt is structured in the more conventional manner, such as the Sterling Bancorp debentures.

DETERMINATION OF THE COUPON

As we have seen, the coupons are based on various benchmarks ranging from short-term rates, such as the prime rate and one-month commercial paper, to one-year and longer Treasury rates, as well as nonfinancial determinants. While we cannot detail how *each* issue's interest rate is determined, we will examine the more important sectors in the market. In many cases, the basic data can be obtained quite easily with few calculations required. For other issues, the coupon setting data are more difficult to obtain, and the investor must rely on the trustee or agent bank to announce the rates. The rates are usually published in a newspaper of general circulation in New York City. However, some note agreements do not require the publication of the new rates but require only that such notice be mailed to the registered holder of the security.

Some of the issues are subject to minimum rates, while a few more are subject to maximums. Crocker National Corporation sold $40 million of Floating Rate Notes due 1994 in August 1974. Due to uncertainty concerning the California usury laws, a maximum rate of 10 percent was placed on the notes. For much of the period since issuance, the interest rate borne by the notes was at the 10 percent ceiling (between February 1, 1976 and January 31, 1979 the coupon ranged between 5.50 percent and 8.2 percent) which encouraged holders to request the company to redeem the notes at par, as the 10 percent rate was not competitive with the alternate investments. At the end of 1979, nearly $30 million worth of these notes had been redeemed, and at the end of 1983, less than $3 million worth of the notes were outstanding. One would have thought that the whole issue would have been retired.

However, this is an extreme example of the ceiling rate. Others with maximum rates include several issues of Texas bank holding companies with a 17 percent ceiling. Many other issues are subject to ceilings as established under New York State law. The limit is currently 25 percent, but this does not apply to issues in which $2.5 million or more has been invested.

LIBOR

Floating rate notes based on the three-month London Interbank Offered Rates (LIBOR) were first issued in the United States in

1983, although Eurodollar LIBOR-based floating rate securities have been of increasing importance in the foreign debt markets for a number of years. LIBOR is the rate at which the major banks in London lend Eurodollar deposits of specific maturities.

Chase Manhattan Corporation's LIBOR-based Floating Rate Subordinated Notes due in 1995 are based on the offered quotations for U.S. dollar deposits as quoted by the London offices of four international banking corporations. The rates are those quoted at approximately 11:00 A.M. (London time) on the second New York business day prior to the commencement of each quarterly interest period. The agent bank collects these rates (rounded upwards, if necessary, to the nearest 1/16 of 1 percent) and takes an arithmetic mean as the new rate. The new rate, the amount of interest (rounded to the nearest full cent) per $1,000 note, and the interest payment date is then promptly published in an authorized newspaper in New York City. Interest is calculated on the basis of the number of days for which it is payable in the applicable interest period divided by 360 days. The interest rate for the period beginning August 13, 1985 through November 13, 1985 and payable November 13 was 8.1875 percent or $20.91 per $1,000 note according to the announcement. A majority of the issues require that a premium of 1/16 to 3/16 of 1 percent be added to the base rate. Also, there are provisions for the calculation of alternate rates in case the agent bank is unable to determine the base rate per the indenture.

91-Day Treasury Bill Auction Rate

Floating rate notes based on this rate first appeared in 1982 and now account for about 18 percent of the market. Interest is usually determined weekly and payable quarterly (the amount of interest payable is usually published retrospectively). Most of the issues have puts at the holders' option. As Citicorp has been the most active issuer in this sector, we will use for our example its $750 million of notes due March 10, 1992. Repayment at the option of the holder can occur on March 10, 1986 and March 10, 1989. The minimum denomination is $110,000 and multiples of $1,000 additional. The interest rate is equal to 100 basis points above the weighted per annum discount rate for the weekly auction of the 91-day Treasury bill, expressed on a bond equivalent basis (this is also known as the investment basis or coupon equivalent) based on a 365-day year. The bond equivalent basis converts a yield quoted on a discount basis to one quoted on a coupon basis. The Treasury bill auctions are normally held each Monday with the interest rate on the notes adjusted on the following day. This rate may be found in the financial sections of many daily newspapers as well as in the weekly report H.15(519)—*Selected Interest Rates*—published by the Board of Governors of the Federal Reserve System. (See Exhibit 3–1, in Chapter 3.)

Three-Month Treasury Bills—Secondary Market

When floaters first came on the market in 1974, the basis for the coupon was the interest yield equivalent of the secondary market yields of three-month Treasury bills calculated on a 360-day year. In these early floaters, interest was payable and the rate adjusted semiannually; these floaters also provided the holder with a put.

Standard Oil of Indiana (now Amoco Corp.) sold $150 million of Floating Rate Notes due August 1, 1989 on August 15, 1974. The basis for the coupon is 1 percent above the interest yield equivalent of the weekly per annum discount rate for three-month U.S. Treasury bills as reported by the Federal Reserve Board of New York during the 21 calendar days immediately preceding the twentieth day of January or July, as the case may be, prior to the semiannual period for which the interest rate on the notes is being determined. At the time of issuance, these rates could be found in Report H.9(511) of the Federal Reserve Board, and they are now carried on page 2 of report H.15(519). The rates are the weekly averages for the weeks ending on a Wednesday. The interest determination periods for the Standard Oil of Indiana notes are December 30 through January 19 and June 29 through July 19 of each year.

Taking the latter period, we first obtain the weekly average for the secondary market for three-month Treasury bills.

Week ended Wednesday, July 4, 1984—9.87 percent
Week ended Wednesday, July 11, 1984—10.03 percent
Week ended Wednesday, July 18, 1984—10.06 percent

The calculations are as follows:

1. Average of the above rates = 9.9867 × $10,000 (face value) = $998.64

2. $998.67 \times 91/360 = 252.44 (the amount of the discount)
3. $10,000 - $252.44 = $9,747.56$ (the original sale price)
4. $252.44 = $9,747.56 = 2.590$ percent
5. 2.590 percent $\times 360 = 91 = 10.246$ percent (the interest yield equivalent of the arithmetic average of the reported per annum discount rates)

We round 10.246 percent to the nearest five hundredths of a percentage point, or 10.25 percent. To this we add the 1 percent differential to arrive at the coupon rate of 11.25 percent for the period from August 1, 1984 through January 31, 1985.

The newer floaters in this category (often rated below investment grade) have a slightly different formula:

$$\frac{\text{three-month discount rate (percent)} \times 365}{360 - (91 \times .01 \times \text{three-month discount rate (percent)})}$$

Some of these issues have an alternate rate (such as the three-month LIBOR), which, if higher than the Treasury bill rate, will become the rate for the interest period (in some cases subject to a maximum rate).

Six-Month Treasury Bills—Secondary Market

What previously were known as second generation floaters—those issued in 1978 and 1979—are based on the interest yield equivalent of the six-month Treasury bill secondary market rates. Again, the base rates are found in the Federal Reserve Report H.15(519), and the calculations are similar to the one shown previously for Standard Oil of Indiana, except a figure of 182 days is substituted for the 91 days shown in that example.

Treasury Constant Maturity

The largest issuer category is based on the Treasury constant maturity yields as reported in Federal Reserve Report H.15(519).[4] While

---

[4] Yields on Treasury securities at "constant maturity" are estimated from the Treasury's daily yield curve. This curve, which relates the yield on a security to its time of maturity, is based on the closing market bid yields on actively traded Treasury securities. The constant yield values are read from the yield curve at fixed maturities, currently 1, 2, 3, 4, 5, 7, 10, 20, and 30 years. This method permits estimation of the yield for a ten-year maturity, for example, even if no outstanding security has exactly ten years remaining to maturity.

some issues are based on a specific constant maturity (e.g., Aluminum Company of America on the five-year rate and Martin Marietta on the two-year rate), others are based on a constant maturity of the issuer's discretion at future reset dates.

Martin Marietta's Adjustable Rate Notes due May 1, 1994 are based on *at least* 103 percent of the two-year constant maturity. The coupon for the initial period from May 7, 1982 through April 30, 1984 was 14.75 percent. The interest rate was changed on May 1, 1984 to 12.25 percent and is applicable through April 30, 1986. The company announced on April 3 that the rate would be 105 percent of the two-year base rate as reported during the interest determination period (i.e., 10 calendar days ending April 15). The Federal Reserve Report for this period was published on April 9 and showed 11.67 percent as the two-year constant maturity for the week ending April 6 (the report for the week ending April 13 would not be published until April 16, one day after the interest determination period). Applying the interest rate determining factor of 105 percent gives a yield of 12.25 percent; this compares with a 12.00 percent yield if the 103 percent minimum factor were used.

The notes have an interesting redemption feature at the option of the holder. They are repayable May 1, 1984 and every two years thereafter at par *unless* Martin Marietta establishes a percentage factor that is 109 percent of the applicable constant maturity rate. In this case, the notes would become optionally repayable on the next May 1 that the rate is changed, regardless of the percentage then established.

Let us look at another example. On September 28, 1983, Xerox Credit Corporation sold $100 million of Extendible Notes due October 1, 1995 with the initial interest rate through September 30, 1985 of 10.75 percent. On September 1, 1985, Xerox Credit will establish the duration of the next interest period which may be one, two, or three years. When the new period nears its termination, another interest period will be selected. The interest rate for each period after the initial one will be at least 102 percent of the comparable Treasury constant maturity. Promptly after September 1 preceding the start of an interest period, the trustee will mail to each registered holder a notice stating the new U.S. Treasury differential percentage, the method used in ascertaining the interest rate for the new interest period, and the interest rate had it been determined as of such September 1. The interest rate is actually determined on September 15 and will be based on the most recent weekly comparable maturity Treasury rate published between August 22 and September 15. The notice of this new rate is to be mailed to all holders with their interest payment checks. The company has the option to establish a rate higher than the one determined by the above method, but it must be done between September 15 and 22. The notice of this change must then be published in the eastern edition of *The Wall Street Journal.*

Holders have the right to redeem their notes on any October 1 following the end of each interest period at 100 percent of the principal amount, with such notice being received by the company or its agent between September 1 and 15. The put is irrevocable unless the company establishes an alternate rate as mentioned previously. If the holder decides to revoke his request for redemption, the revocation notice must be received by the company not later than 5:00 P.M. on the first business day following *The Wall Street Journal* notice. There is very little time for the holder to make a decision. It is important for investors to be alert for these notices, as failure to do so may result in monetary loss.

LOOKING AT
YIELDS—EVALUATION METHODS

Bonds with coupons that remain constant to the next put date should be examined on a yield-to-put basis, whether the put is five months or five years away. Instead of using the maturity date in the calculations, the optional put date is used. This method takes into account any premium or discount amortized or accreted over the remaining term to the put. Nearly one-half of the presently outstanding issues have puts, but only 77 have coupons that are unchanged to the first optional maturity date. These include 6 issues based on the three-month Treasury bill secondary market rate (those originally offered in 1974) and 71 based on the Treasury constant maturity.

Those issues where the coupon varies over the time to put or maturity are more complex. There are numerous calculations used by investors to evaluate the relative attractiveness of such issues, and we will briefly discuss several of them. A more detailed treatment is provided in Chapters 9 and 10. When comparing issues, be sure they have similar coupon reset bases and be consistent with the method used in order to reduce distortions that could occur if issues with dissimilar features were analyzed. Comparing a floater based on a weekly certificate of deposit with a floater based on the quarterly interest payments to a six-month Treasury bill secondary market paying interest semiannually would not be acceptable, nor would using one method of calculation for issue *A* and another for issue *B* be valid. The issue used here is hypothetical, and the terms and results are shown in Table 2–4. It should be noted that there are cases where one bond might appear to be more attractive under one

TABLE 2–4
Hypothetical Issue *A*

Coupon/Maturity	12.15 percent/September 1, 1998
Coupon reset and payment dates	March 1 and September 1
Reset spread	+ 100 basis points (1.00 percent)
Base rate	Six-month U.S. Treasury bill, interest yield equivalent of the secondary market rate
Price	92.625
Today's assumed base rate	10.90 percent
Adjusted reset coupon	11.90 percent
Time remaining to maturity (assuming today is 10/1/84)	13.917 years
Simple current yield	13.12 percent
Adjusted reset current yield	12.85 percent
Adjusted spread to base	195 basis points[*]
Zero coupon basis--spread from base	155 basis points
Simple or positive margin	165 basis points
Reset or adjusted yield to maturity	13.06 percent
Spread or reset yield to maturity over base rate	216 basis points

[*]A basis point is equal to .01 percent.

method or set of assumptions and less attractive under another method. Market participants must live with these complications.

The current yield method (current interest rate divided by market price) is not a satisfactory measurement for floaters, as it only reflects the current point in time, assuming both the coupon and the price remain unchanged. When comparing two similar issues with each other, the current yield would not be helpful in determining relative values, especially when there are different coupon reset dates involved. However, if we readjusted or reset the coupon as of the present time, we would have a better guide to the relative attractiveness (all other things being equal). This is similar to the dividend reset method used in valuing adjustable rate preferred stock. Thus the simple current yield for Issue *A* is 13.12 percent, and the adjusted reset current yield 12.85 percent.

While the contractual reset spread to the base rate is plus (+) 100 basis points, the notes are selling at a discount; and we are really getting a greater spread or margin. Subtracting the assumed reset rate (10.90 percent) from the adjusted reset current yield (12.85 percent) gives us the adjusted spread to base of 195 basis points. If the notes were selling at par, the adjusted reset spread would be 100 basis points (11.90 percent–10.90 percent). Again, this is similar to calculations used in the adjustable rate preferred market.

However, floating rate notes are not perpetual securities as are preferred stocks (or at least most of them). For issues selling below par we pick up the discount at maturity (or put date), and for issues selling above par we lose the premium. Therefore, other calculations are used to analyze floaters. Of course, in relative value analysis, the investor must consider the quality of the debt as well as factors such as call, sinking fund, and subordination provisions, if any.

One such calculation method treats the note as a zero coupon issue, determining the annual "yield" or the value of the discount and adding to that the reset spread (or adjusted average reset spread if it changes over the life of the issue). The result is the locked-in spread. Again, if we are dealing with a premium priced issue we would subtract the "yield" from the reset spread. Note that the coupon does not enter into this calculation except that it is zero—not the current or reset coupon rate. Thus a zero coupon note purchased at 92 5/8 with 13.917 years remaining to maturity yields 0.55 percent. To this we add the reset spread of 1 percent (100 basis points) and arrive at a locked-in spread of 1.55 percent, or 155 basis points.

Another method used by some investors is the simple or positive margin, which gives a margin or spread over the base rate. The formula is simply:

$$\frac{\dfrac{100 - \text{Price of note}}{\text{Time to maturity}} + \text{Reset spread}}{\dfrac{\text{Price of note}}{100}} \times 100 = \begin{array}{c} \text{Simple or positive margin} \\ \text{over base rate} \end{array}$$

The spread calculated with this method is 165 basis points.

The discounted cash flow to maturity basis (preferably called the reset or adjusted yield to maturity method) is yet another way of viewing these securities. Utilizing this yield, we can then establish the margin or spread over the base rate by subtracting from it the base rate (in this case 10.90 percent). Assumptions must be made as to what the base rate (and thus the coupon) will average over the life of the note. The reset yield to maturity (September 1, 1998), assuming an average of 11.90 percent for the coupon, is 13.06 percent, which is a spread of 216 basis points over the base rate.

None of these methods is perfect, but a number of investors prefer the reset yield to maturity method. Again, there are many variations in floating rate debt, and consistency in the method of valuation and among the issues analyzed is important.

MARKET COMMENT

Investors in the first batch of floating rate debt issued in 1974 were rather pleased with the performance of the securities. The prices generally stayed within a few points of par (once the put feature became effective). At worst, they could be viewed as a short-term dated instrument. Thus, when the 1979 issues were sold, they initially met with good market reception. However, these differed from the earlier notes in that they generally lacked puts and thus were only intermediate to long-term instruments with a coupon that was tied to a short-term rate (not necessarily the highest point on the yield curve) and adjusted only every six months. Many of the initial investors apparently failed to take these differences into consideration when purchasing the notes, for they were sorely disappointed by early 1980.

In the last quarter of 1979, interest rates started to rise rather sharply and did not peak until March 1980. These new floaters declined despite upward adjustment of the coupon rate, with some falling to as low as the high 80s. This was due in part to the fact that the reset coupon lagged behind current market rates. Also, these floaters did not have put options that allowed the holder to request the issuer to repurchase the securities every six months as the earlier issues had. Just as rapidly as interest rates rose, they dropped dramatically over the next few months causing an abrupt reversal in the price movement of the notes. Chase Manhattan Corporation Floating Rate Notes (FRNs) of 2009 moved from about 86 to 100 1/8 in 15 weeks, a gain of 16.4 percent; and Citicorp FRNs of 2004 increased 16 percent from around 85 3/4 to 103. Once again, rates reversed direction, and another sharp price decline occurred. By the end of 1980, new lows were recorded. Chase Manhattan 2009s traded as low as 82, and Citicorp 2004s traded at 85 1/2. Without the put feature, the notes failed to hold their own as the market adjusted their yields to compete with returns available on alternate investments. Adding to the pressure on prices was the fact that investors wanted to "get even" after seeing their issues recover in the rally earlier in the year. Only the issues with the puts maintained their value.

Since then, other features have been added to new offerings in order to reduce price volatility. Among these features are more frequent resetting of the coupon rate and, in the case of variable rate notes, more putable issues. In the latter case, the variables would trade as short-term to intermediate-term securities, depending on the period to the put date. Determinants of volatility include the time to maturity or put, the frequency of coupon readjustment, the spread over the base rate, and the spread between the coupon and the current level of interest rates.

Another important factor affecting the aftermarket for these securities (as well as any debt security) is the perceived quality of the issuer. Many of these securities have been downgraded by the rating agencies since they were originally offered. Thus, while a triple-A bank holding company reset spread might have been satisfactory at

100 basis points in 1979, the current rating of double-A might require 125 basis points or more. Of course, if an issue comes under a dark cloud (as Continental Illinois Corporation did in the spring of 1984) investors will dump their bonds into a weak market at steadily declining prices. Despite a put operable on September 15, 1984, Continental's Floating Rate Notes due September 15, 1989 dropped from 96 to 85 in the week ending May 25. Its convertible floaters due in 1987 declined from 87 to 81 at the same time. A month earlier, the putable bonds were at 99 3/4 and the convertibles at 97 3/8. After the Federal Deposit Insurance Corporation stepped in, the notes recovered with most, if not all, of the 1989 issue redeemed at the holders' request in September. The 1987s rose, but not to the levels that existed earlier in the year.

Floating and variable rate debt securities do have a place in investment portfolios. In some cases, they can be regarded as a passive substitute for short-term holdings, especially that part of a short-term portfolio that is consistently maintained. For example, if a short-term portfolio fluctuates between $10 million and $50 million but does not drop below the $10 million level, then floaters can be purchased for a portion of that core of permanent $10 million minimum holding. The variables based on the one-year to seven-year Treasury constant maturity are alternatives to straight intermediate-term issues, as the investor has the option of holding the notes or redeeming them. Despite the poor performance of some of the issues, many have maintained their value and fulfilled the objectives of the investor. They can generally be classified as defensive types of instruments. If short-term rates are expected to remain relatively high or even increase from current levels, then a package of these notes may be held (depending, of course, on the portfolio's goals and parameters). Issues that have frequent resets of the coupon relieve the investor of rolling over short-term paper, and thus save transaction costs.

A FINAL NOTE—LIBOR-BASED FLOATERS

Figure 2-1 compares three-month Treasury bill yields with the three-month LIBOR and shows the spread history since the begin-

Figure 2–1
3-Month Treasury Bill (Line) vs. 3-Month LIBOR (DOT)

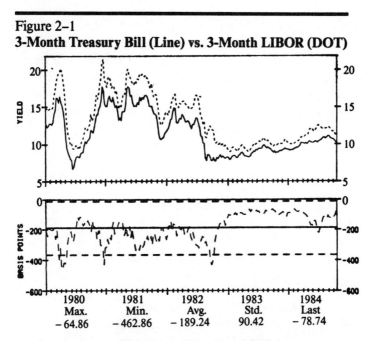

1980	1981	1982	1983	1984
Max.	Min.	Avg.	Std.	Last
– 64.86	– 462.86	– 189.24	90.42	– 78.74

ning of 1980. During periods of generally rising interest rates, the LIBOR-to-bill spread tends to widen as investors, increasingly concerned over credit conditions, move into the relative safety of the bill market. While the spread averaged about 125 basis points in the 1975 to 1978 period, it widened to 250 basis points in the 1979 to 1982 period. As shown in Figure 2–1, the average for 1980 through most of 1984 is 189 basis points.

In May 1984, the banking system in the United States faced problems with its loan portfolios; deposits were withdrawn from some of the banks; and many investors sought refuge in the bill market, restraining yield increases in that sector while longer rates rose. In a five-week period the average yield on three-month Treasury bills rose from 9.64 percent to only 9.76 percent, a mere 12 basis points. During the same period, the seven-year Treasury constant maturity increased 116 basis points from 12.66 percent to 13.82 percent, and the 20-year Treasury constant maturity rose from 12.78 percent to 13.79 percent, a rise of 101 basis points. The three-month LIBOR increased from 11.03 percent to 11.71 percent in the same period with the LIBOR-to-bill spread widening from

139 basis points to 195 basis points. This bolstered the returns on the LIBOR-based issues that reset coupons during that period. Often, floating rate note investors generally would be indifferent regarding LIBOR-based and bill-based issues. However, in the later stages of an interest rate cycle and certain other times when the spreads widen, LIBOR-based floating rate notes would usually provide greater total returns and better performance than their bill-based competitors.

APPENDIX

Listing of Issues by Benchmark Rate[5]
Abbreviations Used in this Appendix

bp	basis point(s)
ECU	European Currency Unit
LIBOR	London Interbank Offered Rate
TCM	Treasury Constant Maturity

Under maturity:

ECN   Equity Commitment Notes
         At maturity the Company may (will) exchange the debt for common stock, preferred stock, or other marketable securities constituting primary capital securities with a market value equal to the principal amount of debt. In some cases, if the debt is called it might be for cash or capital securities at the issuers' option. See the various prospectuses for further details.

Type of Security:

AARN	Annual Adjustable Rate Note
AREN	Adjustable Rate Extendible Note
ARN	Adjustable Rate Note
CD	Certificate of Deposit
CP	Commercial Paper

[5]As the terms of these floating and variable rate issues differ, it is suggested that the reader refer to the individual prospectuses for further details.

CvFRN	Convertible Floating Rate Note
CvSVRN	Convertible Subordinated Variable Rate Note
EFMB	Extendible First Mortgage Bond
EFRN	Extendible Floating Rate Note
EN	Extendible Note
ESN	Extendible Senior Note
FMBES	First Mortgage Bond, Extendible Series
FREN	Floating Rate Extendible Note
FRESSN	Floating Rate Extendible Senior Subordinated Note
FRGSCN	Floating Rate Guaranteed Subordinated Capital Note
FRJr.SN	Floating Rate Junior Subordinate Note
FRMBB	Floating Rate Mortgage-Backed Bonds
FRN	Floating Rate Note
FRSCN	Floating Rate Subordinated Capital Note
FRSN	Floating Rate Subordinated Note
FRSr.N	Floating Rate Senior Note
FRSr.SN	Floating Rate Senior Secured Note
FVRETC	Fixable Variable Rate Equipment Trust Certificate
RN	Reset Note
SEVRD(N)	Subordinated Exchangeable Variable Rate Debenture (Note)
SSEN	Senior Secured Extendible Note
SEVRN	Subordinated Exchangeable Variable Rate Note
SSEVRN	Senior Subordinated Exchangeable Variable Rate Note
V/FRD	Variable/Fixed Rate Debenture
VRN	Variable Rate Note
VRSD	Variable Rate Subordinated Debenture
VRSN	Variable Rate Subordinated Note
VRSSD	Variable Rate Senior Subordinated Debenture
VSFRN	Variable Spread Floating Rate Note

TABLE A–1
Issues Based on the Prime, Commercial Paper, and Other Short-Term Rates

Issue Date	Par Amount ($MM)	Issuer	Type	Final Maturity	Basis for Coupon Adjustment	Approximate Interest Adjustment Dates	Approximate Interest Payment Dates	Put at Holders' Option	Prior Notice Required
5/23/84	250	Citicorp Person-to-Person	FRGSCN	6/1/96 (ECN)	Three-month certificate of deposit (secondary market yield) plus $\frac{1}{8}$ of 1 percent	Weekly	MJSD1	None	–
9/11/84	250	Credit National	EFRN	9/18/96	Prime rate minus 50bp but not more than three-month certificate of deposit plus 40bp (spreads may change on 9/18/87, 90, & 93)	Weekly	MJSD18	9/18/87, 90, 93	15/30 days
2/9/83	100	John Deere Credit Company	FRN	2/12/86	One-month commercial paper rate plus 62.5bp	Every 4 wks	Every 4 wks	None	–
5/3/84	1,500	Sweden, Kingdom of	FRN	5/15/91	Prime rate minus 40bp but not more than three-month certificate of deposit plus 55bp	Weekly	FMAN15 (Arithmetic mean of preceding 13 weekly rates.)	Each May 15	3/15–4/15
1/25/85	100	Wells Fargo & Company	FREN	2/1/88	One-month commercial paper rate plus 20 bp (spread may change 2/1/86 & 87)	Weekly	FMAN1	2/1/86 & 87	15/45 days

TABLE A-2
3-Month LIBOR
(Also see section on 3-month Treasury bill secondary market for some issues subject to 3-month LIBOR criteria)

Issue Date	Par Amount ($MM)	Issuer	Type	Final Maturity	Base Rate Plus	Approximate Interest Adjustment Dates	Approximate Interest Payment Dates	Put at Holders' Option	Prior Notice Required
2/27/85	35	Arizona Bancwest Corporation	FRSCN	3/6/97 (ECN)	$\frac{1}{4}$ of 1%	MJSD 6	MJSD 6	None	–
6/26/84	200	BankAmerica Corporation	FRSCN	7/2/96 (ECN)	$\frac{1}{8}$ of 1%	JAJO 2	JAJO 2	None	–
7/23/84	200	BankAmerica Corporation	FRSCN	8/1/96 (ECN)	Zero	FMAN 1	FMAN 1	None	–
2/2/84	100	Bank of Boston Corporation	FRSN	2/15/96	Zero	FMAN 15	FMAN 15	None	–
7/12/84	75	Bank of New England Corporation	FRSN	7/15/96	$\frac{1}{8}$ of 1%	JAJO 15	JAJO 15	None	–
8/23/84	150	Barnett Banks of Florida	FRSCN	9/1/96 (ECN)	$\frac{1}{8}$ of 1%	Weekly	MJSD 1	None	–
5/16/85	50	Bank of Virginia Company	FRSN	5/15/97	$\frac{1}{8}$ of 1%	FMAN 15	FMAN 15	None	–
11/2/83	350	Chase Manhattan Corporation	FRSN	11/10/95	zero	FMAN 10	FMAN 10	None	–
4/4/84	400	Chase Manhattan Corporation	FRSN	5/3/96	$\frac{1}{8}$ of 1%	FMAN 3	FMAN 3	None	–

Note: Interest of 8 1/2% is payable in common stock and the excess in cash. Holders have the option of having stock sold so they will receive the full interest in cash.

Issue Date	Par Amount ($MM)	Issuer	Type	Final Maturity	Base Rate Plus	Approximate Interest Adjustment Dates	Approximate Interest Payment Dates	Put at Holders' Option	Prior Notice Required
6/5/85	250	Chrysler Financial Corporation	FRJr.SN	6/12/95	100bp	MJSD 12	MJSD 12	None	–
2/20/85	40	Dominion Bankshares Corp.	FRSN	2/27/97	$\frac{1}{8}$ of 1%	FMAN 27	FMAN 27	None	–
4/25/85	50	Fidelcor	FRSN	5/2/97	$\frac{1}{4}$ of 1%	FMAN 2	FMAN 2	None	–
3/12/85	100	Fidelity Federal Savings and Loan Association	FRMBB	4/1/95	$\frac{1}{8}$ of 1%	JAJO 1	JAJO 1	None	–
8/21/84	100	First Atlanta Corporation	FRSCN	8/28/86 (ECN)	$\frac{1}{8}$ of 1%	FMAN 28	FMAN 28	None	–
7/17/84	125	First Chicago Corporation	FRSN	7/24/96 (ECN)	$\frac{1}{8}$ of 1%	JAJO 24	JAJO 24	None	–

TABLE A-2—Continued
3-Month LIBOR
(Also see section on 3-month Treasury bill secondary market for some issues subject to 3-month LIBOR criteria)

Issue Date	Par Amount ($MM)	Issuer	Type	Final Maturity	Base Rate Plus	Approximate Interest Adjustment Dates	Approximate Interest Payment Dates	Put at Holders' Option	Prior Notice Required
4/19/84	100	First City Bancorp. (Texas)	FRSN	4/15/96	$\frac{1}{8}$ of 1%	JAJO 16	JAJO 16	None	–
6/17/85	100	First Interstate Bancorp	FRSN	6/27/97	$\frac{5}{16}$ of 1% (maximum rate 12.75%)	MJSD 25	MJSD 25	None	–
4/10/84	50	First Union Corporation	FRSN	4/16/96	$\frac{1}{8}$ of 1%	JAJO 16	JAJO 16	None	–
6/26/85	100	First Union Corporation	FREN	6/15/05	$\frac{1}{8}$ of 1% to 6/15/95, then at a spread to be determined (on or prior to 5/15/95) for an interest period of at least 1 year.	MJSD 15 to 6/15/95	MJSD 15	6/15/98 and *	15/30 days
1/18/84	50	Fleet Financial Group	FRSN	1/25/96	$\frac{1}{8}$ of 1%	JAJO 25	JAJO 25	None	–
5/9/84	50	Florida National Banks	FRSN	5/16/96	$\frac{1}{8}$ of 1%	FMAN 16	FMAN 16	None	–
11/5/84	50	Gibralter Financial Corporation of California	FRSN	11/15/91	225bp	FMAN 15	FMAN 15	None	–
3/10/83	50	Goodrich (B. F.) Company	FRN	3/30/91	50bp	MJSD 30	MJSD 30	None	–
4/19/85	100	Guardian Savings and Loan Association	FRMBB	3/28/95	zero	MJSD 28	MJSD 28	None	–
5/24/84	100	Hutton (E. F.) Group	FRN	6/7/94	$\frac{1}{8}$ of 1%	MJSD 7	MJSD 7	None	–
9/19/84	100	Hutton (E. F.) Group (Series 2)	FRN	9/27/94	$\frac{3}{16}$ of 1%	MJSD 27	MJSD 27	None	–
3/22/84	75	Irving Bank Corporation	FRSN	3/29/96	zero	MJSD 29	MJSD 29	None	–
5/21/85	50	Key Banks Inc.	FRSN	6/1/97	$\frac{1}{8}$ of 1%	MJSD 3	MJSD 3	None	–
6/24/85	438	Litton Industries, Inc.	FRSN	7/1/00	125bp	JAJO 1	JAJO 1	None	–
3/6/85	150	McDermott Incorporated	FRN	3/13/92	$\frac{1}{8}$ of 1%	MJSD 13	MJSD 13	None	–
11/21/84	75	Meridian Bancorp, Inc.	FRSCN	12/1/96 (ECN)	$\frac{1}{8}$ of 1%	MJSD 1	MJSD 1	None	–

1/22/85	75	National City Corporation	FRSN	1/30/97	$\frac{1}{8}$ of 1%	JAJO 30	JAJO 30	None	–
1/15/85	100	Norstar Bancorp Inc.	FRSCN	1/23/97 (ECN)	$\frac{1}{8}$ of 1%	JAJO 23	JAJO 23	None	–
10/31/84	25	Northern Trust Corporation	FRN	11/8/96	$\frac{1}{8}$ of 1%	FMAN 8	FMAN 8	None	–
8/14/84	50	Ogden Corporation	FRESSN	8/15/96	$\frac{5}{8}$ of 1% to 8/14/87, then new spread may be determined	Weekly	FMAN 15	8/15/87 90 & 93	7/15–7/31
3/28/85	2,105	Phillips Petroleum Company	FRSr.N	3/15/95	150bp	MJSD 15	MJSD 15	None	–
12/11/84	100	Pima Savings and Loan Assn.	FRMBB	12/1/94	$\frac{1}{8}$ of 1%	MJSD 1	MJSD 1	None	–
3/7/84	50	Republic New York Corp.	FRN	3/14/04	zero	MJSD 14	MJSD 14	None	–
8/7/84	250	Security Pacific Corporation	FRSCN	8/15/96 (ECN)	zero	Weekly	FMAN 15	None	–
1/24/85	75	Sovran Financial Corporation	FRN	1/30/97	$\frac{1}{8}$ of 1%	JAJO 30	JAJO 30	None	–
11/15/84	75	Union Bancorp	FRSN	12/1/96	$\frac{1}{8}$ of 1%	MJSD 1	MJSD 1	None	–
5/20	1,850	Unocal Corporation	FRSr.SN	5/15/91	325bp	FMAN 15	FMAN 15	None	–
2/10/84	100	Wells Fargo & Company	FRSN	2/15/96	zero	FMAN 15	FMAN 15	None	–
7/20/84	150	Wells Fargo & Company	FRSCN	8/1/96	$\frac{1}{16}$ of 1%	Weekly	FMAN 1	None	–

Note: Under certain circumstances the rate may be increased by 200bp.

*Interest adjusted at the end of any subsequent interest period which will be determined by the issuer. Also, in the case of "puttable" bonds, the put option may be exercised on the dates indicated and at the end of each subsequent interest period, subject to appropriate prior notification.

TABLE A-3
Twelve-Month LIBOR

Issue Date	Par Amount ($MM)	Issuer	Type	Final Maturity	Base Rate Plus	Approximate Interest Adjustment Date	Approximate Interest Payment Date	Put at Holders' Option	Prior Notice Required
8/9/84	125	Ford Motor Credit Company	AARN	8/22/94	$\frac{1}{4}$ of 1% to 8/18/89 percentage may be changed or eliminated on 8/18/89	8/18	8/18	8/18/89	15/30 days
5/30/85	100	Ford Motor Credit Company	AARN	6/14/99	$\frac{3}{16}$ of 1% to 6/10/92. At that time the percentage may be changed or eliminated and a new interest period announced (but to be no later than 6/12/98)	6/6	6/6	6/10/92 and *	15/30 days

*Interest adjusted at the end of any subsequent interest period which will be determined by the issuer. Also, in the case of "puttable" bonds, the putoption may be exercised on the dates indicated and at the end of each subsequent interest period, subject to appropriate prior notification.

91-Day Treasury Bill Auction Rate
(Bond Equivalent Basis)

Issue Date	Par Amount ($MM)	Issuer	Type	Final Maturity	Base Rate Plus	Approximate Interest Adjustment Dates	Approximate Interest Payment Dates	Put at Holders' Option	Prior Notice Required
6/28/85	100	Baltimore Gas & Electric	FRN	7/1/95	110bp (collar: 8%/12%)	JAJO1	JAJO1	None	–
11/21/83	300	Chase Manhattan Corporation	FREN	11/28/92	55bp	Weekly	FMAN 28	11/28/86 & 89	15/30 days
12/13/82	100	Citicorp	FRN	12/1/87	100bp	Weekly	MJSD 10	None	–
3/13/85	100	Citicorp	FRN	4/1/88	75bp	Weekly	JAJO 10	None	–
3/18/82	100	Citicorp	FRN	3/10/89	100bp	Weekly	MJSD 10	None	–
3/3/83	750	Citicorp	FRN	3/10/92	100bp	Weekly	MJSD 10	3/10/86 & 89	30/60 days
3/15/83	150	Citicorp	FRN	4/10/92	75bp	Weekly	JAJO 10	4/10/86 & 89	30/60 days
4/4/85	150	Citicorp	FREN	4/1/00	65bp	Monthly	JAJO 10	4/1/88 and *	4/15 days
		Note: Spread may change 4/1/88 and on each subsequent election date which shall be 1, 2, 3, 4 or 5 years following 4/1/88.							
5/3/84	150	Citicorp Person-To-Person	FRGSCN	5/10/96 (ECN)	125bp	Weekly	JAJO 10	None	–
6/15/83	75	Clark Equipment	FRN	6/15/91	120bp to 6/14/87, the new spread may be determined.	Weekly	MJSD 15	6/15/87 & 89	at least 30 days
5/8/85	150ECU =104US$	Denmark, Kingdom of	FRN	5/15/90	70bp notionally hedged into ECU utilizing spot and 3-month forward US$/ECU exchange rates.	FMAN 15	FMAN 15	None	–
3/14/84	150	John Deere Credit Company	FRN	3/21/93	75bp Spread may change on 3/21/87 & 90	Weekly	MJSD 21	3/21/87 & 90	15/45 days
6/9/83	100	First City Bancorp. (Texas)	FRN	6/1/86	62½bp	Weekly	MJSD 1	None	–
4/26/83	50	First Interstate Bancorp.	FRN	5/1/92	62½bp	Weekly	FMAN 1	5/1/86 & 89	30/50 days
3/11/82	100	Household Finance Corporation	FRN	3/1/87	90bp (Spread may be increased each 3/1)	Weekly	MJSD 10	3/1/86 & 87	15/30 days

TABLE A-4—*Continued*
91-Day Treasury Bill Auction Rate
(Bond Equivalent Basis)

Issue Date	Par Amount ($MM)	Issuer	Type	Final Maturity	Base Rate Plus	Approximate Interest Adjustment Dates	Approximate Interest Payment Dates	Put at Holders' Option	Prior Notice Required
4/17/84	150	International Bank for Reconstruction & Development	FRN	5/1/89	50bp	Weekly	FMAN 1	None	–
1/10/85	150	International Bank for Reconstruction & Development	FRN	1/15/90	55bp	Weekly	JAJO 15	None	–
3/14/85	150	International Bank for Reconstruction & Development	FRN	4/1/90	50bp	Weekly	JAJO 1	None	–
8/31/84	100	Lomas & Nettleton Financial	FREN	9/1/98	75bp (Spread may change 9/1/86, 89, 92 & 95)	Weekly	MJSD 1	9/1/86, 89, 92 & 95)	15/30 days
3/18/83	250	Manufacturers Hanover Corp.	FRN	10/7/90	62½bp	Weekly	JAJO 7	10/7/85 & 4/7/88	30/60 days
3/14/83	150	Manufacturers Hanover Corp.	FRN	4/7/92	75bp	Weekly	JAJO 7	4/7/86 & 89	30/60 days
4/8/85	200	Manufacturers Hanover Corp.	FREN	4/15/97	65bp (Spread may change 4/15/88, 91 & 94)	Monthly	JAJO 15	4/15/88, 91 & 94	15/22 days
5/19/83	35	Maryland National Corp.	FREN	6/1/92	62½bp (Spread may change 6/1/86 & 89)	Weekly	MJSD 1	6/1/86 & 89	30/60 days
4/18/85	150	Mellon Financial Company	FREN	4/30/00	65bp (Spread may change 4/30/88 and any subsequent election date)	Weekly	JAJO 30	4/30/88 and *	10/20 days
8/10/83	200	Merrill Lynch & Co.	FRN	8/23/91	60bp (Spread may change on 8/23/85 & 88)	Weekly	FMAN 23	8/23/85 & 88	15/30 days
5/12/83	200	Merrill Lynch & Co.	FRN	5/10/92	60bp (Spread may change on 5/10/86 & 89)	Weekly	FMAN 10	5/10/86 & 89	15/30 days
4/15/85	150	Merrill Lynch & Co.	FRN	10/15/93	70bp (Spread may change on 10/15/87 and any subsequent election date)	Weekly	JAJO 15	10/15/87 and *	10/20 days

Date	Amount	Issuer	Type	Date	Spread	Reset Frequency	Payment Dates	Call Dates	Days
3/6/84	200	Merrill Lynch & Co.	FRN	3/14/95	62½bp (Spread may change on 3/14/86, 89 & 92)	Weekly	MJSD 14	3/24/86, 89 & 92	15/25 days
10/31/84	500	New Zealand	AREN	11/1/94	To date rate has based on T-bill auction plus a spread either fixed or a % of 3-mo. LIBOR over T-bills. However, issuer may elect any rate for future periods.	3, 6 or 9 mos. or 1 to 9 yrs.	At end of any repayment date but semiannual if more than 6 mos.	At the end of extension period which may be 3, 6, or 9 mos., or 1 to 9 years.	7/15 days
12/19/84	100	Nordic Investment Bank	VSFRN	12/27/04	the greater of (a) 55% of the amount by which 3-mo. LIBOR exceeds the base rate or (b) 35 bp. Base rate is on a CD equivalent basis.	Quarterly	MJSD 27	Any interest payment date	10/20 days
4/8/83	100	PNC Funding Corp.	FRN	4/14/92	62½bp	Weekly	JAJO 14	4/14/86 & 89	30/60 days
10/25/83	100	PNC Funding Corp.	FRN	10/14/95	50bp (Spread may change 10/14/86, 89 & 92)	Weekly	JAJO 14	10/14/86, 89 & 92	30/60 days
3/28/84	100	Rainier Bancorporation	FRN	4/1/96	65bp (Spread may change 4/1/87, 90 & 93)	Weekly	JAJO 1	4/1/87, 90 & 93	15/25 days
3/18/82	200	Student Loan Marketing Assn.	FRN	3/31/89	75bp	Weekly	JAJO 10	None	--
3/18/85	450	Student Loan Marketing Assn. Series "D"	FRN	3/7/89	50bp	Weekly	JAJO 10	None	--
6/20/83	100	Sweden Export Credit Corp.	FREN	6/30/95	75bp (spread may change 6/30/86, 89 & 92)	Monthly	MJSD 30	6/30/86, 89 & 92	30/90 days
2/16/84	100	Texas Commerce Bancshares	FRN	2/15/96	50bp (Spread may change 2/15/87, 90 & 93)	Weekly	FMAN 15	2/15/87, 90 & 93	30/60 days
5/11/83	100	Wells Fargo & Company	FREN	5/15/92	75bp (Spread may change 5/15/86 & 89)	FMAN 15	FMAN 15	5/15/86 & 89	30/60 days
5/11/83	50	Wells Fargo & Company (2nd Series)	FREN	5/15/92	62½bp (Spread may change on 5/15/86 & 89)	FMAN 15	FMAN 15	5/15/86 & 89	30/60 days
12/1/83	150	Wells Fargo & Company	FREN	12/1/92	70bp (Spread may change 12/1/86 & 89)	Weekly	MJSD 1	12/1/86 & 89	15/45 days
11/21/83	50	Wells Fargo Mortgage & Realty Trust	FREN	11/15/98	80bp (Spread may change 11/15/86, 89, 92 & 95)	Weekly	FMAN 15	11/15/86, 89, 92 & 95	15/30 days

TABLE A–5
3-Month Treasury Bill Secondary Market Rate (Interest Yield Equivalent Basis)

Issue Date	Par Amount ($MM)	Issuer	Type	Final Maturity	Base Rate Plus	Interest Adjustment Dates	Interest Payment Dates	Put at Holders' Option	Prior Notice Required
4/2/85	100	AMAX Inc.	SEVRN	Notes will be exchanged on or before 4/15/90 into Fixed Rate Notes due 4/15/95.	Higher of (a) 3-mo. T-bill + 375bp or (b) 3-mo. LIBOR + 250 bp. Minimum 14¼% to 10/15/85	JAJO 15	JAJO 15	None	-
8/15/74	150	Amoco Corp. (formerly Standard Oil of Indiana)	FRN	8/1/89	100bp	F&A 1	F&A 1	Each F&A 1	30/60 days
10/3/74	30	AmSouth Bancorporation	FRN	9/1/99	100bp	M&S 1	M&S 1	Each M&S 1	30/60 days
8/2/74	200	Chase Manhattan Corp.	FRN	6/15/99	100bp	J&D 15	J&D 15	Each J&D 15	45/90 days
8/1/84	200	Chrysler Financial Corp.	SEVRN	Notes will be exchanged 8/1/89 for Fixed Rate Notes unless exchanged earlier at company's option.	Highest of (a) 3-mo. Treasury + plus 300bp, (b) 3-mo. LIBOR + 175bp, (c) 104% of 10-yr. TCM	FMAN 1	FMAN 1	None	-
7/24/74	650	Citicorp.	FRN	6/1/89	100bp	J&D 1	J&D 1	Each J&D 1	30/60 days
4/22/80	250	Citicorp.	FRN	5/1/10	102.5% of the interest differential between 3-mo. T-bill and 3-mo. CD.	Monthly	M&N 1	Each M&N 1	30/60 days
8/9/84	600	Coastal Corporation	SEVRN	8/15/94 unless exchanged at company's option prior to 8/15/99.	Higher of (a) 3-mo. T-bill + 300 bp or (b) 3-mo. LIBOR + 175bp, subject to maximum of LIBOR + 250bp. Spreads may change 8/15/89.	FMAN 15	FMAN 15	None	-
8/14/84	50	Columbia Savings & Loan	SEVRN	9/1/94. At company's option may be exchanged from 9/1/85 to 9/1/88 into Fixed Rate Notes.	Higher of (a) 3-mo. T-bill + 200bp, or (b) 3-mo. LIBOR + 200bp, subject to maximum of 3-mo. T-bill + 400bp.	MJSD 30	MJSD 30	None	-
9/14/84	30	Far West Savings and Loan Association	SSEVRN	9/15/94. At company's option may be exchanged from 9/15/85 to 9/15/88 into Fixed Rate Notes.	Higher of (a) 3-mo. T-bill + 350bp, or (b) 3-mo. LIBOR + 225bp, subject to maximum of 3-mo. T-bill + 400bp.	MJSD 15	MJSD 15	None	-

Date	Amount	Company	Type	Terms	Rate			Call	
8/9/84	100	First City Properties	SSEVRN	8/15/94 unless exchanged at company's option for Fixed Rate Notes.	Higher of (a) 3-mo. T-bill + 200bp, or (b) 3-mo. LIBOR + 200bp, subject to maximum of 3-mo. T-bill + 400bp.	FMAN 15	FMAN 15	None	—
9/17/74	30	First Security Corp.	FRN	9/1/99	125bp	M&S 1	M&S 1	Each M&S 1	30/60 days
6/26/84	65	First Texas Savings Assn.	VRSSD	7/15/91	450bp	JAJO 15	JAJO 15	None	—
10/26/84	40	The Foothill Group, Inc.	SSEVRN	Notes will be exchanged for 5-yr. Fixed Rate Notes on or before 11/6/89.	Higher of (a) 3-mo. T-bill + 390bp or (b) 3-mo. LIBOR + 275bp	FMAN 1	FMAN 1	None	—
2/11/83	100	Gelco Corporation	VRN	2/15/90	300bp	FMAN 15	FMAN 15	None	—
11/9/84	65	Frank B. Hall & Co. Inc.	SEVRN	11/15/94. Exchangeable at company's option on or prior to 11/15/89 into 5-yr. Fixed Rate Notes.	Higher of (a) 3-mo. T-bill + 300bp or (b) 3-mo. LIBOR + 275bp.	FMAN 15	FMAN 15	None	—
9/19/84	125	Kaufman and Broad Inc.	SSEVRN	Notes will be exchanged on or prior to 9/15/89 into Fixed Rate Notes due 9/15/94.	Higher of (a) 3-mo. T-bill + 325bp or (b) 3-mo. LIBOR + 200bp subject to a maximum of LIBOR + 200bp.	MJSD 15	MJSD 15	None	—
11/8/84	180	Lear Petroleum Corp.	SSEVRN	Notes will be exchanged on or prior to 11/15/89 into 5-yr. Fixed Rate Notes.	Higher of (a) 3-mo. T-bill + 375bp or (b) 3-mo. LIBOR + 250bp subject to a maximum of LIBOR + 375bp.	FMAN 15	FMAN 15	None	—
8/16/84	100	LTV Corporation	SEVRN	8/15/95 Exchangeable at LTV's option prior to 8/15/90 into Fixed Rate Notes.	Higher of (a) 3-mo. T-bill + 325bp or (b) 3-mo. LIBOR + 200bp subject to maximum LIBOR + 275bp.	FMAN 15	FMAN 15	None	—
7/18/84	75	McCrory Corporation	SSEVRN	7/15/94 Exchangeable at company's option prior to 7/15/88 into Fixed Rate Notes.	Higher of (a) 3-mo. T-bill + 350bp or (b) 3-mo. CD + 250bp. CD + 250bp.	JAJO 15	JAJO 15	None	—
12/6/84	30	MacAndrews & Forbes Group, Incorporated	SSEVRN	Notes will be exchanged on or prior to 12/1/89 into Fixed Rate Notes due 12/1/94.	Highest of (a) 3-mo. T-bill + 400bp, (b) 3-mo. LIBOR + 275bp, (c) 100% of 10-yr. TCM, (d) Prime Rate + 175bp.	MJSD 1	MJSD 1	None	—
6/22/84	110	M.D.C. Corporation	SEVRN	7/1/94 Exchangeable at company's option into Fixed Rate Notes on and after 10/1/86.	300bp	JAJO 1	JAJO 1	None	—

TABLE A-5—*Continued*
3-Month Treasury Bill Secondary Market Rate
(Interest Yield Equivalent Basis)

Issue Date	Par Amount ($MM)	Issuer	Type	Final Maturity	Base Rate Plus	Interest Adjustment Dates	Interest Payment Dates	Put at Holders' Option	Prior Notice Required
8/22/74	90	Mellon National Corp. ("Old")	FRN	6/1/89	100bp	J&D 1	J&D 1	J&D 1	30/60 days
7/19/84	500	Mesa Petroleum Corp.	SEVRN	Notes will be exchanged for Fixed Rate Notes on or before 7/15/89.	Higher of (a) 3-mo. T-bill + 300bp or (b) 3-mo. LIBOR + 175bp, subject to maximum of LIBOR + 225bp.	JAJO 15	JAJO 15	None	–
11/29/84	335	Metromedia Broadcasting Corporation	SEVRD	Debs will be exchanged for Fixed Rate Debs due 12/1/96 on or before 12/1/89 in whole or multiples of $50 MM.	Highest of (a) 3-mo. T-bill + 375bp, (b) 3-mo. LIBOR + 250bp, or (c) 107% of 10-yr. TCM.	MJSD 1	MJSD 1	None	–
8/10/84	60	Nortek, Inc.	SEVRN	Notes will be exchanged for 5-yr. Fixed Rate Note on or before 8/15/89.	Higher of (a) 3-mo T-bill + 375bp or (b) 3-mo. LIBOR + 250bp. The spread will be reduced upon conversion of 75% of company's 10¼% Cv. Debs. due 2004.	FMAN 15	FMAN 15	None	–
4/2/84	350	Occidental Petroleum Corp.	Cv.SVRN	Notes will be convertible into 6-yr. Fixed Rate Notes on or before 3/15/88.	275bp	MJSD 15	MJSD 15	None	–
9/28/84	25	OXOCO INC.	SSEVRN	Notes will be exchanged on or prior to 10/1/89 into 5-yr. Fixed Rate Notes.	Higher of (a) 3-mo. T-bill + 425bp or (b) 3-mo. LIBOR + 300bp.	JAJO 1	JAJO 1	None	–

Note: Company is in default on its debt obligations and is presently soliciting a debt exchange for this issue and other publicly held notes and debentures.

Date	Amount	Company	Security	bp	Rate formula				
6/22/84	20	Petroleum Heat and Power Co.	SEVRN 7/1/94 unless exchanged at company's option for 5-yr. Fixed Rate Notes on or before 7/1/88.	325bp		JAJO 1	JAJO 1	None	–
5/10/84	100	Southmark Corporation	VRSN 5/15/94 unless exchanged at company's option for 5-yr. Fixed Rate Notes on or before 5/15/88.	300bp		FMAN 15	FMAN 15	None	–
9/28/84	60	Templeton Energy, Inc.	SSEVRN Notes will be exchanged on or prior to 10/1/89 into 5-yr. Fixed Rate Notes.		Highest of (a) 3-mo. T-bill +425bp, (b) 3-mo. LIBOR +300bp or (c) 113% of 10-yr. TCM.	JAJO 1	JAJO 1	None	–
9/11/84	100	Trans World Airlines	SEVRN 9/14/94 unless exchanged at company's option for Fixed Rate Notes due 1994 on or before 9/15/89.		Higher of (a) 3-mo. T-bill +375bp or (b) 3-mo. LIBOR + 250bp.	MJSD 15	MJSD 15	None	–
7/6/84	100	Triangle Industries, Inc.	SSEVRN 7/15/94 unless exchanged at company's option on or before 7/15/88 for 5-yr. Fixed Rate Notes.		Higher of (a) 3-mo. T-bill + 350bp or (b) 3-mo. LIBOR + 225bp.	JAJO 15	JAJO 15	None	–
10/25/84	17	World Airways, Inc.	FVRETC Due on the 10th anniversary of the Fixed Interest Rate Date.		Higher of (a) 3-mo. T-bill + 425 bp or (b) 3-mo. LIBOR + 275bp. The interest rate will become fixed on or before 10/15/88 and will be equal to 142% of 10-yr. TCM.	JAJO 15	JAJO 15	None	– Note: Semi-annual sinking fund of $250M 4/15/85–10/15/87 and at 4.75% of ETCs outstanding on 10/15/87 4/15/88 to maturity.

TABLE A-6
Six-Month Treasury Bill Auction Rate (Bond Equivalent Basis)

Issue Date	Par Amount ($MM)	Issuer	Type	Final Maturity	Base Rate Plus	Approximate Interest Adjustment Date	Approximate Interest Payment Date	Put at Holders' Option	Prior Notice Required
4/22/83	200	Citicorp	FRN	5/1/95	70bp	M&N1	M&N1	5/1/86, 89, & 92	30/60 days
5/13/83	150	Citicorp	FRN	5/15/98	65bp	M&N15	M&N15	5/15/86, 89, 92, & 95	30/60 days
8/4/83	125	Citicorp	FRN	8/10/98	30bp spread may change on 8/10/86, 89, 90, & 92.	Weekly	FMAN10	8/10/86, 89, 92, & 95	4/15 days

TABLE A-7
Six-Month Treasury Bill Secondary Market Rate (Interest Yield Equivalent)

Issue Date	Par Amount ($MM)	Issuer	Type	Final Maturity	Base Rate Plus	Approximate Interest Adjustment Date	Approximate Interest Payment Date	Put at Holders' Option	Prior Notice Required
5/30/79	200	Beneficial Corporation	Cv.FRN	8/1/87	50bp	F&A 1	F&A 1	None	–
4/26/79	300	Chase Manhattan Corp.	Cv.FRN	5/1/09	55bp to 4/30/89, then 50bp	M&N 1	M&N 1	None	–
4/6/79	100	Chemical New York Corp.	FRN	5/1/04	100bp to 4/30/89, then 75bp	M&N 1	M&N 1	None	–
7/26/78	200	Citicorp	FRN	9/1/98	100bp to 8/31/88, then 75bp	M&S 1	M&S 1	None	–
1/31/79	500	Citicorp	FRN	5/1/04	100bp to 4/30/89, then 75bp	M&N 1	M&N 1	None	–
4/19/79	200	Continental Illinois Corp.	Cv.FRN	5/1/87	50bp	M&N 1	M&N 1	None	–
5/18/79	125	First Bank System, Inc.	FRN	5/15/89	50bp	M&N 15	M&N 15	None	–
9/27/79	150	Georgia-Pacific Corp.	Cv.FRN	10/1/87	50bp	A&O 1	A&O 1	Only if the company elects to force conversion into 8¼% debentures due 10/1/09. Company's option expires 3/31/87. Notice of "put" must be received by company at least 15 days prior to conversion date.	–
7/18/79	16.5	Imperial Bancorp.	Cv.FRN	8/1/99	100bp to 7/31/86, then 75 bp	F&A 1	F&A 1	None	–
4/25/79	100	Interfirst Corporation (formerly First International Bancshares, Inc.)	Cv.FRN	8/1/97	50bp	F&A 1	F&A 1	None	–

TABLE A-7—*Continued*
Six-Month Treasury Bill Secondary Market Rate (Interest Yield Equivalent)

Issue Date	Issuer	Par Amount ($MM)	Type	Final Maturity	Base Rate Plus	Approximate Interest Adjustment Date	Approximate Interest Payment Date	Put at Holders' Option	Prior Notice Required
4/20/79	Irving Bank Corporation (formerly Charter New York Corporation)	90	FRN	5/1/04	100bp to 4/30/89, then 75bp	M&N 1	M&N 1	None	–
4/27/79	Manufacturers Hanover Corp.	150	Cv.FRN	5/1/87	50bp	M&N 1	M&N 1	None	–
3/12/79	MCorp. (formerly Mercantile Texas Corp.)	35	FRN	6/15/99	100bp to6/14/89,	J&D 15	J&D 15	None	–
5/25/79	Mellon National Corporation (formerly The Girard Company)	50	Cv.FRN	5/15/87	65bp	M&N 15	M&N 15	None	–
6/19/79	Mellon National Corporation*	200	Cv.FRN	6/15/89	50bp	J&D15	J&D15	None	–
5/18/79	Norwest Corporation (formerly Northest Bancorporation)	100	Cv.FRN	5/1/89	50bp	M&N1	M&N1	None	–
4/26/79	RepublicBank Corporation (formerly Republic of Texas Corporation)	75	FRN	5/1/04	100bp to 4/30/89, then 75bp	M&N1	M&N1	None	–

*This issue is convertible at the option of the company into fixed rate debentures between 6/15/80 and 6/15/88. The rate will be the higher of $8\frac{1}{2}$% or 65bp above the Treasury 30-year constant maturity.

TABLE A-8
One-Year and Longer Treasury Constant Maturity

Issue Date	Par Amount ($MM)	Issuer	Type	Coupon	Final Maturity	Minimum Basis for Coupon Adjustment	Interest Adjustment Dates	Interest Payment Dates	Put at Holders' Option	Prior Notice Required
7/26/84	50	American Can Company	EN	13.25	8/1/96	102.5% of 1, 2, 3, 4 or 5 yr.	8/1/87 and *	F&A 1	8/1/87 and *	7/1-15/87 and *
7/20/82	100	Associates Corporation of North America	EN	12.54	8/1/87	103% of 1 yr.	8/1/85 & 86	F&A 1	8/1/85 & 86	7/1-15/85 & 86
10/26/81	250	BankAmerica Corporation	ARN	11.25	11/1/89	105% of 2 yr.	11/1/85 & 87	M&N 1	11/1/85 & 87	15/30 days
4/26/84	150	BankAmerica Corporation	EN	12.125	5/1/94	101% of 1, 2, 3, 4 or 5 yr.	5/1/86 and *	M&N 1	5/1/86 and *	4/1-15/86 and *
11/17/83	200	BankAmerica Corporation	EN	11.50	11/15/95	102% of 3 yr.	11/15/86, 89 & 92	M&N 15	11/15/86, 89 & 92	15/30 days
1/26/84	200	BankAmerica Corporation	EN	11.375	2/1/96	102% of 3 yr.	2/1/87, 90 & 93	F&A 1	2/1/87, 90 & 93	15/30 days
6/18/84	100	BarclaysAmerican Corp.	EN	13.00	7/1/96	101% of 1, 2, 3, 4 or 5 yr.	7/1/86 and *	J&J 1	7/1/86 and *	10/20 days
8/2/84	75	BarclaysAmerican Corp.	EN	12.00	8/1/99	101% of 1, 2, 3, 4 or 5 yr.	8/1/87 and *	F&A 1	8/1/87 and *	10/20 days
3/17/82	75	Borg-Warner Acceptance	EN	11.20	3/15/92	105% of 2 yr.	3/15/86, 88 & 90	M&S 15	3/15/86, 88 & 90	15 days
6/7/85	50	Borg-Warner Acceptance	EN	8.875	6/15/97	101% of 3yr.	6/15/88, 91 &94	J&D 15	6/15/88, 91 &91	15 days
6/24/85	125	Burroughs Corporation	EN	9.25	7/1/95	to be determined	7/1/87 and *	J&J 1	7/1/87 and *	15/30 days
3/19/85	125	Carolina Power & Light	FMBES	11.125	4/1/95	to be determined (minimum 1 yr.)	4/1/87 and *	A&O 1	4/1/87 and *	3/1-15
7/19/82	150	Caterpillar Tractor Co.	EN	10.10	7/15/97	102% of 3 yr.	7/15/88, 91, & 94	J&J 15	7/15/88, 91, & 94	6/15-7/1/88, & 94
						Note: Coupon effective 7/1/85 is based on 109% of the 3 yr. TCM.				
7/22/82	100	Champion International	EN	9.92	7/15/94	103% of 3 yr.	7/15/88, 91	J&J 15	7/15/88, 91	6/15-7/1/88 & 91
						Note: Coupon effective 7/1/85 is based on 107% of the 3 yr. TCM.				
6/12/85	250	Chase Manhattan Corp.	EN	9.00	6/15/97	to be determined (1 to 5 yrs.)	6/15/87 and *	J&D 15	6/15/87 and *	5/15-31
4/4/85	300	Chrysler Financial Corp.	EN	11.50	4/15/97	101% of 1, 2, 3, 4 or 5 yr.	4/15/88 and *	A&O 15	4/15/88 and *	3/15-31
6/6/85	100	C.I.T. Financial Corp.	EN	8.875	6/1/97	to be determined (30 days to 6/1/97)	6/1/88 and *	J&D 1	6/1/88 and *	5/12-22

TABLE A–8—Continued
One-Year and Longer Treasury Constant Maturity

Issue Date	Par Amount ($MM)	Issuer	Type	Coupon	Final Maturity	Minimum Basis for Coupon Adjustment	Interest Adjustment Dates	Interest Payment Dates	Put at Holders' Option	Prior Notice Required
12/19/84	300	Citicorp	EN	10.25	12/15/94	101% of 1 yr. to 8 yr.	12/15/86 and *	J&D 15	12/15/86 and *	4/15 days
2/6/83	250	Citicorp	EN	11.30	12/15/95	102% of 1, 2, 3, 4 or 5 yr.	12/15/85 and *	J&D 15	12/15/85 and *	4/15 days
6/1/84	150	Citicorp	EN	13.75	6/1/96	101% of 1, 2, 3, 4 or 5 yr.	6/1/87 and *	J&D 1	6/1/87 and *	4/15 days
7/19/84	200	Citicorp	EN	13.625	8/1/96	101% of 1, 2, 3, 4 or 5 yr.	8/1/86 and *	F&A 1	8/1/86 and *	4/15 days
10/19/84	250	Citicorp	EN	11.875	11/1/96	101% of 1, 2, 3, 4 or 5 yr.	11/1/86 and *	M&N 1	11/1/86 and *	4/15 days
6/14/84	250	Citicorp	EN	13.60	6/15/99	101% of 1, 2, 3, 4 or 5 yr.	6/15/86 and *	J&D 15	6/15/86 and *	4/15 days
7/13/84	100	Credithrift Financial	ESN	13.00	1/15/94	101% of 1, 2, 3, 4 or 5 yr.	1/15/86 and *	J&J 15	1/15/86 and *	10/20 days
5/21/85	120	Delta Air Lines, Inc.	EN	9.75	5/15/00	to be determined	5/15/88 and *	M&N 15	5/15/88 and *	15/30 days
5/10/85	50	First Fidelity Bancorp.	EN	11.75	5/15/05	101% of 1 to 10 tr.	5/15/95 and *	M&N 15	5/15/95 and *	15/30 days
8/23/84	150	First Interstate Bancorp	EN	13.00	9/1/99	101% of 1, 2, 3, 4 or 5 yr.	9/1/86 and *	M&S 1	9/1/86 and *	4/15 days
7/12/84	75	Fleet Financial Group	EN	13.00	7/15/91	102% of 1, 2, 3, 4 or 5 yr.	7/15/85 and *	J&J 15	7/15/85 and *	6/15–30/85 and *
3/21/84	50	Fleet Financial Group	EN	12.25	4/1/99	102% of 1, 2, 3, 4 or 5 yr.	4/1/87 and *	A&O 1	4/1/87 and *	3/1–15/87 and *
9/21/83	100	Ford Motor Credit Company	EN	12.25	9/15/98	102.5% of 5 yr.	9/15/88 & 93	M&S 15	9/15/88 & 93	8/15–31/88 & 93
1/26/84	100	Ford Motor Credit Company	EN	12.00	2/1/99	102% of 5 yr.	2/1/89 & 94	F&A 1	2/1/89 & 94	1/1–13/89 & 1/1–14/94
4/18/85	200	Ford Motor Credit Company	EN	10.375	4/15/00	to be determined (not later than 10/15/99)	4/15/88 and *	A&O 15	4/15/88 and *	15/30 days
2/19/81	85	General Felt Industries	VRSSD	10.489	2/15/01	1.32x 20 yr. (minimum rate 8.012% maximum rate 15.97%)	Quarterly	FMAN 15	None	

11/13/80	200	General Motors Acceptance Corporation	ARN	12.90	11/15/90	107.2% of 10 yr.	Annually 11/15	M&N 15	None	2/15–3/1/88
3/15/83	100	GTE Corporation	EN	11.00	3/15/93	103% of 5 yr.	3/15/88	M&S 15	3/15/88	None
5/24/79	250	Gulf Oil Corporation	V/FRD	11.45	6/1/09	30 yr. plus 35bp	J&D 1	J&D 1	None	
		Note: Automatically converts to 8.375% Fixed Rate Debenture due 2009 if the 30 year TCM drops to 8.00% or lower.								
7/26/84	100	Holiday Inns, Inc.	EN	13.25	8/1/99	102% of 1, 2, 3, 4 or 5 yr.	8/1/87 and *	F&A 1	8/1/87 and *	7/1–15/87 and *
9/22/82	50	Hormel (Geo. A.) & Co.	EN	13.25	9/1/94	102% of 3 yr.	9/1/85, 88 & 91	M&S 1	9/1/85, 88	On or before 8/17/85, 88 & 91
8/2/84	75	Hospital Corporation of America	EN	13.00	8/1/99	102% of 1, 2, 3, 4 or 5 yr.	8/1/87 and *	F&A 1	8/1/87 and *	7/1–15/87 and *
9/18/84	50	Household Finance Corp.	RN	12.55	10/1/92	2 yr. plus 45bp	10/1/86, 88 & 90	A&O 1	None	
3/14/85	200	Household Finance Corp.	EN	11.25	4/1/95	to be determined (not later than 10/1/94)	4/1/87 and *	A&O 1	4/1/87 and *	15/20 days
12/5/84	300	IBM Credit Corporation	EN	10.75	12/15/96	to be determined (one or more whole years)	12/15/87 and *	J&D 15	12/15/87 and *	11/15–30
5/2/83	50	Kroger Co.	EN	11.00	5/1/95	102.5% of 2 yr.	5/1/87, 89, 91 & 93	M&N 1	5/1/87, 89, 91 & 93	On or before 4/15/87, 89, 91 & 93
6/15/84	150	Manufacturers Hanover Corporation	EN	13.70	6/15/90	101% of 2 yr.	6/15/86 & 88	J&D 15	6/15/86 & 88	30/60 days
12/17/84	100	Manufacturers Hanover	EN	10.50	12/15/90	101% of 1, 2, 3 or 5 yr.	12/15/86 and *	J&D 15	12/15/86 and *	15/20 days
5/7/82	75	Martin Marietta Corp.	ARN	12.25	5/1/94	103% of 2 yr.	5/1/86, 88, 90 & 92	M&N 1	5/1/86, 88, 90 & 92 unless the new rate is exactly 109% of 2 yr. TCM.	4/1–15/86, 88, 90 & 92
10/11/84	200	Merrill Lynch & Co., Inc.	EN	12.30	10/15/94	101% of 1, 2, 3, 4 or 5 yr.	10/15/86 and *	A&O 15	10/15/86 and *	10/20 days
4/2/85	200	Merrill Lynch & Co., Inc.	EN	11.25	4/15/97	to be determined (4/15/89–96)	4/15/88 and *	A&O 15	4/15/88 and *	10/20 days
6/4/85	125	Merrill Lynch & Co., Inc.	EN	9.375	6/1/97	to be determined (6/1/89–96)	6/1/88 and *	J&D 1	6/1/88 and *	10/20 days
3/26/84	250	Merrill Lynch & Co., Inx.	EN	10.625	4/1/99	102% of 1, 2, 3, 4, 5, 6 or 7 yr.	4/1/86 and *	A&O 1	4/1/86 and *	10/20 days

TABLE A-8—Continued
One-Year and Longer Treasury Constant Maturity

Issue Date	Par Amount ($MM)	Issuer	Type	Coupon	Final Maturity	Minimum Basis for Coupon Adjustment	Interest Adjustment Dates	Interest Payment Dates	Put at Holders' Option	Prior Notice Required
8/20/82	100	NL Industries	EN	12.50	8/15/87	103% of 1 yr.	8/15/85 & 86	F&A 15	8/15/85 & 86	7/15–8/1/85 & 86
6/11/84	100	Penney (J. C.) Company	EN	13.625	6/15/99	101% of 1 through 11 yr.	6/15/88 and *	J&D 15	6/15/88 and *	5/15–6/1/88 and *
10/22/84	100	Pillsbury Company	EN	12.00	10/15/99	101% of 1, 2, 3, 4 or 5 yr.	10/15/89 and *	A&O 15	10/15/89 and *	9/15–30
11/15/84	75	Portland General Electric	FMBES	11.625	11/15/99	102% of 1, 2, 3, 4 or 5 yr.	11/15/87 and *	M&N 15	11/15/87 and *	10/15/–11/1
6/21/84	75	Puget Sound Power * Light	EFMB	14.00	7/1/96	103% of 1, 2, or 3 yr.	7/1/87 and *	J&J 1	7/1/87 and *	6/1–15/87 and *
11/5/84	100	Ryder System, Inc.	EN	11.50	11/15/99	101% of 1, 2, 3, 4 or 5 yr.	11/15/87 and *	M&N 15	11/15/87 and *	10/16–31
9/27/84	150	Security Pacific Corp.	EN	12.50	10/1/96	101% of 1, 2, 3, 4 or 5 yr.	10/1/87 and *	A&O 1	10/1/87 and *	15/30 days
11/26/84	150	Security Pacific Corp.	EN	10.75	12/1/99	101% of 1, 2, 3, 4 or 5 yr.	12/1/86 and *	J&D 1	12/1/86 and *	15/30 days
4/13/84	200	Sears, Roebuck & Co.	EN	12.00	4/15/99	101% of 1, 2, 3, 5 or 7 yr.	4/15/87 and *	A&O 15	4/15/87 and *	4/15 days
1/28/82	40	Southmark Corporation	VRSN	14.61	2/1/87	1.315 × 5 yr.	Quarterly	FMAN 1	None	–
7/30/84	50	Squibb Corporation	EN	12.875	8/1/93	102.5% of 1, 2, 3, 4, 5 or 6 yr.	8/1/87 and *	F&A 1	8/1/87 and *	7/1–15/87 and *
10/30/84	50	Squibb Corporation	EN	11.50	11/15/99	101% of 1, 2, 3, 4 or 5 yr.	11/15/87 and *	M&N 15	11/15/87 and *	10/15–31 and *
6/5/84	500	Texaco Capital Inc.	EN	13.25	6/1/99	101% of 1 through 12 yr.	6/1/87 and *	J&D 1	6/1/87 and *	5/1–15/87 and *
12/5/84	500	Texaco Capital Inc.	EN	10.75	1/15/00	101% of 1 through 12 yr.	1/15/88 and *	J&J 15	1/15/88 and *	12/15–31 and *
2/27/85	300	Texaco Capital Inc.	EN	11.25	3/1/00	to be determined (1–11 yrs.)	3/1/89 and *	M&S 1	3/1/89 and *	2/1–15 and *

Date	Amount	Issuer	Type	Rate	Maturity	Call Provision		Pay		
9/14/84	125	Transcontinental Gas Pipe Line Corporation	EN	12.50	9/15/99	102% of 1, 2, 3, 4 or 5 yr.	9/15/87 and *	M&S 15	9/15/87 and *	8/15–9/1/87 and *
5/23/85	125	Transcontinental Gas Pipe Line Corporation	EN	9.875	5/15/00	to be determined for 1, 2, 3, 4 or 5 yrs.	5/15/88 and *	M&N 15	5/15/88 and *	4/15–5/1/1 and *
5/20/84	1,156	Unocal Corporation	SSEN	13.50	5/15/97	120% of 3 yr.	5/15/88, 91 & 94	M&N 15	5/15/88, 91 & 94	4/15–5/1/88, 91 & 94

Note: Under certain circumstances the interest rate may be increased by 175bp.

Date	Amount	Issuer	Type	Rate	Maturity	Call Provision		Pay		
10/31/84	50	Valley National Corp.	EN	11.875	11/1/93	102% of 1, 2, 3, 4, 5 or 6 yr.	11/1/87 and *	M&N 1	11/1/87 and *	10/1–15 and *
3/19/84	100	Westinghouse Credit Corp.	EN	11.875	3/15/96	102% of 1, 2, 3, or 5 yr.	3/15/87 and *	M&S 15	3/15/87 and *	2/15–3/1/87 and *
8/3/84	100	Westinghouse Credit Corp.	EN	12.875	8/1/99	101% of 1, 2, 3, 4 or 5 yr.	8/1/86 and *	F&A 1	8/1/86 and *	7/1–15/86 and *
8/25/83	100	Xerox Corporation	EN	11.25	9/1/98	102% of 1, 2, 3, or 5 yr.	9/1/86 and *	M&S 1	9/1/86 and *	8/1–15/86 and *
6/22/82	100	Xerox Credit Corporation	EN	8.55	6/15/87	102% of 1 yr.	6/15/86	J&D 15	6/15/86	5/15–6/1/86
9/28/83	100	Xerox Credit Corporation	EN	10.75	10/1/95	102% of 1, 2, or 3 yr.	10/1/85 and *	A&O 1	10/1/85 and *	9/1–15/85 and *
3/12/84	100	Xerox Credit Corporation	EN	11.75	3/15/99	102% of 1, 2, 3 or 5 yr.	3/15/87 and *	M&S 15	3/15/87 and *	2/15–3/1/87 and *

TABLE A-9
Nonfinancial Benchmarks

Issue Date	Par Amount ($MM)	Issuer	Type	Coupon Percent	Final Maturity	Basis for Coupon Adjustment	Interest Adjustment Dates	Interest Payment Dates	Put at Holders' Option	Prior Notice Required
6/25/80	52	Petro-Lewis Corporation	VRSD	13.00	7/1/00	Based on percentage change in west Texas crude oil. Minimum rate 13.00%; maximum rate 15.50%.	Each 7/1	J&J 1	None	–
7/18/84	25	Rooney, Pace Group Inc.	FRN	18.00	8/1/94	Based on average trading volume of NYSE stocks. 18.00% if volume is between 85MM and 100MM. Positive interest adjustment of 0.2% for each 1MM sharers above 100MM; negative interest adjustment 0.2% for each 1MM shares below 85MM. Minimum rate 17.00%; Maximum rate 22.00%.	2/1/86 and each F&A 1 thereafter.	F&A 1	None	–
4/12/85	50	U.S. Home Corporation	RN	11.25	4/15/00	The interest rate will be adjusted on 4/15/90 to a rate established by the company but in no event will it be less than 13⅜%.	4/15/90	A&O 15	4/15/90; notice must be received by the company between 3/15 & 3/13/90.	

CHAPTER 3

ADJUSTABLE RATE PREFERRED STOCKS

Richard S. Wilson[*]
Vice President
Fixed Income Research Department
Merrill Lynch Capital Markets

BACKGROUND

Adjustable rate preferred stocks (ARPS) first came to the public market in May, 1982, and by mid-1985 slightly more than $10.4 billion had been issued by 94 companies.[1] The 112 issues range in size from $10 million to $400 million. Nine of these stocks with a

---

[*]The author wishes to thank Victoria C. Kess, CFA, Vice President of Merrill Lynch Capital Markets, for her helpful comments and suggestions. Of course, any errors or oversights remain the responsibility of the author.

[1]In 1978 AMAX Inc. privately placed an issue of preferred stock with quarterly dividends based on one-half of the U.S. dollar London Interbank Offered Rate (LIBOR) plus 1.25 percent, with the dividend limited on a cumulative basis to an annual rate of $5 per share. The stated redemption value of this Series "D" stock is $50 per share.

In March 1980, Chemical New York Corporation issued $50 million and Citicorp issued $40 million of adjustable rate preferred stock to subsidiaries of a Texas insurance holding company. The stocks had an initial period at a fixed rate, and then the dividends were to be adjusted every three years to 90 percent of the interest rate on certain adjustable rate notes.

In March 1981, a $16 million issue of variable rate preferred stock was sold

TABLE 3-1
Adjustable Rate Preferred Stocks—Financing Statistics to 6/30/85

Industry	Total ($ MM) (no. of issues)	1982	1983	1984	1985 6/30/85
Banks	$5,200.11	$1,847.00	$2,321.95	$727.36	$303.80
no. of issues	51	16	23	10	2
Electric	1,050.00	40.00	460.00	365.00	185.00
no. of issues	22	1	11	7	3
Finance	460.00		460.00		
no. of issues	4		4		
Gas	335.00	185.00	50.00	100.00	
no. of issues	5	3	1	1	
Industrial	1,059.56	200.00	493.02	366.54	
no. of issues	10	1	6	3	
Insurance	786.21	551.21	100.00	135.00	
no. of issues	5	3	1	1	
Savings & Loan	1.071.73		134.03	887.70	50.00
no. of issues	12		1	10	1
Transportation	356.94		356.94		
no. of issues	1		1		
Telephone	85.04			85.04	
no. of issues	2			2	
Total	$10,404.59	$2,823.21	$4,375.94	$2,666.64	$538.80
no. of issues	112	24	48	34	6

par value totalling slightly more than $1.6 billion were issued in conjunction with mergers or acquisitions. One company, for example issued an adjustable rate convertible preferred stock amounting to some $250 million as part of an acquisition.[2] Three other stocks were issued as a result of debt for equity swaps.

As Table 3-1 shows, bank holding companies have been the

privately by Weyerhaeuser Real Estate Company. As is often the case with financial innovations, the private placement market is the first to test the new ideas.

[2] This will be discussed later in this chapter. This was not the first issue, as on September 12, 1980, Landmark Bancshares Corporation made a rights offering to its common shareholders inviting them to subscribe to 36,364 shares of Series "I," variable rate cumulative convertible preferred stock, $1 par value, at $55 per share. The dividend rate was based on the prime rate of the Chase Manhattan Bank, subject to a minimum of 9.00 percent and a maximum rate of 13.25 percent on the $55 stated value ($4.95 to $7.29 per share). Each share was convertible into 2.25 shares of common stock. The author is not aware of any earlier adjustable rate convertible issues, although there could very well be some extant.

largest issuers of ARPS. They are more familiar with variable rate assets and liabilities than are many industrial and utility companies and thus are more likely to take advantage of variable rate equities. In addition, regulatory authorities permit bank holding companies to include perpetual preferred stock as part of primary capital. This allows banks to strengthen their capital positions without resorting to common equity sales at a time when bank stocks are selling at low market prices in relation to stated book values.

WHAT ARPS ARE AND ARE NOT

In general, adjustable rate preferred stocks are perpetual equity securities (a few of the issues have provisions for sinking funds) whose dividends are fixed quarterly at a predetermined spread (*dividend reset spread*) from the highest of three points (*benchmark rate*) on the Treasury yield curve (see "Dividends and Dividend Determination Period"). A few issues have the dividend based on only the 3-month U.S. Treasury bill. Because *it* is not tied to either a short-term or long-term rate (as is the case with floating rate and variable rate debt securities), the investor is provided with income riding the crest of the yield curve. A *fixing* based on only one benchmark rate could prove to be a disadvantage when the shape or slope of the yield curve changes. The dividend rates are subject to minimum and maximum levels called *collars,* with the maximum rate labeled a *cap.*

A large majority of the presently outstanding issues cannot be redeemed at the option of the issuer during the first five years after issuance, although the redemption protection period ranges from two to seven years. The normal redemption price is 103 percent of par or stated value for the sixth through tenth year, dropping to 100 percent in the eleventh year. Redemption may be made in whole or in part; some issues provide for earlier redemption in the event of certain circumstances such as changes in the Federal tax laws or mergers and acquisitions. A typical redemption provision might read as follows:

> The shares of Adjustable Rate Preferred Stock are not redeemable prior to May 1, 1987. On and after that date, the shares will be redeemable in whole or in part at the option of the Company, upon not less than 30 not (sic) more than 60 days' notice by mail, at a redemption price (i) in the case of a redemption occurring on or after

May 1, 1987 and prior to May 1, 1992, of $51.50 per share and (ii) in the case of a redemption occurring on or after May 1, 1992, of $50.00 per share, plus in each case accrued and unpaid dividends to the date fixed for redemption.[3]

Of course, if the dividends are in arrears, the preferred stock may not be redeemed in part.

Some of the utility preferred stocks have call/refunding provisions similar to those on their debt issues. In these cases the ARPS is currently callable at par plus the dividend rate, scaled down *annually* to par at the start of the eleventh year. However, the preferred stock may not be redeemed in the first five years, directly or indirectly, from the proceeds of or in anticipation of any refunding involving the issuance of debt or preferred stock (ranking on a parity) having an effective interest cost or dividend rate of less than the initial dividend rate. This protection against refunding is not as strong nor as absolute as an outright prohibition against redemption.

ARPS are *not* money market instruments and are *not* substitutes for short-dated paper. They possess more of the characteristics of equities than of debt instruments, such as voting rights in certain events, and liquidation rights superior to those of common and other junior securities but inferior to those of debt. Also, unlike most debt cases, failure to meet a dividend or sinking fund payment is not an event of default. And, in contrast to the case of floating rate debt, ARPS do not enjoy the "magical drawing power" or "magnetism" of an approaching maturity. With a few exceptions, they do not give the holder the right to put the stock back to the issuer for cash. Thus, unless selling above the call price, ARPS will normally be valued on a current yield basis similar to any perpetual instrument.

DIVIDENDS AND DIVIDEND DETERMINATION PERIOD

The dividend rate for adjustable rate preferred stocks is determined from statistics published in *Federal Reserve Statistical Release*

---

[3] Prospectus for 4,000,000 shares of Chemical New York Corporation, adjustable rate preferred stock (stated value, $50 per share), May 11, 1982, p. 11.

H.15(519) Selected Interest Rates during what is called the dividend determination period (DDP). The DDP is generally, but not always, 14 calendar days (the "calendar period") immediately prior to the last ten calendar days preceding the start of a dividend payment period. *Report H.15* is normally released every Monday and may be obtained through the various Federal Reserve Banks and by subscription from the Board of Governors of the Federal Reserve System.

The index basis (also known as the base rate or benchmark rate) for the calculation of the dividend rate is the highest of the two-week average of the following rates as published in *H.15* during the dividend determination period:

- Three-month Treasury bills—market discount rate,

- Ten-year Constant Maturity Rate,

- Twenty-year Constant Maturity Rate.[4]

To this benchmark rate (usually rounded to the nearest five–hundredths of a percentage point) an adjustment is made in order to arrive at the applicable dividend rate. This adjustment factor, also known as the dividend determination spread or the dividend reset spread, is usually a fixed basis point premium or discount (although it can be stated as a percentage of the base rate). Normally this applicable dividend rate will be published in a newspaper of general circulation in New York City prior to the commencement

---

[4] Description of the Treasury Constant Maturity Series from the *Federal Reserve Statistical Release H.15(519) Selected Interest Rates:*

Yields on Treasury securities at 'constant maturity' are estimated from the Treasury's daily yield curve. This curve, which relates the yield on a security to its time to maturity, is based on the closing market bid yields on actively-traded Treasury securities in the over-the-counter market. These market yields are calculated from composites of quotations reported by five leading U.S. Government securities dealers to the Federal Reserve Bank of New York.

The constant yield values are read from the yield curve at fixed maturities, currently 1, 2, 3, 4, 5, 7, 10, 20, and 30 years. This method permits estimation of the yield for a 10-year maturity, for example, even if no outstanding security has exactly 10 years remaining to maturity.

of the new dividend period to which it applies. In some cases, the rate is not published by the issuer and in other cases it might appear after the start of the dividend period. Also, the company will send notice of the new rate with the dividend payment check to holders of record. The record date is usually not more than 30 days preceding the dividend payment date.

Let us look to see how the dividends for several issues have been determined. The issues with their reset spreads are:

Aetna Life & Casualty Company	90 basis point discount
Chemical New York Corporation Series "A"	50 basis point premium
Chemical New York Corporation Series "B"	65 basis point discount
J. P. Morgan & Co. Incorporated	487.5 basis point discount
Student Loan Marketing Association	450 basis point discount

The dividend determination period for these issues is ". . . the Calendar Period immediately prior to the last ten calendar days of March, June, September, or December, as the case may be, prior to the dividend period for which the dividend rate . . . is being determined." Since the calendar period is defined as a period of 14 calendar days, the dividend determination periods are March 8 to 21, June 7 to 20, September 7 to 20, and December 8 to 21. From *Report H.15* released during the calendar period (issues of September 9 and September 18, 1985—see Figure 3–1) and applicable for the fourth quarter's dividend (October, November, and December and payable December 31) we find the following:

3-month Treasury Bill	7.31%	week ending Sept. 6
(Secondary Market)	7.42%	week ending Sept. 20
Average	7.37%	
10-year Treasury Constant Maturity	10.29%	week ending Sept. 6
	10.48%	week ending Sept. 20
Average	10.39%	
20-year Treasury Constant Maturity	10.71%	week ending Sept. 6
	10.89%	week ending Sept. 20
Average	10.80%	

The highest of the averages of these rates is 10.80 percent provided by the 20-year Treasury Constant Maturity. This average,
when necessary, is rounded to the nearest 5 basis points (.05); the
benchmark rate is 10.80 percent. The new dividend rates for the
fourth quarter of 1985 for the above issues are:

Aetna Life & Casualty	10.80% minus 90 basis points = 9.90%
Chemical New York "A"	10.80% plus 50 basis points = 11.30%
Chemical New York "B"	10.80% minus 65 basis points = 10.15%
J.P. Morgan & Co.	10.80% minus 487.5 basis points = 5.925%
Student Loan Marketing Association	10.80% minus 450 basis points = 6.30%

It should be emphasized that the dividend benchmark rate is determined by the publication date of *Report H.15* falling within that
DDP. The daily rates used to arrive at the weekly averages may start
prior to the commencement of the dividend determination period.
In the examples above the daily rates covered the period from September 2 through September 13.

The dollar amount of the dividends payable each dividend period
is computed by dividing the applicable rate by 4 in the case of $100
par or stated value issues, by 8 in the case of $50 par issues, and by
16 in the case of $25 par issues. Thus, the quarterly dollar dividend
for a stock with a 12.80 percent dividend rate is $3.20 for $100 par,
$1.60 for $50 par, and $0.80 for $25 par shares. The dividends are
computed on the basis of a 360-day year consisting of four 90-day
quarters and 30-day months. The dollar dividends to be paid on
September 30 for the above issues are:

Aetna Life & Casualty ($50)	9.90%	$1.2375
Chemical New York "A" ($50)	11.30%	$1.4125
Chemical New York "B" ($50)	10.15%	$1.26875
J.P. Morgan & Co. ($100)	6.30%	$1.48125
Student Loan Market Association ($50)	8.95%	$0.7875

Although the dividend rate has been determined, it cannot be
paid unless another step is taken. It is necessary for the Board of
Directors of the company to declare the dividend out of assets

Figure 3-1

FEDERAL RESERVE statistical release

H.15 (519)

SELECTED INTEREST RATES
Yields in percent per annum

For immediate release
SEPTEMBER 16, 1985

Instruments	SEPT 9	SEPT 10	SEPT 11	SEPT 12	SEPT 13	Week ending SEPT 13	Week ending SEPT 6	AUG
FEDERAL FUNDS (EFFECTIVE) 1/	7.95	7.83	8.03	7.95	7.77	7.80	7.88	7.90
COMMERCIAL PAPER 2/3/								
1-MONTH	7.83	7.87	7.93	7.95	7.95	7.91	7.74	7.73
3-MONTH	7.86	7.88	7.93	7.97	7.96	7.92	7.75	7.72
6-MONTH	7.92	7.94	7.98	8.02	8.02	7.98	7.76	7.74
FINANCE PAPER PLACED DIRECTLY 2/								
1-MONTH	7.86	7.84	7.94	7.97	7.98	7.92	7.79	7.70
3-MONTH	7.64	7.66	7.75	7.73	7.76	7.71	7.58	7.58
6-MONTH	7.64	7.67	7.67	7.68	7.68	7.67	7.49	7.55
BANKERS ACCEPTANCES (TOP RATED) 2/								
3-MONTH	7.87	7.85	7.90	7.95	7.92	7.90	7.78	7.68
6-MONTH	7.97	8.00	8.00	8.03	7.97	7.99	7.79	7.68
CDS (SECONDARY MARKET)								
1-MONTH	7.90	7.90	7.95	7.98	7.99	7.94	7.84	7.77
3-MONTH	7.95	7.95	8.03	8.05	8.05	8.00	7.87	7.81
6-MONTH	8.18	8.18	8.25	8.30	8.31	8.24	8.02	7.97
BANK PRIME LOAN 1/4/	9.50	9.50	9.50	9.50	9.50	9.50	9.50	9.50
DISCOUNT WINDOW BORROWING 1/5/	7.50	7.50	7.50	7.50	7.50	7.50	7.50	7.50
U.S. GOVERNMENT SECURITIES								
TREASURY BILLS								
AUCTION AVERAGE 2/ 6/								
3-MONTH	7.22					7.22	7.16	7.18
6-MONTH	7.39					7.39	7.30	7.35
1-YEAR								7.60

AUCTION AVERAGE (INVESTMENT) 6/								
3-MONTH	7.46				7.21	7.46	7.35	7.41
6-MONTH	7.78				7.39	7.78	7.69	7.74
SECONDARY MARKET 2/								
3-MONTH	7.25	7.23	7.24	7.24	7.24	7.23	7.14	7.14
6-MONTH	7.44	7.41	7.43	7.43	7.43	7.42	7.31	7.32
1-YEAR	7.64	7.61	7.64	7.63	7.57	7.62	7.49	7.48
TREASURY CONSTANT MATURITIES 7/8/								
1-YEAR	8.22	8.19	8.23	8.21	8.14	8.20	8.04	8.05
2-YEAR	9.13	9.10	9.13	9.15	9.03	9.11	8.97	8.94
3-YEAR	9.53	9.52	9.53	9.54	9.43	9.51	9.36	9.31
5-YEAR	9.97	9.96	9.98	9.97	9.87	9.95	9.76	9.81
7-YEAR	10.37	10.35	10.39	10.40	10.29	10.36	10.18	10.20
10-YEAR	10.49	10.48	10.51	10.52	10.40	10.48	10.29	10.33
20-YEAR	10.91	10.90	10.92	10.91	10.80	10.89	10.71	10.73
30-YEAR	10.73	10.71	10.73	10.73	10.62	10.70	10.52	10.56
COMPOSITE								
OVER 10 YEARS (LONG-TERM) 9/	10.78	10.77	10.79	10.79	10.69	10.76	10.57	10.59
CORPORATE BONDS								
MOODY'S SEASONED								
AAA	11.11	11.12	11.14	11.17	11.12	11.13	10.94	11.05
BAA	12.51	12.49	12.53	12.55	12.50	12.52	12.41	12.50
A-UTILITY 10/					11.92	11.92	11.77	11.77
STATE & LOCAL BONDS 11/				9.26		9.26	9.07	9.08
CONVENTIONAL MORTGAGES 12/					12.24	12.24	12.15	12.19

1. Weekly figures are averages of 7 calendar days ending on Wednesday of the current week; monthly figures include each calendar day in the month.
2. Quoted on bank-discount basis.
3. Rates on commercial paper placed for firms whose bond rating is AA or the equivalent.
4. Rate charged by banks on short-term business loans.
5. Rate for the Federal Reserve Bank of New York.
6. Auction date.
7. Yields on actively traded issues adjusted to constant maturities. Source: U.S. Treasury.
8. Unweighted average of all issues outstanding of bonds neither due nor callable in less than 10 years, including several very low yielding "flower" bonds.
9. Estimate of the yield on a recently-offered, A-rated utility bond with a maturity of 30 years and call protection of 5 years; Friday quotations.
10. Bond buyer index, general obligation, 20 years to maturity, mixed quality; Thursday quotations.
11. Contract interest rates on commitments for fixed-rate first mortgages and A-utility bonds.
NOTE: Weekly and monthly figures are averages of daily rates, except for state and local bonds, which are based on Thursday figures, and conventional mortgages and A-utility bonds, both of which are based on Friday figures.
** As of the H. 15 release date of June 24, 1985, treasury bill auction averages will be reported on the auction date instead of the issue date.

METHODIST COLLEGE LIBRARY
Fayetteville, N.C.

legally available for payment thereof.[5] If the dividend is not declared, it then accumulates. If there are arrearages then the adjustable rate preferred stock may not be redeemed in part and the company may not purchase or acquire any shares of the preferred stock otherwise than pursuant to a purchase or exchange offer made on the same terms to all holders of the stock. Obviously, if dividends are not paid on the ARPS then cash dividends cannot be paid on the common shares or other stock ranking junior to the preferred.

Voting rights among the ARPS issues vary, but most do not carry the voting privilege except in special circumstances. Usually, if the issuer is in arrears by six quarterly payments, then the preferred stock may vote for some members of the Board of Directors until all dividends in arrears have been paid.

DIVIDEND COLLARS OR CAPS

One of the features of adjustable rate preferred stocks is the minimum and maximum rates (known together as collars) that the issuer is permitted to pay. While the minimum rate has not come into play, the maximum rate or "cap" on some issues became effective in mid-1984 due to rising interest rates. For example, the dividend rate for Gulf States Utilities Company Series B, $100 par value adjustable rate preferred stock for the three-month period ending June 15, 1984 was 12.5 percent. The new dividend for the quarter payable September 15 was set at 13.5 percent, the maximum rate permitted under the terms of the issue (the collar was 7 percent and 13.5 percent). The benchmark rate for the dividend determination period of May 22 to June 4, 1984 was 13.75 percent. Adding the dividend reset spread of 70 basis points gives a new dividend rate of 14.45 percent or 95 basis points greater than the cap. According to

[5] In the dividend notice for Continental Illinois Corporation's adjustable rate preferred stock, Series 1, which appeared in the press on June 28, 1984, it was stated: "Pursuant to an agreement with the Federal Deposit Insurance Corporation, payment of this dividend on September 30, 1984, is subject to the approval of that governmental agency." The dividend rate is 12.45 percent, equal to $1.55625 per share. Arrearages through September 30, 1985 totalled $6.925 a share.

the Amendment to the Restated Articles of Incorporation of the company under which the shares were issued, however, the maximum rate applicable to the stock is 13.5 percent, so that the dividend was set at that maximum rate.[6] Figure 3–2 shows what the applicable quarterly rate for this issue would have been, based on the same collars and reset spread, if it had been offered at the end of 1973 instead of early 1984. In that ten-year period the 13.5 percent cap would have been in effect for eight quarterly payments; the 7 percent minimum rate would have been utilized only once.

The interest rate level at which the collars become effective can easily be determined. To the maximum rate we add (subtract) the discount (premium)—ignoring the plus or minus sign—used as the reset spread. In the Gulf States case the maximum collar is 13.5 percent and the dividend reset spread is a premium of 70 basis points, resulting in 12.8 percent (13.5 percent minus 0.7 percent). Thus, if the level of interest rates used to determine the dividend is 12.8 percent or higher, the maximum dividend collar is in effect. For an issue with a reset spread that is a 70 basis point discount from the benchmark rate we would get 13.5 percent plus 0.7 percent or 14.2 percent. To find the interest rate level that brings the minimum collar into effect we would add (subtract) the reset discount (premium), which then gives the effective minimum level to which rates have to fall before the minimum collar becomes effective. For this Gulf States issue the minimum rate will become effective when the benchmark rate declines to 6.3 percent or lower (7 percent less 0.7 percent).

The ceiling on the dividend obviously restricts an investor's yield on the stock. In a rising interest rate environment, the dividend rates cannot rise above the maximum rate. Therefore, to counter the effect of the lid and to keep the yields in line with other ARPS issues, the market will value the capped stock at a lower price. Investors will anticipate the capping of the dividend rate either by reducing their bids or by selling these issues prior to the date the cap becomes effective. Such stocks will start to trade more as though they were straight (non-adjustable rate) preferreds. Alternatives to

[6] It is interesting to note that the collar confused the company. In the dividend announcement dated June 14, 1984, the incorrect rate of 14.45 percent was given. This was corrected the next day to 13.50 percent.

Figure 3–2

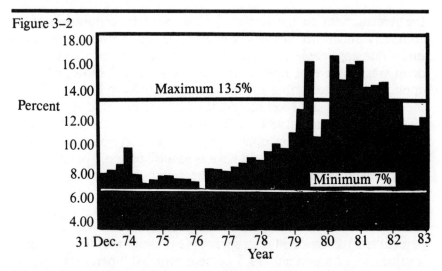

Source: Prospectus dated January 24, 1984 for Gulf States Utilities Company, Adjustable Rate Cumulative Preferred Stock, Series B-$100 Par Value.

these lower maximum collar issues include higher capped stocks or straight preferreds. Again, when interest rates decline to levels where the .nimum dividend rates provide a floor, the ARPS will trade in a manner similar to that of straight issues but are likely to be at premium prices.

SEARCHING FOR RELATIVE VALUES: THE DIVIDEND STRIP AND YIELD TO CALL

In order to compare the various ARPS with one another it is necessary to place them on a more comparable footing through some minor adjustments to the price and the dividend rate. This results from the fact that, as the ex-dividend date approaches, the price of the stock reflects the accrual or build-up of the dividend from the last ex-dividend date. In contrast, bonds normally trade on a price basis with the accrued interest added on. Equities trade flat, i.e., without the accreted dividend added to the purchase or sale price. The dividends for the various issues are also set at different times throughout the year and at diverse rates. Even if the dividend rates were the same, the price of the preferred stock would reflect a different amount of accrued dividend, as the issues probably have different ex-dividend dates. Only when the dividend amounts and ex-dividend dates are the same will the amount of the dividend accruals be the same also.

The first step that an investor in these issues should take is to remove the accrual of the dividend, to "strip" the dividend from the price of the shares. Dividends are usually computed on the basis of a 360-day year, four 90-day quarters, and 30-day months. If the dividend on a $100 par value stock is at the rate of 12 percent or $3 quarterly, and it is one month after the ex-dividend date and two months prior to the next ex-dividend date, we should subtract $1 ($3 × 1/3) from the preferred price to get the stripped or adjusted price. One month later the market price of the stock will reflect two-thirds of the $3 dividend or an accrual of $2 per share. The stock actually accretes the dividend at $0.333 a day.

Table 3–2 gives five examples of the dividend strip. Looking at the preferred of Company "A" we see that the price on June 29, 1984 was $55 per share. The dividend is at the rate of 11.5 percent ($1.4375) payable on September 30. The ex-dividend date for the dividend paid on June 30 was June 8. Buyers of the shares on and after that date would not be entitled to receive the June 30 dividend payment; therefore the price dropped by the amount of that payment. The current price reflects the build-up of the dividend due to be paid on September 30, a 22-day accretion amounting to $0.35 a share. Subtracting the $0.35 accrual from the current market price results in an adjusted price of $54.65.

Now that we have eliminated the effect of the dividend build-up, we must reset the dividend rates so that they, too, are on a comparable footing. For this purpose we assume that the base rate on June 29 was 13.85 percent. From this rate we can establish the adjusted or reset dividend rate, and by dividing this figure by the adjusted price we arrive at the new adjusted current yields. Thus, both the numerator and the denominator of the equation have been adjusted to the analysis date. This makes the comparison between the issues easier, and aids the investor in determining which issues offer more attractive values, taking, of course, quality differentiations into account.

In looking at the preferreds of Companies "B" and "C" we note that the initial reset rates are minus 200 and minus 400 basis points,

TABLE 3–2
Examples of the Adjustable Rate Preferred Dividend Strip

	Company				
	A	B	C	D	E
Current Dividend Rate	11.50%	11.10%	9.10%	12.90%	11.75%
Quarterly Dividend Amount	$1.4375	$1.3875	$2.2750	$1.6125	$1.46875
Next Dividend Date	9/30	8/31	8/31	9/30	9/30
Next Ex-dividend Date	9/10	8/3	8/3	9/11	9/11
6/29/84 Current Price	55	42	$71\frac{1}{2}$	$51\frac{1}{2}$	$50\frac{1}{2}$
Current Yield	10.46%	13.21%	12.73%	12.52%	11.63%
Estimated Dividend Accrual[a]	0.35 (22)	0.88 (57)	1.44 (57)	0.34 (19)	0.31 (19)
Adjusted Price[b]	54.65	41.12	70.06	51.16	50.19
Reset Rate	– 90 bp	– 200	– 400	+ 50	– 65
Adjusted or Reset Dividend Rate	12.95%	11.85%	9.85%	14.35%	13.20%
Current Yield Based on Adjusted Price/ Dividend	11.85%	14.41%	14.06%	14.03%	13.15%
Yield to Call	10.14%	NM	NM	NM	NM
Adjusted Reset Spread	– 200 bp	+ 56	+ 21	+ 18	– 70

Notes: [a]Estimated dividend accrual is based on thirty–day months, actual number of days in month, from the last ex-dividend date. Figure in parentheses is the number of days of the accrual. We are assuming that the last ex-dividend dates were June 8, May 4, May 4, June 11, and June 11, respectively. The accrual is rounded to two decimal places.

[b]Adjusted price is the current price less the dividend accrual.

Adjusted reset spread is (1) adjusted current yield less (2) new or assumed base rate.

Adjusted dividend rate is based on an assumed base or benchmark rate on June 29 of 13.85 percent. This is not an actual rate but a theoretical rate for purposes of this table.

NM = Not meaningful as stock is selling below call price.

Adjusted reset spread based on yield to call is minus 371bp.

a 200 basis point difference. However, the market has greatly narrowed the reset spreads. If we subtract the new reset base rate from the adjusted current yield rate, we arrive at the adjusted dividend reset spread. The new market spread is a 56 basis point premium for issue "B" compared with the stated discount of 200 basis points (14.41 − 13.85). The effective market spread for issue "C" is now a 21 basis point premium, and the difference between the two issues is no longer 200 basis points but only 35 basis points. For the issues that are selling at a premium to the original offering price, the adjusted reset spreads have also changed and are less attractive than they were at the original offering. They are now minus 200 basis points, plus 18 basis points and minus 70 basis points for stocks "A", "D", and "E", respectively, compared with minus 90 basis points, plus 50 basis points and minus 65 basis points at issue.

Another very important calculation must be made for issues selling above their call prices, and that is to obtain the yield-to-call. The adjusted current yield for issue "A" of 11.85 percent overstates the return. If things remain unchanged, the stock is vulnerable to call at the issuer's first opportunity, and the investor can lose the difference between the market price and the call price. A call would be probable if the issuer could refinance the preferred stock at more advantageous terms. The issuer has the option to call or redeem the shares so that the stockholder can only be assured of owning the preferred stock until the call date. The lesser of the current yield or the yield-to-call is the appropriate measurement to use.

Stock "A" is callable on July 1, 1987 at $51.50 a share, 3 1/2 points below today's market and $3.15 below the adjusted or stripped price. As we do not know what the future dividend rates will be, we have to assume that the 12.95 percent ($1.61875 quarterly) rate will remain unchanged over the life of the issue. As most professional investors have access to bond calculators or various yield programs for computers, they would normally calculate the yield-to-call on these machines. Adjusting the prices to make them comparable with bonds, i.e. on a percentage of par basis, we would input $109.30 as the market price and $103 as the call price with July 1, 1987 as the call date. The yield-to-call is 10.14 percent, 171 basis points less than the current yield.

With respect to bonds, the term yield-to-maturity implies the reinvestment of the coupon at the purchase yield, and yield-to-call implies the reinvestment of the interest coupon at the yield-to-call rate, both on a semiannual basis. With preferreds, the generally accepted current yield calculation is simple and does not take compounding or reinvestment into account. Preferred stocks also pay on a quarterly basis. Therefore, some investors might want to perform an internal rate of return (IRR) calculation to examine the cash flow stream of investment. Many pocket calculators are programmed for these internal rate of return computations.

With stock "A" we have a cash outflow (investment) of $54.65 (adjusted or stripped price) on June 29 and cash inflows (dividends) of $1.61875 quarterly from September 30, 1984 to March 31, 1987. On July 1, 1987 we receive another dividend plus the call price of $51.50 for a total of $53.11875. The internal rate of return turns out to be 10.18 percent.

AFTER-TAX YIELDS AND PRETAX EQUIVALENTS

Because preferred dividends qualify for the 85 percent intercorporate dividends received deduction,[7] the appeal of these investments for corporations lies in the after-tax returns. The Deficit Reduction Act of 1984 requires that preferred stocks acquired after the date of the law's enactment be held at least 46 days (increased from 16 days under previous regulations) in order for a corporation to take the dividends received deduction. Taxable corporations, whether large or small, should consider these instruments as part of their intermediate term (three to five years) portfolio. Because only 15 percent of the dividend is subject to income taxes, corporations in a 46 percent marginal tax bracket will be able to keep 93.1 percent of the income

[7] All preferred dividends of industrial and finance companies, railroads, banks, utility holding companies, and many operating utility companies are eligible for the 85 percent dividends received deduction. For operating utilities, this deduction applies to "new money" preferred stocks, i.e. those issues offered on and after October 1, 1942, for purposes other than that of refunding. Preferreds issued prior to that date, and those issued after that date for purposes of refunding bonds, debentures, or other preferred issues prior to October 1, 1942, are "old money" issues that qualify only for a 60.208 percent dividends received deduction. The taxable portion of the dividend is 39.792 percent. All of the ARPS are "new money" issues.

generated from a preferred stock investment. Investors in lower marginal tax brackets may retain an even larger amount of the dividends.

Below are the formulae used in computing the current yield, after-tax yield, and the pretax or taxable equivalent yield.

$$\text{Current yield} = \frac{\text{Dollar amount of dividend}}{\text{Price of the preferred stock}}$$

$$\text{After-tax yield} = \text{Current yield} \times [1 - (\text{Marginal tax rate} \times DT)]$$

where DT = percent of dividend subject to income tax.

$$\text{Pretax or taxable equivalent yield} = \frac{\text{After-tax yield}}{(1 - \text{Marginal tax rate})}$$

The pretax or taxable equivalent yield indicates the yield that is necessary before taxes on an alternative investment in order to match the preferred stock's after-tax yield.

Preferred stock "C" from Table 3–2 will be used to illustrate the application of these formulae. Preferred stock "C", on an adjusted basis, is selling at $70.06 a share, has a dividend rate of 9.85 percent, and an annual dividend of $9.85. Assume that the investor is a corporate investor subject to a 46 percent marginal tax rate, and that only 15 percent of the dividends are subject to income tax. The three yields are computed as follows:

$$\text{Current yield} = \frac{\$9.85}{\$70.06}$$

$$= .1406 = 14.06\%$$

$$\text{After-tax yield} = .1406 \, [1 - (.46 \times .15)]$$

$$= .1406 \, [1 - .069]$$

$$= .1406 \times .931$$

$$= .1309 = 13.09\%$$

$$\text{Pretax equivalent yield} = \frac{.1309}{1 - .46}$$

$$= \frac{.1309}{.54}$$

$$= .2424 = 24.24\%$$

Thus, the current yield on the adjusted or reset basis is 14.06 percent. After taxes, a corporate investor in the 46 percent marginal tax bracket gets a return of 13.09 percent. For this investor to match the preferred stock's after-tax yield of 13.09 percent, a fully taxable investment yielding 24.24 percent would be necessary.

Table 3–3 shows the pretax equivalent yields, the preferred stock yields, and the fully taxable yields for dividend rates from 5 percent to 15 percent at 50 basis point increments. Again, a preferred stock with a 13 percent current yield provides a 12.1 percent after-tax yield to an investor in the 46 percent tax bracket, and a 12.22 percent yield to an investor with a 40 percent marginal tax rate. To match these yields, the investor would have to obtain a pretax yield of 22.41 percent in the 46 percent bracket or 20.37 percent in the 40 percent bracket. On the other hand, an investment in a fully taxable instrument yielding 13 percent pretax would only provide after-tax yields of 7.02 percent and 7.8 percent for the 46 percent and 40 percent tax rate investor.

VARIATIONS OF ADJUSTABLE RATE PREFERRED STOCKS

While the bulk of this chapter concerns straight run-of-the-mill ARPS, a few words should be stated about the other types of issues, those with "wrinkles" or out-of-the-ordinary variable rate preferred stocks. Most have features designed to minimize price fluctuations and loss of principal by allowing the stock to trade around the initial offering price under normal market conditions.

Treasury Indexed Preferred Stock (TIPS)

Banco de Ponce, a Puerto Rican banking corporation sold a small ($10 million) issue in June 1984 having the quarterly dividend rate tied to the higher of (1) 115 percent of the six-month Treasury bill bond equivalent rate or (2) 85 percent of the five-year Treasury constant maturity rate. The notice of this quarterly rate is to be published in a newspaper of general circulation in San Juan, Puerto Rico. The issue was structured for investment by corporations that could take advantage of the 85 percent dividend credit under the

TABLE 3–3
Comparison of Preferred Stock and Other Yields for a Corporate Investor*

zero	Preferred Stock Yields (%) Marginal Income Tax Rate			Pre-tax Yield Needed to Equal After-Tax Return on Preferreds (%) Marginal Income Tax Rate			Fully Taxable Alternative Investment Yields (%) Marginal Income Tax Rate		
	40%	46%	50%	40%	46%	50%	40%	46%	50%
5.00	4.70	4.66	4.63	7.83	8.63	9.26	3.00	2.70	2.50
5.50	5.17	5.12	5.09	8.62	9.48	10.18	3.30	2.97	2.75
6.00	5.64	5.59	5.55	9.40	10.35	11.10	3.60	3.24	3.00
6.50	6.11	6.05	6.01	10.18	11.20	12.02	3.90	3.51	3.25
7.00	6.58	6.52	6.48	10.97	12.07	12.96	4.20	3.78	3.50
7.50	7.05	6.98	6.94	11.75	12.93	13.88	4.50	4.05	3.75
8.00	7.52	7.45	7.40	12.53	13.80	14.80	4.80	4.32	4.00
8.50	7.99	7.91	7.86	13.32	14.65	15.72	5.10	4.59	4.25
9.00	8.46	8.38	8.33	14.10	15.52	16.66	5.40	4.86	4.50
9.50	8.93	8.84	8.79	14.88	16.37	17.58	5.70	5.13	4.75
10.00	9.40	9.31	9.25	15.67	17.24	18.50	6.00	5.40	5.00
10.50	9.87	9.78	9.72	16.45	18.11	19.44	6.30	5.67	5.25
11.00	10.34	10.24	10.18	17.23	18.96	20.36	6.60	5.94	5.50
11.50	10.81	10.71	10.64	18.02	19.83	21.28	6.90	6.21	5.75
12.00	11.28	11.17	11.10	18.80	20.69	22.20	7.20	6.48	6.00
12.50	11.75	11.64	11.56	19.58	21.56	23.12	7.50	6.75	6.25
13.00	12.22	12.10	12.03	20.37	22.41	24.06	7.80	7.02	6.50
13.50	12.69	12.57	12.49	21.15	23.28	24.98	8.10	7.29	6.75
14.00	13.16	13.03	12.95	21.93	24.13	25.90	8.40	7.56	7.00
14.50	13.63	13.50	13.41	22.72	25.00	26.82	8.70	7.83	7.25
15.00	14.10	13.97	13.87	23.50	25.87	27.74	9.00	8.10	7.50

*Assumes only 15 percent of the dividend is subject to income tax.

Income Tax Act of Puerto Rico and those corporations having elected "possessions" corporation status under the United States Internal Revenue Code.

Price Adjusted Rate Preferred Stock (PARS)

PARS, which sounds better than PARPS, implies stability around the par level. Only one issue has been marketed, Citicorp's Fourth Series of preferred stock offered in February 1984 at $100 per share. The dividend rate for the initial period ending March 31, 1984 was 8 percent. This is equal to 86.5 percent (applicable percentage) of the bond equivalent yield of the three-month U.S. Treasury bill secondary market discount rate immediately prior to the February 2, 1984 offering. The dividend rate for subsequent periods is the product of the index rate and the applicable percentage. The index rate is the arithmetic average (expressed on a bond equivalent basis) of the two-weekly-per-annum secondary market discount rates for three-month Treasury bills as published during the interest determination period. The applicable percentage is the product of the applicable percentage and the market price adjustment ratio for the immediately preceding dividend period. The price ratio is obtained by dividing $100 by the average market price of the preferred stock for the last five trading days of the dividend determination period. This market price adjustment increases the dividend rate if the stock trades below par, and decreases the dividend if it trades above par.

Multiple Adjustable Rate Preferred Stock (MARS)

Huntington Bancshares, the only issuer of MARS, sold 500,000 shares at $50 each on April 8, 1983. The determination of the base dividend rate is the same as that of the mundane ARPS (50 basis point discount from the highest of the three benchmark rates) except that it is adjusted upwards by 1 percent if the market price of the stock during the specified period immediately preceding the dividend period is less than $45 per share. If the stock trades above $55 per share, the dividend would be decreased by 1 percent. If the average market price is between $45 and $55 then the adjustment factor is the same as in the immediately preceding dividend period. The adjustment factor has not been applied to the dividend because the stock has traded within the $45 to $55 range since it was first issued.

Controlled Adjustable Rate Preferred Stock (CARPS)

This name has been given by Standard & Poor's Corporation to adjustable rate preferred stock issued by special purpose subsidiaries of savings institutions. These subsidiaries have as their main purpose the issuance of adjustable rate preferred stock and the management of pledged assets such as Government National Mortgage Association fully modified pass-through mortgage-backed certificates, Federal Home Loan Mortgage Corporation mortgage participation certificates, Federal National Mortgage Association mortgage pass-through certificates, U.S. Treasury securities, and short-term money market instruments. The assets are valued monthly and the asset coverage for each share of preferred stock must be at least equal to the liquidation price of the preferred stock. If the required asset coverage is deficient, then the issuer must acquire additional required assets, purchase stock in the open market, or redeem stock so as to restore the asset coverage to the proper level. The high quality of the assets and the structure of the corporations and the preferred stocks provide for prime ratings and thus enable the subsidiaries to raise capital at advantageous rates. In other respects the terms of these preferred stocks and regular ARPS are similar.

Adjustable Rate Convertible Preferred Stock and Convertible Adjustable Preferred Stock (ARCPS and CAPS)

The adjustable preferred market has two types of ARPS with similar names—adjustable rate convertible preferred stock and convertible adjustable preferred stock—and similar dividend determination features, but with different conversion terms. The former has more appeal to the normal buyer of convertible securities while the latter is of interest to the ARPS investor.

The adjustable rate convertible preferred stock is the same as other normal convertible preferred stocks except that the dividend fluctuates with changes in the level of interest rates. The stock is convertible into a fixed number of common shares (subject to antidilution provisions) at a fixed price and is an alternative to a direct investment in the company's common stock. The market price of the preferred stock is more affected on the up side by the price performance of the underlying common shares. For example, American General Corporation issued a regular ARPS and an adjustable rate convertible issue at the same time when it acquired NLT Corporation in 1982. The regular dividend of the ARPS was set at the benchmark rate (no premium or discount) and the convertible stock's dividend was set at 75 basis points below the benchmark rate. The convertible stock can be exchanged for 2.6787 common shares. In 1983, when the common stock reached a price of $26.25, the convertible preferred stock sold for about $71.50. The high price for the regular ARPS for 1983 was $58.75. The low price for the common stock in 1983 was $18.25, the convertible stock $54, and the straight ARPS $50.125.

Convertible adjustable preferred stock is convertible at the holder's option on any quarterly dividend payment date into a *fixed dollar amount* of common stock (usually $50 worth) subject to a maximum number of shares per preferred share issued. This type of convertible preferred stock is *not* an alternative way to invest in the common equity of a company as it does not participate in the price movements of the underlying common stock. The corporation has the right to pay cash in lieu of issuing common shares. If it pays cash for less than all shares tendered, then the payment must be made on a pro rata basis. The issuers have the right to change the maximum number of shares that may be issued upon conversion. The conversion feature thus provides a floor to the risk an investor assumes with adjustable rate preferred stocks. Of course, if the common stock price declines to a point where the conversion worth is less than $50, and the company does not increase the maximum number of shares for conversion, the floor disappears and the necessary support is gone. The new support areas would be the higher of the new conversion worth or the level where straight ARPS with comparable dividend reset rates and collars trade.

How has this conversion privilege worked in practice? Of the eight issues outstanding in mid-1985, only one issuer, AMF Incorporated, had holders exercise the conversion option. On November 22, 1983 AMF offered 700,000 shares of convertible adjustable preference stock at $50 per share with settlement for November 30. The net proceeds to the company after expenses is estimated at $48.08 per share. The shares are convertible into $50 market value of common subject to a maximum of 6.15 shares. The initial dividend rate was 9.25 percent and the dividend reset spread was minus 280 basis points. The shares were listed on the New York Stock Exchange at the beginning of 1984, but volume was nil in the week ending January 6 (the conversion period). In the author's opinion, the shares had been placed in weak hands; that is, with investors who did not want to hold the stock as a longer term investment. The conversion feature provided an excellent way to dispose of a large number of shares without any loss, especially in view of the thin market for the stock. On January 14, a little more than 6 weeks after settlement of the new offering, holders of 274,300 shares (39.2 percent of the original 700,000 shares) tendered their stock, and AMF exercised its option to purchase the shares for cash. This turned out to be an expensive proposition for the company. After all, just a month and a half earlier it had received (after underwriting discounts, commissions, and estimated expenses) $48.08 a share. AMF paid out $50 per share *plus* the initial 59 cent dividend.

MARKET REVIEW

The first four ARPS issued in May, 1982 were well received in the marketplace, especially in view of the novelty of the security. The dividend reset rate was plus 50 basis points over the base rate for double-A issues, and plus 75 basis points for the single-A name. They soon rose to 3 or 4 point premiums above the initial offering prices when the next batch of issues began to enter the market in late July. Dividend reset spreads were reduced for high grade names to the range of minus 35 basis points to minus 100 basis points between July 22 and October 15. Dividend reset spreads then dropped to minus 200 basis points with the October 22 offering of BankAmerica Corporation Series "A" stock, and minus 225 basis points with Irving Bank's November 18 sale. Investor demand was broad enough to accept medium grade issues, with 10 stocks selling between August and mid-December. Again, demand was such that the reset spreads on these issues were substantially below Republic New York Corporation's Series "A" sold in May at plus 75 basis points.

At the start of 1983, the market appeared to be in good shape with substantial investor demand. The price index of seven issues closed at 116.36 percent of par on December 31, 1982, and rose to a high of 122.29 percent of par on February 11, 1983. This proved to be the all-time high and a turning point in the market. Enthusiasm quickly cooled when 13 issues with a par value of $1.8 billion were rushed to the offering table. Reset rates went to even larger discounts—minus 300 basis points, minus 400 basis points, and minus 412.5 basis points on the high grades—down 450 basis points, down 487.5 basis points on the prime names. Medium grade issuers also benefitted from the trend with resets between minus 250 basis points and minus 275 basis points. Collars were also reduced to as low as J.P. Morgan's 5 percent to 11 percent range. Some issues also had less call protection, declining to three years from the general five years. But some sweeteners were added in the form of a longer initial dividend rate period. In other cases the initial dividend rate was extended nine months to a year after the offering date. This was in addition to a rate that was higher than it would have been if it had been determined solely on the basis of the reset rate and the base rate in effect at the time of the initial offering.

From the February high, the index closed the end of March at 110.14. The J.P. Morgan issue with a reset spread of minus 487.5 basis points, initially offered at $100 on February 23, 1983, found few takers at that price; much of the stock was finally sold by the underwriters at much lower prices. Trades took place at $75 and somewhat lower. After the so-called "February Massacre," high grade and prime issuers withdrew from the market. New issue activity declined, and medium grade and non-investment grade names had the primary market to themselves as reset rates reversed the trend and approached or rose above the base rate. While this market action unnerved some investors, others felt that it presented opportunities. Prices had adjusted to create an effective narrowing of the reset spread at the current market levels. For the balance of the year, new issue supply met the demand and the market did not suffer from congestion. Initial pricing became more realistic. Some gimmicks or new variations in the terms of the issues were tried, the most successful being the convertible adjustable rate preferred stock. The price index closed at 109.61 on December 31, 1983.

In 1984 the second major decline occurred. In the first part of the year the market rose moderately to 113.39 on May 18. This time new issue pricing and market congestion were not the culprits; there were three other causes that converged about the same time:

- Rising interest rates brought a general malaise to all sectors of the senior securities markets, with investors and dealers lowering their bids and reducing positions. It was not the time to assume an aggressive market stance and play the role of a hero. Higher interest rates created additional pressure on ARPS with low dividend ceilings or caps, as the maximum dividend rates for a number of issues started to become effective in mid-May.

- For many months corporate investors had concerns about proposed changes in the tax law and the effect on preferred stock investment. Some investors postponed purchases, further weakening the market. Many viewed changes in the Tax Reform Act of 1984 as having no significant market impact.

- Probably of greatest influence on investor psychology were the ripples (more like a tidal wave!) caused by the problems at the Continental Illinois Corporation and the Latin American loan situation. Large money center bank holding company issues suffered the greatest declines, in general, although almost all issues were impacted. Some ARPS issues declined even more than the common equity.

The price index dropped to 95.32 percent of par in a seven-week period before investors, overcoming their many fears, stepped in. Prices quickly rebounded, though not to the former levels. At the end of July the index stood at 103.21.

As long as there are no major changes in the taxation of intercorporate dividends, the market for ARPS is expected to expand. Investors have learned that, while the income from these instruments is somewhat insulated from changes in interest rates, the stocks are still subject to the forces of the market, rational or not. It is likely that more issues will be designed so as to reduce or limit the effects of the markets. The convertible adjustable rate preferred stock is one of these new concepts.

CHAPTER 4

MONEY MARKET PREFERRED* STOCK

Richard S. Wilson
Vice President
Merrill Lynch Capital Markets

In 1984, the designers of financial instruments developed a new variety of variable rate preferred stock—the Money Market Preferred (MMP), Short Term Auction Rate (STAR), Preferred or Dutch Auction Rate Transferable Securities (DARTS)[1] —for corporate money managers. The instrument is not for the small or unsophisticated investor as the shares are priced from $100,000 to $500,000 each. The manager of "temporarily" idle corporate funds, however, might well find this an attractive alternative to money market instruments and other types of preferred stocks. The dividends, payable every seven weeks, are determined by bids from current holders and potential buyers and should be reflective of the money markets at the time of the bidding auction. Dividends on other adjustable rate preferreds are determined quarterly. The more frequent dividend setting mechanism, as it is not set on any predetermined spread from a base rate, will allow the dividends (subject

---

*Money Market Preferred and MMP are trademarks of Shearson Lehman/American Express Inc.

[1] Dutch Auction Rate Transferable Securities and DARTS are trademarks of Salomon Brothers Inc.

to certain maximum rates) to be based on the current credit perceptions of the issuer. All purchases and sales conducted through the
auction process are at the liquidation value, so far either $100,000
or $500,000 per share.

In this chapter we will look at how the dividends are determined
through the auction process, how the shares are transferred, and
make a general review of the issues. However, investors would be
well advised to refer to the original prospectuses for further information, as there are some minor differences between issues.

THE CURRENT MARKET

As of June 1985, 24 issues have been offered by 14 companies. The
outstanding shares total only 8,650, but the funds raised (before
underwriting discounts, commissions, and expenses) equal
$1,825,000,000. The first issue, offered in two series on August 27,
1984, raised $150,000,000. In the first three weeks of November
another five offerings raised $400,000,000. Table 4–1 summarizes
the issues.

Investors apparently like the maintenance of the value of the
stock at the issue price although it comes at a cost. If these offerings
were conventional adjustable rate preferreds the dividend would be
200 to 300 basis points more. But then, MMP shares are for the
temporary investment of corporate cash while a longer term view
should be taken of ARPS. Table 4–2 (pp. 82–83) compares the dividend rate on money market preferreds with various alternate investments at the date of offering. The MMP investor comes out ahead of
fully taxable investors in the other securities. Of course, it should be
mentioned that MMP is a perpetual equity security ranking lower
in the capitalization order than commercial paper.

Table 4–3 (p. 84) compares the preferred stock yields, the pretax
equivalent yield, and the fully taxable yields for dividend rates from
5 percent to 15 percent in 50 basis point increments. We show the
effect of the current 46 percent marginal tax rate and include a 33
percent tax rate which has been mentioned as a possible future
corporate rate. Although we do not know how intercorporate dividends might be treated in any future tax legislation, this table

TABLE 4-1
Selected Data on Money Market Preferreds

Issue Date	Ratings M	Ratings S&P	No. of Shares	Gross Proceeds ($ Million)	Issuer	Initial Offering Price	Initial Dividend Rate	Dividend Rate at 6/30/85
8/27/84	aa3	AA–	150	75	American Express "A"	$500,000	9.00%	5.61%
8/27/84	aa3	AA–	150	75	American Express"B"	500,000	9.00	5.40
11/2/84	baa3	BBB	150	75	United States Steel "A"	500,000	9.00	8.00
11/8/84	aaa	AAA	150	75	City Capital Funding	500,000	8.00	6.88
11/13/84	a1	AA	1000	100	Lincoln National Corp. "B"	100,000	8.00	5.84
11/19/84	aa3	AA–	150	75	American Express "C"	500,000	7.15	5.60
11/21/84	aaa	AAA	150	75	Coast Credit Corp.	500,000	7.875	6.75
1/24/85	aaa	AA	125	62.5	United States Steel"S-A"	500,000	6.50	5.75
1/24/85	aaa	AA	125	62.5	United States Steel "S-B"	500,000	6.50	6.02
2/13/85	aa3	AA–	150	75	American Express "D"	500,000	6.00	5.248
2/22/85	aaa	AAA	150	75	Glenfed Finance	500,000	6.75	6.38
3/27/85	aaa	AAA	750	75	Goldome Florida Funding	100,000	6.25	8.444
4/18/85	aaa	AAA	1000	100	First Nationwide Capital	100,000	6.30	6.90
4/18/85	aaa	AA	125	62.5	United States Steel "S-C"	500,000	6.00	5.85
5/08/85	aaa	AAA	150	75	Glenfed Finance II	500,000	6.55	6.55
5/17/85	aaa	AAA	750	75	Dollar Finance	100,000	6.375	6.375
6/05/85	a2	A–	750	75	Transamerica Corp.	100,000	5.75	5.75
6/07/85	aa1	A+	200	100	Citicorp "5A"	500,000	5.50	5.50
6/07/85	aa1	A+	200	100	Citicorp "5B"	500,000	5.50	5.50
6/07/85	aaa	AA	125	62.5	United States Steel "S-D"	500,000	5.75	5.75
6/26/85	a1	AA–	500	50	Lincoln National Corp. "C"	100,000	6.25	6.25
6/26/85	a1	AA–	500	50	Lincoln National Corp. "D"	100,000	6.25	6.25
6/27/85	aaa	NR	400	100	AMCAP Corporation	250,000	6.90	6.90
6/27/85	aaa	AAA	750	75	USAT Finance	100,000	7.25	7.25

assumes that the 85 percent dividends received deduction will remain.

REDEMPTION FEATURES

All of the shares are currently redeemable at the option of the issuer, in whole or in part on any dividend payment date, at 103 percent of the offering price for the first year, 102 percent for the second year, 101 percent for the third year, and at 100 percent thereafter. These premiums are in line with regular adjustable rate preferred stock (ARPS) but, as there is expected to be less incentive for refunding MMP than ARPS, the deferred call period has been abandoned.[2] However, the issuer does have an out in the event that the dividend rate reaches certain levels. If the dividend rate is equal to or exceeds the AA commercial paper rate, the MMP may be redeemed in whole at 100 percent on any dividend payment date. Notice of redemption must be given at least 30 days and not more than 45/60 days prior to the redemption date. Several issues of thrift institutions also have provisions for mandatory redemption in the event the minimum asset coverage test is not satisfied, or if the distributions made in any calendar year exceed the current and accumulated earnings and profits of the company for Federal income tax purposes.

STOCK CERTIFICATES, SECURITIES DEPOSITORY, SETTLEMENT

All existing holders and prospective purchasers of MMP have to sign a *Purchaser's Letter* which states, among other things, that as long as the dividends are determined by auction, the ownership of the shares will be maintained in book entry form by a securities depository and no certificates will be issued. Currently, the Depository Trust Company is such a depository and Cede & Co. is its nominee and the holder of record of such shares. Cede & Co. will maintain records of the beneficial owners. Settlement of purchases

[2] ARPS are discussed in Chapter 7.

TABLE 4–2
Comparison of Money Market Preferred Yields at Issuance with Other Instruments

Issue Date	Dividend Rate (%)	After Tax Return/46% Marginal Rate	Pretax Return Needed to Equal After Tax Preferred Return	60–Day Commercial Paper Rate (Pretax) (%)
08/27/84	9.000	8.38	15.52	11.44
11/02/84	9.000	8.38	15.52	9.62
11/08/84	8.000	7.45	13.79	9.28
11/13/84	8.000	7.45	13.79	9.24
11/19/84	7.150	6.66	12.33	9.29
11/21/84	7.875	7.33	13.58	9.12
1/24/85	6.500	6.05	11.21	8.01
2/13/85	6.000	5.59	10.34	8.75
2/22/85	6.750	6.28	11.64	8.69
3/27/85	6.250	5.82	10.78	8.83
4/18/85	6.300	5.87	10.86	8.36
4/18/85	6.000	5.59	10.34	8.36

Note: The 60–day commercial paper rate is the certificate of deposit equivalent yield for commercial paper of corporate issuers whose bonds are rated AA. This rate is released by the Federal Reserve Bank of New York.

The 60– to 89–day municipal commercial paper rate is the certificate of deposit equivalent yield. This rate is released by the Merrill Lynch Tax Exempt Money Markets Department.

and sales of shares will be made on the first business day following the dividend auction through the securities depository. In the case when the dividend is not determined at auction, the beneficial owner may obtain a certificate for his shares.

DIVIDENDS

Dividends, payable at every seven weeks, are determined by a Dutch auction process held on the first business day prior to the

TABLE 4–2—*Continued*
**Comparison of Money Market Preferred Yields at Issuance
with Other Instruments**

60 -Day Commercial Paper Rate (after tax) (%)	60- to 89-Day $A - 1 + /P - 1$ Municipal Commercial Paper (%)	MMP After Tax Dividend as % of Pretax Commercial Paper Rate	MMP After Tax Dividend % of After Tax Commercial Paper Rate	MMP After Tax Dividend % of Muni Commercial Paper Rate
6.18	6.80	73.22%	135.59%	123.22%
5.20	5.50	87.08	161.26	152.35
5.01	5.63	80.25	148.61	132.41
4.99	5.63	80.61	149.27	132.41
5.02	5.80	71.64	132.66	114.77
4.92	5.90	80.43	148.94	124.26
4.32	4.63	75.60	139.99	130.84
4.72	4.75	63.87	118.28	117.60
4.69	4.50	72.28	133.86	139.65
4.77	5.05	65.91	122.06	115.22
4.51	5.13	70.16	129.92	114.44
4.51	5.13	66.82	123.74	109.00

start of a dividend period. The current dividend period is set at 49 days in order to comply with the 46-day holding period requirement, under which a corporate stockholder is entitled to take the 85 percent dividends received deduction. If the dividend payment date is not a business day then it will be paid on the next business day with the payment date reverting to the original schedule for the next payment date. If the law changes the minimum holding period the issuer may change the dividend period to equal or exceed (but not by more than nine days) the new holding requirement, provided that the new period will not be longer than 98 days. Any new dividend period must be evenly divisible by seven.

The amount of the dividend for each period is obtained as follows:

$$\frac{\text{Number of days in dividend period}}{360} \times \text{Dividend rate} \times \text{Share price}$$

TABLE 4–3
Comparison of Preferred Stock and Other Yields

Preferred Stock Yields			Pretax Yield Needed to Equal After-Tax Return on Preferreds		Fully Taxable Alternative Investment Yields	
Zero%	33%	46%	33%	46%	33%	46%
5.00	4.75	4.66	6.96	8.63	3.35	2.70
5.50	5.23	5.12	7.64	9.48	3.69	2.97
6.00	5.70	5.59	8.34	10.35	4.02	3.24
6.50	6.18	6.05	9.03	11.20	4.36	3.51
7.00	6.65	6.52	9.73	12.07	4.69	3.78
7.50	7.13	6.98	10.42	12.93	5.03	4.05
8.00	7.60	7.45	11.12	13.80	5.36	4.32
8.50	8.08	7.91	11.81	14.65	5.70	4.59
9.00	8.55	8.38	12.51	15.52	6.03	4.86
9.50	9.03	8.84	13.19	16.37	6.37	5.13
10.00	9.51	9.31	13.90	17.24	6.70	5.40
10.50	9.98	9.78	14.50	18.11	7.04	5.67
11.00	10.46	10.24	15.28	18.96	7.37	5.94
11.50	10.93	10.71	15.96	19.83	7.71	6.21
12.00	11.41	11.17	16.67	20.69	8.04	6.48
12.50	11.88	11.64	17.37	21.56	8.38	6.75
13.00	12.37	12.10	18.06	22.41	8.71	7.02
13.50	12.83	12.57	18.76	23.28	9.05	7.29
14.00	13.31	13.03	19.45	24.13	9.38	7.56
14.50	13.78	13.50	20.15	25.00	9.72	7.83
15.00	14.26	13.97	20.85	25.87	10.05	8.10

If the issuer does not pay the full amount of the dividend and/or the redemption price on time to the dividend paying agent, the auctions will then be discontinued and the applicable rate will be equal to LIBOR plus a premium.

Not all issues have this type of provision. For example, on each dividend payment date, City Capital is required to deposit with the dividend paying agent and to maintain on deposit until the next dividend payment date sufficient cash and/or short-term securities to pay the dividends that will accrue on the stock during that period.

Coast Credit has a dividend coverage provision that requires the company to value, as of each evaluation date (each dividend payment date and each 25 days preceding the next dividend payment date), its cash and short-term securities maturing within 49 days, in order to ensure that the total value is at least equal to the amount of 49 days of dividends at the current applicable rate. Several of the issues are backed by standby obligations of major insurance companies under which a specially organized standby company is obligated to purchase the shares if certain events occur. These include the issuer's failure to pay the dividend, honor a share redemption, or if the Dutch auction fails due to the expiration of the surety bonds.

The maximum dividends are of the floating variety, not fixed as with ARPS. That is, they are based on a percentage of the AA composite commercial paper rate. This rate is the interest yield equivalent of the 60-day rate on commercial paper issued by corporations whose bond ratings are AA or equivalent. It is made available by the Federal Reserve Bank of New York on a discount basis. Provisions are included in the terms of the preferred for alternate commercial paper rates if the Federal Reserve Bank does not make such a rate available. Also, if the dividend period is increased, the commercial paper rate definition will be changed to reflect the longer dividend period.

AUCTION PROCEDURES

The auction for the determination of the dividend takes place on the first business day prior to the start of a dividend period. Each existing holder or prospective purchaser must sign a Purchaser's Letter which requires the signer to abide by the procedures set forth in the prospectus. The issuer will have entered into an agreement with a trust company (currently Manufacturers Hanover Trust Company) which will run the auction and determine the applicable dividend rate, among other things. The three types of orders that may be entered are:

- **Hold order** The number of shares that an existing holder wishes to continue to hold *without regard* to the applicable rate for the next dividend period.

- **Bid** The number of shares that an existing holder wishes to continue to hold provided that the applicable rate for the next dividend period is not less than the rate specified by the holder. Also, an order by a potential holder willing to purchase shares at a dividend rate not less than that specified or by an existing holder who wishes to purchase additional shares.

- **Sell order** The number of shares that an existing holder wishes to sell without regard to the applicable rate for the next dividend period.

On or prior to the auction date the existing holders will submit their hold orders, bids, and sell orders to a broker-dealer who will, in turn, submit them to the trust company prior to 1:00 P.M. New York City time on each auction date. Prospective holders may also submit their bids through broker-dealers at that time.

Bids are subject to certain conditions. Any bid by an existing holder with a rate higher than the maximum rate allowed will be treated as a sell order and any similar bid by a potential holder will not be accepted. All bids with rates above that determined by the auction and all sell orders by existing holders constitute irrevocable offers to sell. A bid by a potential holder is an irrevocable offer to purchase shares. The number of shares purchased or sold may be subject to proration procedures. If an existing holder does not submit any order then the trust company will deem that a hold order has been entered on behalf of the holder.

The trust company will assemble all orders and determine if sufficient clearing bids have been made (i.e., if the number of shares of MMP that are the subject of submitted bids by potential holders equals or exceeds the number of shares that are the subject of submitted sell orders). For example, if 75 shares are subject to bids and 25 shares are the subject of sell orders, then clearing bids exist. If submitted clearing bids have been made then the winning bid rate will be determined and will become the applicable rate for the next dividend period. The winning bid rate is the lowest rate which would result in existing holders continuing to hold stock which, when added to shares to be purchased by potential holders, equals the available money market preferred (the number of shares of stock not subject to hold orders). Thus, if hold orders amount to 25 shares with 100 shares outstanding, available shares will be 75.

To illustrate the auction process, consider the following:

Existing Holders	No. of Shares	Order
Bidder		
#1	25	Hold
2	25	Continue to hold if new rate is at least 8%
3	25	Continue to hold if new rate is at least 8.20%
4	15	Continue to hold if new rate is at least 8.35%
5	10	Sell

Potential Holders	No. of Shares	Order
Bidder		
#6	10	Buy if new rate is at least 8%
7	25	Buy if new rate is at least 8.10%
8	30	Buy if new rate is at least 8.25%
9	25	Buy if new rate is at least 8.35%
10	20	Buy if new rate is at least 8.40%

100 shares outstanding less 25 shares subject to hold orders equals 75 shares that are available. There are bids for 110 shares which exceeds the 10 shares subject to a sell order; thus there are sufficient clearing bids. The winning bid is 8.20 percent (and the dividend rate for the next dividend period) because at the next lowest bid of 8.10 percent only 60 shares would continue to be held or purchased and that is less than the available MMP of 75 shares. Bidder no. four sells his 15 shares as his bid of 8.35 percent was greater than the winning bid and bidder no. 5 sells his 10 shares as he was a seller at any rate.

Bidder #1 continues to hold 25 shares	
#2 continues to hold 25 shares	(bids were below
#6 buys 10 shares	the winning bid
#7 buys 25 shares	of 8.20%)

At this point only 15 MMP shares are available (75 initially available less the 60 shares purchased). Therefore, bidder no. 3 continues to hold 15 shares and must sell 10 shares as the winning bid rate was equal to his bid of 8.20 percent.

At settlement on the day after the auction the following transactions take place:

Bidder #3 sells 10 shares	Bidder #6 buys 10 shares
#4 sells 15 shares	#7 buys 25 shares
#5 sells 10 shares	
Total 35 shares sold	Total 35 shares purchased

After settlement the ownership of the shares will be as follows:

Bidder #1 holds 25 shares
#2 holds 25 shares
#3 holds 15 shares
#4 holds 0 shares
#5 holds 0 shares
#6 holds 10 shares
#7 holds 25 shares
Total 100 shares held

If sufficient clearing bids exist (as in the above example) the applicable rate for the next dividend period is equal to the winning bid. If sufficient clearing bids do not exist (other than due to all outstanding shares being subject to hold orders) the applicable rate will be equal to the maximum rate. This is a *failed* auction. If all of the shares are the subject of hold orders, the applicable rate for the next dividend period will be the minimum rate.

Under the auction procedures there are instances when a holder wanting to sell stock might not be able to sell any or all of his shares. This could occur when there are not bids for a sufficient amount of shares.

SUMMARY

The Money Market Preferred Stock has earned its place among preferred stock market participants. While the instrument is somewhat more complicated than regular adjustable rate preferreds, it offers some advantages not held by ARPS including minimal fluctuation of principal value (at least to date) and, in some cases, a backup or standby commitment by a third party insurance company. However, these advantages come at a cost, namely reduced yield compared with other types of preferred stock. Each investor must weigh the needs of his portfolio against the risks and rewards of MMPs compared to other financial instruments.

CHAPTER 5

EURODOLLAR FLOATING RATE NOTES

Sarah Allen
International Fixed Income Analyst
Fixed Income Research
Merrill Lynch Capital Markets
(London)

and

Lizabeth L. Palumbo, C.F.A.
Vice President
Fixed Income Research
Merrill Lynch Capital Markets
(New York)

INTRODUCTION

The purpose of this chapter is to discuss the structure and operation of the Eurodollar floating rate note market. The chapter sequentially defines the instrument and size of the market; describes the terms of the instrument accompanied by a comparison to the U.S. domestic floating rate note market; discusses the price behavior on the primary and secondary markets; compares the rates of return on money and capital market instruments; and, finally, considers strategies to improve portfolio returns.

90

During the 1970s and 1980s, large and unpredictable shifts in interest rates encouraged borrowers and lenders alike to minimize the accompanying risk exposure, providing an optimal arena for the development of the Eurodollar floating rate note market. As lenders relaxed their short-term maturity preferences when provided variable coupons, banks, with continual and large demands for funds, increasingly utilized variable rate instruments in their liability management. Further acceleration of growth came with the entrance of sovereign and state entities, prompted by borrowing costs competitive to alternative funding vehicles.

Similarly, on the U.S. domestic market variable rate and/or short-term instruments took hold. However, in contrast to the Eurodollar market, the floating rate note sector did not show parallel growth, as alternative funding sources and lack of homogeneity discouraged borrowers and lenders alike from participating in this market. Recently, U.S. domestic floating rate notes with terms analogous to Eurodollar floating rate instruments have met with favorable response, giving rise to the further development of this market.

Further growth is envisioned as interest rate swaps and other financial developments continue to provide an impetus to this market.

Floating rate notes are short-term to long-term debt instruments that carry a variable rate of interest that, for each interest period, is set in advance at a specified margin with respect to a reference market rate or index.

Floating rate notes issued in the dollar sector of the Eurobond market are referred to as Eurodollar floating rate notes. Accordingly, Eurodollar floating rate notes are U.S. dollar-denominated debt instruments typically underwritten and sold simultaneously in a number of national markets and offshore centers by international syndicates of investment banks. In general, Eurodollar floating rate notes have their coupons fixed at a stated margin over rates in the London interbank market for Eurodollar deposits of a similar interest period.

Eurodollar floating rate notes were first issued in 1970 but became prominent in the second half of the 1970s, when they accounted for 21 percent of all gross Eurodollar bond financings (see

TABLE 5-1
Gross Borrowings

PUBLICLY PLACED BOND MARKET	Amounts in $ Billions											
	1974	1975	1976	1977	1978	1979	1980	1981	1982	1983	1984[1]	Total 1974–1983
Eurodollar Market												
Straight	2.8	4.4	8.1	9.0	4.3	6.1	6.8	12.0	26.2	19.1	28.2	98.8
Floating Rate	.2	.2	1.1	1.7	2.3	3.7	4.4	7.0	11.2	17.9	29.7	49.7
Convertible	.1	.3	.8	.8	.3	.7	2.1	2.2	1.3	7.2	4.0	15.8
Total	3.1	4.9	10.0	11.5	6.9	10.5	13.3	21.2	38.7	44.2	61.9	164.3
Domestic Corporate Market												
Straight	24.1	31.1	25.6	23.7	19.2	22.4	36.7	33.2	39.9	38.3	56.7	294.3
Floating Rate	1.3	–	–	–	.2	2.7	.6	.3	1.1	3.0	10.5[2]	9.2
Convertible	.5	1.5	.9	.5	.4	.7	4.3	4.6	3.2	6.0	4.2	22.6
Foreign (Yankee)	3.5	6.8	10.6	7.7	6.4	4.4	2.7	7.6	6.0	4.5	2.8	60.2
Total	29.4	39.4	37.1	31.9	26.2	30.2	44.3	45.7	50.2	51.8	74.2	386.3

Percent

	1974	1975	1976	1977	1978	1979	1980	1981	1982	1983	1984[1]	Total 1974–1983
Eurodollar Market												
Straight	90	90	81	78	63	58	51	56	68	43	46	60
Floating Rate	7	4	11	15	33	35	33	33	29	40	48	30
Convertible	3	6	8	7	4	7	16	11	3	17	6	10
Total	100	100	100	100	100	100	100	100	100	100	100	100
Domestic Corporate Market												
Straight	83	79	69	74	73	74	83	73	80	74	76	76
Floating Rate	4	–	–	–	1	9	1	–	2	6	14	2
Convertible	1	4	2	2	2	2	10	10	6	11	6	6
Foreign (Yankee)	12	17	29	24	24	15	6	17	12	9	4	16
Total	100	100	100	100	100	100	100	100	100	100	100	100

[1]January through November annualized rate.

[2]Includes foreign (Yankee) totaling $2.8 billion annualized.

Source: Federal Reserve Bulletin, OECD Financial Trends, and Merrill Lynch Capital Markets.

Table 5–1). By 1983, this figure had risen to 40 percent, and for the first 11 months of 1984 floating rate notes accounted for 48 percent of all Eurodollar bond financings, or $27.2 billion of gross borrowings versus $25.8 billion for straight securities.

Floating rate notes issued on the national market of the United States are referred to as U.S. domestic floating rate notes. Accordingly, publicly placed U.S. domestic floating rate notes are U.S. dollar-denominated debt instruments, registered with the Securities and Exchange Commission (SEC), and underwritten and sold primarily, but not exclusively, to U.S. residents by syndicates of investment banks on the national market of the United States. Typically, U.S. domestic floating rate notes have their coupons fixed at a stated premium to a U.S. Treasury index; however, on occasion they have been tied to other short-term money market rates of a similar interest period and, more recently, to the London interbank rate for deposits.

Primary market activity of U.S. domestic floating rate notes varies significantly from year to year and, as shown in Table 5–1, gross borrowings are significantly below that of the larger Eurodollar floating rate market.

TERMS OF EURODOLLAR FLOATING RATE NOTES

The Instrument

The terms on most instruments on the Eurodollar floating rate market are similar, creating a market of like instruments, particularly with regard to the coupon refixing mechanism. Consequently, Eurodollar floating rate notes may be described according to terms shared by the majority of issues, or according to variations or exceptions.

Eurodollar floating rate notes are typically issued in minimum denominations of $1,000, $5,000, $10,000 and, on occasion, $50,000 to $500,000. They vary in the following aspects:

Maturity. At issue, most floating rate notes have a maturity between 5 and 15 years. Recent offerings by some borrowers, typically banks, have been perpetuals.

Reference Market. The London interbank market for Eurodollar deposits is the main reference market for Eurodollar floating rate notes; however, the infrequent so-called Asian dollar floating rate notes are normally indexed to the Singapore interbank deposit market for U.S. dollars. As the interbank market for deposits is perfectly arbitraged, the two markets are effectively one and the same.

Reference Rates. Floating rate note reference rates are typically indexed to the London interbank offered rate for period deposits (LIBOR), the bid (LIBID) or the arithmetic mean (referred to as LIMEAN). Some recent issues have the coupon referenced to, for example, the three-month or six-month interbank rates but have the coupon refixed every month, three months, or, in some instances, every week with payment on a quarterly or semiannual basis.

The reference rate is calculated by averaging the specified deposit rates (rounded to the nearest 1/16 of 1 percent) quoted by the designated banks (usually three) at 11:00 A.M. local time in London two business days prior to the start of the interest period. The determination of the coupon two days prior is meant to coincide with lenders' funding in the interbank market where funds are borrowed for two-day value.

Basic Margin over Reference Rates. Margins of 1/8 of 1 percent to 1/4 of 1 percent were typical, but lower margins of 1/16 of 1 percent or less have recently been the trend. The influential factors determining the margin are the perceived quality of the issuer, the respective margins available on the syndicated loan and revolving underwriting facility (RUF) markets at the time of issue, and market conditions.

Interest Period. Coupons on floating rate notes are generally reset either on a semiannual basis and tied to six-month deposit rates, or on a quarterly basis and tied to three-month deposit rates.

Minimum and Maximum Coupons. Most floating rate notes have a minimum coupon below which the coupon may not be fixed with maximum coupons less frequently specified (referred to as capped). The minimum is typically set at a rate between 5 percent and 10 percent—usually 5 1/4 percent.

Variations of the Instrument

As noted, there are exceptions to these general terms, and although they are few in number, these exceptions do demonstrate the many possibilities available in setting terms on floating rate notes. In this context, it is important to recognize that floating rate notes of similar terms *do* prevail, resulting in a market homogeneous in most respects.

For example, instruments may differ with regard to reference rates and/or basic margins. Basic margins have ranged between less than 1/2 of 1 percent and 2 percent, with some margins variable during the term of the borrowing as established at the time of the offering. Other examples follow.

> The $200 million Kingdom of Denmark Floating Rate Note due August 1999 has the coupon reset weekly at the higher of one-week LIBOR or six-month LIMEAN payable semiannually. This mismatching is designed to provide protection against an inverted yield curve.

> The $250 million World Bank Floating Rate Note due February 1994 has the coupon reset quarterly at 0.35 percent above the money market (360 days) yield of 91-day Treasury bills at the most recent auction preceding the relevant interest period.

> The $100 million Merrill Lynch Overseas Capital N. V. Floating Rate Note due May 1987 has the quarterly coupon set at the higher of 1/8 of 1 percent above three-month LIBOR or a rate specified by the borrower.

Other infrequent variations on floating rate notes include convertible and drop-lock bonds. In both, the interest rate is variable but may be fixed at some point during the borrowing term. With the *convertible* bond, the holder has the option to convert to a fixed rate basis during designated time periods. With the *drop-lock* bond, the interest rate is automatically fixed if stated criteria for fixing are met. Accordingly, these variations may allow for enhanced returns during periods of prolonged declines in interest rates.

Some floating rate note offerings include warrants that entitle the holder to purchase straight debt and, again, if interest rates decline during the exercise period, returns could be enhanced. Others include warrants entitling the holder to subscribe to shares.

Finally, a more recent offering incorporates a long-term sterling conversion option. With the $100 million borrowing by Credit d'Equipement des Petites et Moyennes Enterprises (CEPME) guaranteed by the Republic of France due 1996, the lender is entitled to take repayment in sterling at a rate of L1 = $1.3770 on 20 percent of the principal value on redemptions at specified dates prior to maturity (five, eight, and ten years from offering date) or on 100 percent of the principal value at maturity date. Should the dollar depreciate to the extent that lenders prefer sterling assets, the borrower exchanges a dollar liability for a sterling liability—a favorable exchange should the French franc/sterling rate at minimum move together. The price for this conversion option is reflected in the terms of the coupon fixing (i.e., 1/2 of 1 percent below six-month LIBOR).

Redemption Provisions

The month and year of maturity is set at issue date with the exact day of redemption determined by the rollover of the interest periods during the borrowing term. For example, interest accrues for a given period (typically, six months or three months from the last payment date), but should the interest payment date fall on a non-business day, it is postponed to the next business day, thus extending the number of days in that particular interest period. All subsequent payment dates are adjusted accordingly, and the cumulative effect is reflected in the setting of the redemption date. An exception generally occurs when the payment date falls in the next calendar month, in which case the payment date is set for the last business day of the month.

Maturities of floating rate notes range from five years onwards, seven to twelve years being the norm. Maturities have lengthened of late, as demonstrated in Table 5-2 and illustrated by the $500 million borrowing by the Kingdom of Sweden due 2024 and perpetual borrowings by National Westminster, Banque Paribas, and the Kingdoms of Denmark, Sweden, and Belgium to name a few. Furthermore, the Bank of England allows banks to issue perpetual debt

TABLE 5–2
Redemption[1] Profile Weighted by Amount Borrowed (Percent)

	1977	1978	1979	1980	1981	1982	1983	1984[2]
Less than 5 years	1	2	3	2	8	–	1	2
5–6 years	39	11	10	14	8	20	37	8
7–9 years	55	28	23	39	54	49	20	12
10 years	5	8	20	18	21	11	21	4
Over 10 years	–	51	44	27	9	20	21	74
	100	100	100	100	100	100	100	100

[1]Redemption is the term to first put, if applicable, or maturity date.
[2]January through November.

that counts as primary capital (if prescribed characteristics are attached). This has given rise to several large borrowings of this type by the British clearing banks.

Three recent undated offerings have provided lenders with a conversion feature to a floating rate note with a final maturity referred to as a "flip flop." For example, a $300 million Kingdom of Belgium Floating Rate Note with no maturity date attached to the borrowing and with the coupon refixed at 1/4 of 1 percent over six-month LIBOR entitles the lender to convert the notes from August 1986, and on any August coupon date thereafter, into a four-year floating rate note fixed over LIMEAN. Likewise, holders of the LIMEAN floating rate note can convert back into the undated floating rate note on any August coupon date.

Floating rate notes often contain provisions, referred to as put options, which entitle the holder to redeem the notes at par on a set date(s) prior to maturity. This allows some lenders (e.g., central banks) to meet maturity parameters on assets (e.g., five years). The Kingdom of Denmark $500 million Floating Rate Note, for example, entitles the holder to require early repayment of principal on October 13, 1988 at par.

Mandatory redemption via sinking or purchase funds are sometimes featured in floating rate borrowings. A redemption provision generally available to borrowers occurs when withholding or other taxes are imposed. In this regard, the borrower has the option to call the issue at par or, in some instances, to increase the interest payment so that the net payment after the tax deduction is exactly equal to the previous gross payment.

Optional call by the borrower at par is attached to most offerings, with recent issues typically providing one-year call protection. Table 5–3 lists the floating rate notes redeemed by this provision from 1981 to 1984 and indicates that in general borrowers have infrequently called floating rate notes for early redemption. Typically, borrowers redeem outstanding floating rate notes when the terms on reissue are finer (e.g., the margin over LIBOR is lower) which has occurred frequently of late or when less expensive funding from alternative instruments are available (e.g., revolving underwriting facilities). In other instances, borrowers recourse to early redemption is motivated by changes in the intended use of proceeds and, accordingly, is specific to the borrower.

Capital requirements imposed by regulators may shape the practice of some banks. For example, under French banking regulations, loan capital and deposits of less than two years are not included in calculating the ratio de transformation (capital adequacy ratio) or, similarly, the Bank of England requires United Kingdom banks to reduce capital, with respect to loan capital of five years to maturity, by the straight-line amortization of the principal value. By the systematic exclusion of funds from a bank's capital base, these regulations may effectively increase the cost of funding and may lead borrowers to seek relief by early redemption of outstanding debt.

Other redemption features at the holder's discretion include the extendible, retractable, and putable perpetual. For example, the $250 million Societe Generale Floating Rate Note due March 1995 is retractable to March 1990 and requires holders to exercise the option by March 1985. Those electing not to do so receive an additional flat fee of .375 percent. The latter is exemplified by the $200 million Citicorp Overseas Finance Corporation Limited Quarterly Refixed Floating Rate Note, which has no fixed redemption date but is redeemable at the option of the holder on the October and April interest payment dates commencing two and one-half years from offering date.

TABLE 5-3
Floating Rate Notes Redeemed by Borrower Prior to Maturity

Call Date	Issue-Maturity Dates	Amount	Borrower	Call Price (%)
1984				
11/16	1983–93	$1,200	Kingdom of Sweden	100
10/15	1979–87	50	The Industrial Bank of Japan	100
9/24	1978–85	25	Frab-Bank International	100
9/14	1988	50	Industrial Bank of Japan	100
9/14	1987	50	Industrial Bank of Japan	100
8/16	1980–85	25	Bank of Communications	100
8/14	1979–85	10	Charterhouse Japhet International Finance	100
5/31	1982–86	20	Bank of Helsinki Ltd.	100
5/25	1977–87	50	Midland Bank Ltd.	100
5/23	1980–86	100	BBL International NV	100
5/18	1978–88	25	Gotabanken	100
5/15	1979–89	40	Eurofima	100
5/91	1978–85	45	Credit Commercial de France	100
4/30	1979–91	50	Banco di Roma International	100
1/27	1978–85	40	Banque de L'Indochine et de Suez	100

1983				
12/19	Caisse Nationale de Credit Agricole	50	1977–84	100
11/18	Bank of Tokyo	60	1977–84	100
8/08	Trade Development Financial Services	40	1979–86	100
5/24	Security Pacific Ovs Fin NV	110	1981–88/91	100
4/22	International Westminster Bank	120	1977–84	100
4/22	American Express International Fin Corp NV	40	1978–82/85	100
4/01	Societe Generale	60	1977–84	100
1/13	Credit Commercial de France	30	1976–83	100
1/13	Credit Commercial de France	35	1977–83	100
1982				
8/24	Midland Bank Ltd.	50	1976–83	100
7/26	Kansalles-Osaka-Pankki	30	1977–83	100
5/18	Midland Bank Ltd.	50	1975–82	100
4/30	The Industrial Bank of Japan Fin	50	1977–82	100
2/26	Williams & Glyn's Bank Ltd.	40	1977–84	100
1/29	African Development Bank	40	1978–83	100
1981				
12/81	Societe Franciere Pour Les Telecommunications et L'Electronique	50	1974–84	100
9/16	Sumitomo Heavy Industries Ltd.	25	1978–83	100
3/12	Banque Louis-Dreyfus	20	1977–83	100
6/24	Hydrocarbons Bank Ltd.	75	1977–82	100
2/04	Societe Nationale des Chemins de Fer	50	1977–85/97	100

MARKET PARTICIPANTS AND
THE SECONDARY MARKET

Borrowers

Although nonfinancial institutions were the first to tap the floating rate note market, financial institutions, especially banks, were the engineers of its development and expansion, participating both as borrowers and as lenders of funds. Large, medium, and small banks alike, typically nondollar-based from major developed countries, have had recourse to this market (see Table 5–4), with the large banks typically dominating its activity.

There are several reasons why floating rate notes are an attractive financing instrument for banks. First, they generally provide banks with funds for longer periods than deposit sources of funds, interbank or otherwise. From 1970 to 1977, most floating rate notes had maturities from five to seven years. In the last several years, maturities have generally increased to seven to ten years and longer. Second, floating rate notes may provide banks with a means of matching part of their medium-term loan portfolio with medium-term finance. Third, floating rate notes may provide banks with an increased capital base. For example, floating rate notes of U.S. holding companies can be classified on the balance sheet as equity capital, provided there are arrangements to finance the retirement of the notes from equity proceeds as prescribed by banking regulations, the maximum maturity is 12 years, and the debt is subordinate. Bankers Trust International Capital N. V. recently borrowed $200 million on such a basis. When redeemed at maturity in 1996, the floating rate notes can be exchanged for Bankers Trust common stock or other primary capital at 105 percent of principal value or, alternatively, for cash generated by a secondary offering of Bankers Trust common stock at the maturity period at par. Also, as mentioned previously, if structured properly, British banks may include perpetuals in the calculation of their primary capital. Fourth, since floating rate notes may rank equally with rather than subordinately to deposit liabilities, depending upon the specific issuer and country of domicile, as is the case with Japanese, French, and German banks, they may be viewed as broadening the banks' deposit source

TABLE 5–4
Borrowers by Country of Domicile (Percent)

	1981			1982		
	Bank	Sovereign	Other	Bank	Sovereign	Other
U.S.	6	–	3	9	–	1
Europe	30	15	4	26	30	5
U.K.	15	–	0	1	–	1
France	6	5	–	19	16	2
Sweden	2	–	–	1	6	1
Denmark	–	–	–	–	4	–
Other	7	10	4	5	4	1
Japan	5	–	–	1	–	–
Australia & New Zealand	–	2	–	–	5	1
Canada	5	–	1	6	–	–
Other	8	9	12	4	5	7
Supranational	–	–	–	–	–	–
Total	54	26	20	46	40	14

	1977			1978		
	Bank	Sovereign	Other	Bank	Sovereign	Other
U.S.	17	–	–	9	–	–
Europe	25	11	3	32	8	2
U.K.	–	–	–	17	–	–
France	22	6	3	9	6	–
Sweden	–	–	–	2	–	–
Denmark	2	–	–	–	–	–
Other	11	5	–	4	2	2
Japan	13	–	–	13	–	2
Australia & New Zealand	–	–	–	–	4	–
Canada	–	–	–	–	–	–
Other	4	–	17	16	6	6
Supranational	–	–	–	–	–	2
Total	69	11	20	70	18	12

TABLE 5–4—*Continued*
Borrowers by Country of Domicile (Percent)

	1983			1984[1]		
	Bank	Sovereign	Other	Bank	Sovereign	Other
U.S.	2	–	–	15	–	1
Europe	23	45	4	34	31	1
U.K.	2	–	–	11	–	–
France	10	16	–	12	3	–
Sweden	0	15	–	–	6	–
Denmark	–	6	–	–	5	–
Other	11	8	4	11	17	4
Japan	0	–	–	3	–	–
Australia & New Zealand	–	–	–	–	–	2
Canada	0	–	–	2	–	1
Other	1	9	2	2	3	1
Supranational	–	–	14	–	–	–
Total	26	54	20	56	34	10

	1979			1980		
	Bank	Sovereign	Other	Bank	Sovereign	Other
U.S.	20	–	4	8	–	5
Europe	29	8	3	34	18	–
U.K.	12	–	1	18	–	–
France	10	2	–	7	–	–
Sweden	–	4	–	1	–	–
Denmark	–	–	–	–	–	–
Other	7	2	2	8	18	–
Japan	7	–	–	8	–	–
Australia & New Zealand	–	–	–	–	–	–
Canada	–	–	–	4	–	–
Other	11	11	6	12	4	7
Supranational	–	–	1	–	–	–
Total	67	19	14	66	22	12

[1]January through November.

of funds. Fifth, some banking regulations favor floating rate notes. For example, there are French regulations that exclude from current credit controls any lending funded by bond issues. Finally, the early redemption clauses of most floating rate notes provide banks with flexibility in liability management, which allows them to seek access to alternative sources of funds, if so desired.

From 1982, nonfinancial institutions, particularly governments and their agencies, raised significant sums on this market (see Figure 5–1) as an alternative to tapping the medium-term syndicated credit market or fixed rate bond market. Relative to some bank credit agreements, floating rate notes with extended maturities may offer borrowers better protection against nonavailability of funds in the future; and, for some borrowers, significant sums can be raised at a lower cost (see Table 5–5). Also, lower quality borrowers in these categories (e.g., LDC governments and agencies) at times enjoy much easier access to funds in the floating rate note market than

Figure 5–1
Borrower's Profile

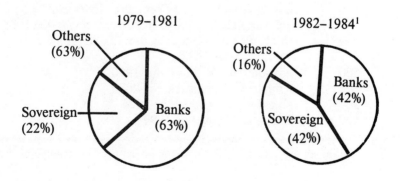

1 January through August

TABLE 5–5
Amounts Outstanding by Size
(in Millions)

By Borrower[1]	
$4,350	Kingdom of Sweden
2,425	Banque Nationale de Paris
2,838	Credit Lyonnais
2,150	Kingdom of Denmark
1,800	European Economic Community
1,500	Kingdom of Belgium
By Issue	
$1,800	European Economic Community due 1990
1,200	Kingdom of Sweden due 1993
1,000	Kingdom of Sweden due 2003
1,001	Republic of Italy due 1994
850	Malaysia due 1993
750	Kingdom of Sweden undated
650	Kingdom of Sweden due 1989
600	Banque Francaise du Commerce Exterieur (guaranteed by the Republic of France) due 1999
600	Barclays undated
600	Industrial Penole due 1889
600	Kingdom of Denmark undated
500	Banque Francaise du Commerce Exterieur (guaranteed by the Republic of France) due 1988
500	Credit Foncier (guaranteed by the Republic of France) due 1993
500	Kingdom of Denmark due 1990
500	Kingdom of Denmark due 2004
500	Kingdom of Sweden due 2024
500	Republic of Italy due 1999

[1]Not including an estimated $5.5 billion guaranteed by the Republic of France.

in the straight bond market. Finally, the penalties attached to the prepayment of borrowings in the floating rate note market can be less onerous than those attached to prepayment of borrowings in the bank credit or bond markets.

In general there has been an increase in the amount borrowed from the $75 million offerings in the late 1970s to large offerings of

TABLE 5–6
Offering Size Profile
(Percent)

Amounts (Millions)	1977	1978	1979	1980	1981	1982	1983	1984[1]
< $75	88	80	71	80	54	39	33	21
$75–124	12	13	21	7	28	29	23	28
$125–199	–	7	5	3	11	8	11	18
≧ $200	–	–	3	10	7	24	33	33
	100	100	100	100	100	100	100	100
Number of Issues	36	46	65	40	76	91	66	155

[1] January through November.

$200 million or more in the 1980s (see Table 5–6), particularly by sovereigns and supranationals as previously noted. For example, the United Kingdom recently borrowed $2.5 billion with a maturity date of October 1992 and put option of 1990.

Investors

Available information indicates that financial institutions, primarily banks, are also major lenders to the market, providing an estimated 70–80 percent of total funds. Floating rate notes generally provide banks with an attractive alternative outlet for funds to the interbank market and in particular give smaller banks the opportunity to participate in a medium-term variable rate instrument that may otherwise be unavailable to them in the syndicated credit market. However, in this context, the Bank of England, concerned with the implications of inter-bank investment in subordinated loan capital, issued guidelines in May 1984 that require U.K.-authorized banks to deduct these respective amounts (e.g., floating rate notes, if subordinated loan capital of the borrower) in the assessment of capital adequacy. Further inducement to bank investment in floating rate notes are marketability providing greater flexibility in asset management and the possibility of purchase below par, thus increasing the spread over the reference rate.

Table 5–7 gives some indication as to the extent banks participate in the floating rate note market. Japanese banks are particularly important. For these investors, floating rate notes are favored instruments as they are not subject to the maturity matching requirements set by the Ministry of Finance on assets and liabilities.

Other lenders include financial institutions other than banks, such as business corporations, central monetary institutions, governmental or quasi-governmental agencies, and individuals. The floating rate note market is particularly attractive to such lenders in periods of rising interest rates because it protects them from the capital losses that would otherwise accrue in the fixed income market; yet, because of the easy marketability provided by regular bank participation on the buy side of the market, the investors' option for switching into straight bonds, if and when interest rate expectations change, is left intact.

Major U.S. participants include international banks, investment advisors, corporations, thrifts, insurance companies, and regional and money center bank fund managers. With respect to U.S. individuals, in general, transactions in non-SEC-registered securities during primary distribution are not possible.

Secondary Market

The secondary market in floating rate notes is active and characterized by large dealing size, a function of active bank participation.

TABLE 5–7
Floating Rate Note Holdings of Banks in the United Kingdom (in Billions)

Total	7.9	8.5	10.1	11.7	13.1
Japanese banks	4.5	5.2	5.8	7.3	8.6
American banks	0.7	0.5	0.9	0.7	0.9
British banks	0.6	0.6	0.8	0.7	0.9
Consortium banks	0.6	0.6	0.7	0.8	0.4
Other overseas banks	1.4	1.5	1.9	2.2	2.3

Source: Bank of England

Currently, there are over 40 market makers trading issues from the bulk of the market. In normal market conditions, most of the active issues are traded in amounts ranging from $500,000 to $10 million principal value, with a 15- to 20-basis point spread between bid and offered prices. Some of the large issues trade on a spread as low as five basis points between the bid and offered prices. Since coupons are refixed periodically, prices tend to trade close to par.

Trading is done on a net price basis usually for seven-day settlement; however, it is possible to settle for two-day value. Accrued interest is figured from (but not including) last coupon date to (and including) settlement date on an actual-day (360 days per year) basis. Transactions are cleared through Euroclear or Cedel, independent clearing agents owned by shareholder banks. In general, the two systems operate in the same manner, that is, bonds are held in depository banks with transactions between system members affected by book entry transfers of securities and cash at one central location. Physical delivery is possible with additional fees and extended settlement.

COMPARISON TO U.S. DOMESTIC FLOATING RATE NOTES

The Instrument

A significant difference between Eurodollar and U.S. domestic floating rate notes is the lack of homogeneity in the terms of the coupon fixing in the latter market, as described in Table 5–8 and in the following discussion on the key characteristics.

U.S. domestic floating rate notes are typically issued in minimum denominations of $1,000 and/or occasionally $5,000, $110,000, or $100,000. They vary from one another as to:

1. *Maturity.* The term to maturity typically is between 8 and 12 years.
2. *Reference Market.* Traditionally, the coupon is referenced to the U.S. Treasury market and, of late, to the London interbank market for deposits.

TABLE 5-8
Summary of Coupon Terms

Reference Market	Eurodollar Floating Rate Notes*		
	Reference Rate	Spread (Basis Points)	Interest Rate Adjustment Period
London Interbank Market for Deposits	Offered (LIBOR)	12.5–75	Quarterly
		minus 50–100	Semiannually
		minus 25–0	Quarterly
	Bid (LIBID)	12.5–37.5	Quarterly
	Mean (LIMEAN)	12.5–25	Semiannually
		0	Weekly
Treasury Market	3-Month Treasury Bill Auction (Interest Yield Equivalent)	35	Quarterly

U.S. Domestic Floating Rate Notes

Reference Market	Reference Rate	Spread (Basis Points)	Interest Rate Adjustment Period
Treasury Market	91-Day Treasury Bill Auction (Bond Equivalent Basis)	55–125	Weekly
	3-Month Treasury Bill Secondary Market (Interest Yield Equivalent)	275–300	Quarterly
	6-Month Treasury Bill Auction (Bond Equivalent Basis)	100–125	Semiannually
	6-Month Treasury Bill Secondary Market (Interest Yield Equivalent)	30	Weekly
	Treasury Constant Maturity Yield	65–70	Semiannually
		50–100	Semiannually
Money Market	3-Month Certificate of Deposit	Various	Various
	1-Month Commercial Paper	12.5–55	Weekly
	Prime Rate	62	Every four weeks
		minus 40	Weekly
London Interbank Market for Deposits	Offered (LIBOR)	0–125	Quarterly
		0	Weekly

* Reflects terms on instruments presently outstanding and does not indicate the most common terms attached to the instruments.

3. *Reference Rates.* There are several reference rates used with regard to the Treasury market, whereas the offered rate (LIBOR) has generally been the rate used when referencing the London interbank deposit market.

4. *Basic Margins over Reference Rates.* The margin differs according to the reference market and frequently may be variable over the term of the borrowing. On occasion some are quoted as a percentage of the reference rate (e.g., 105 percent).

5. *Interest Period.* Interest periods typically match the period of the reference rate, with the exception of floating rate notes tied to the 91-day Treasury bill auction rate. In this instance, the coupon is generally refixed weekly and paid quarterly.

6. *Minimum and Maximum Coupons.* Generally, there are provisions setting minimum coupons on U.S. domestic floating rate note instruments, typically at 6.00 percent to 7.25 percent. Maximum coupon rates are less frequently included.

While the domestic market, in general, is not homogeneous, the fast growing LIBOR-based sector of the market is characterized by similarity in the terms of the instruments. Moreover, this sector tends to replicate the instruments available on the significantly larger Eurodollar market. This gives rise to similar instruments on both markets, often by the same issuer.

Redemption Provisions

Maturities typically range from 8 to 12 years, shortened from the 8 to 25 years prevalent in the 1970s but consistent with the current norm of 7 to 12 years on Eurodollar floating rate notes. Actual maturities on some will be shorter than the stated maturity, if optional or mandatory redemption features are provided.

Optional redemption by borrowers and/or lenders is, at times, provided through call or put features. On recent offerings, call protection of three to four years is not uncommon, in contrast to borrowings made in 1982 and 1983 when these securities were typically noncallable. With respect to put features, usually there are provisions entitling holders to receive payment on dates specified, typically every three years from offering date. These optional redemption provisions allow some lenders (e.g., savings and loans) to meet asset maturity parameters set by their respective regulatory bodies (e.g., Federal Home Loan Bank).

In contrast to 1979 offerings, there is usually no sinking fund provisions nor features extending final maturity when holders convert to fixed rate instruments.

Borrowers

The profile of borrowers on the publicly placed U.S. domestic market contrasts with that of borrowers on the Eurodollar market. Borrowers on the U.S. domestic market are typically U.S.-domiciled entities, dominated by financial institutions and concentrated with regard to specific borrowers (e.g., Citibank, Chase, Merrill Lynch, and Wells Fargo).

Banks and financial institutions have the most frequent recourse to the market and generally borrow in amounts of $50 to $400 million. Industrial, sovereign, and supranational borrowers account for the remaining amounts outstanding. With respect to the former sector, there are numerous corporate offerings in amounts between $35 and $50 million, whereas the sovereign and supranational public placement sector includes four offerings—a $1.5 billion Swedish offering, a $100 million borrowing by Swedish Export Credit, $150 million by the World Bank, and a recent $250 million offering by Credit National.

On some borrowings by bank holding companies, the borrower arranges for principal amount and, in some instances, interest to be paid from funds generated from the sale of primary capital as described in the indenture. This allows for the borrowing to be included in primary capital and has been a significant reason why banks participate in this market. For example, the $100 million Bank of Boston Floating Rate Subordinated Note due 1996 provides for a trustee to hold amounts representing proceeds from issuances of capital of the corporation in a note fund from which it is anticipated that the notes will be paid. The $400 million Chase Manhattan Corporation Floating Rate Subordinated Notes due 1996 provides for the notes to be issued as so-called capital notes or stock notes. Interest is payable in common shares of the company at the rate of 8 1/2 percent per annum, with the remaining excess payable in cash.

Accordingly, shares paid as interest on capital notes are automatically sold so that holders receive the full amount of interest in cash, whereas shares paid as interest on stock notes are automatically credited to accounts established under the company's dividend reinvestment plan, as more fully described in the prospectus.

Investors

Like Eurodollar floating rate notes, U.S. domestic floating rate notes traditionally were tailored to the needs of particular institutional lenders. However, the traditional lenders on the domestic market are U.S. financial institutions (e.g., savings and loans and banks). For these lenders, coupons referenced to Treasury bills or interbank rates can be matched against their respectively based liabilities. Other lenders, including insurance companies, trust funds, and investment advisory accounts, participate in the market when floating rate instruments meet their investment parameters.

Secondary Market

In general, U.S. domestic instruments are classified into three representative groups differentiated by their coupon reference rates:

The six-month Treasury bill rate,
The 91-day Treasury bill rate, and
The London interbank offered rate (LIBOR).

Secondary market prices typically tend to reflect money market rates by selling at discounts (premiums) to par when the coupon on the floating rate note is below (above) alternative money market instruments. This is particularly noticeable with notes referenced to the Treasury bill market when spreads favoring higher yielding money market instruments are widening or narrowing. This tends to make Treasury bill-referenced notes significantly more price volatile than LIBOR-based domestic or Eurodollar floating rate notes.

In normal market conditions, U.S. domestic floating rate notes typically trade in units of $1 million principal value with a 1/2 point spread between bid and offered rates. LIBOR-referenced floating rate notes trade generally with 10–25 points between bid and offered rates. Trades are done on a net price basis with five business days for settlement and payment against delivery in New York at the designated clearing/custodian bank. Interest typically accrues from (but not including) coupon date to (and including) settlement date on a 30-day month, 360-days-per-year basis.

PRICE BEHAVIOR OF EURODOLLAR FLOATING RATE NOTES

Primary Market

With respect to the primary market, the issue procedure for publicly placed floating rate notes usually consists of four stages:

1. The lead manager receives a mandate from the borrower on set terms and begins the necessary documentation for the borrowing, typically including an offering circular commonly referred to as a prospectus.
2. Syndicate members (i.e., managers, underwriters, and selling groups members) inform lenders of the terms of issue, referred to as the offering or selling period.
3. The lead manager allocates the notes among syndicate members and notifies each of their respective allotment by telex.
4. The issue is signed and subsequently closed with syndicate members compensated in accordance with a schedule of fees (each fixed in percent of the principal amount differing from issue to issue) and the borrower receiving the net proceeds on the designated payment date.

The issue price and terms on the primary market are set by the lead manager, with the first coupon fixed two business days prior to the designated payment date. Syndicate members, once notified of their respective allocations, typically develop market liquidity by making bid and offered prices for the note. In this regard, the deal is judged to be a so-called success if it trades above the price at which underwriters receive their allotments.

Secondary Market

Secondary market transactions are defined as those that settle one day or more after the payment date. In general, prices of floating rate notes on the secondary market have similar characteristics. First, prices tend to trade near par; second, prices trade within a narrow range with small price variations; and last, prices have exhibited a declining trend in volatility over the past several years.

Nevertheless, differences in price behavior between issues do occur and are affected by the following:

1. *Maturity.* Banks, the major players abiding by lending and funding policies, typically participate in arbitrage activities at the short end of the market. Consequently, prices on floating rate notes with short terms to maturity, in general, tend to be more stable at higher average values compared to medium-term and long-term maturities (see Table 5–9).

2. *Reference Market.* Floating rate notes tied to the larger London interbank deposit market are typically more liquid and marketable compared to those of smaller deposit markets.

3. *Interest Period.* Generally, the revision of coupons in line with changing short-term interest rates keeps price fluctuations of floating rate notes within relatively close limits of par value, particularly at or near rollover (i.e., refixing) dates. Consequently, floating rate notes with quarterly coupon resets and, accordingly, more frequent coupon revisions typically trade at higher average prices, within a narrower price range, and with lower price volatilities.

   This apart, relative price movements between floating rate notes tend to reflect the timing of coupon revisions. There is a tendency for investors to switch into those floating rate notes with the nearest and/or most frequent coupon revision dates when interest rates are rising and into those floating rate notes with farthest coupon revision dates when interest rates are falling. For example, Figure 5–2 indicates that over a period of increasing interest rates, floating rate notes with semiannual coupon revisions show greater price depreciation than those with quarterly coupon revi-

TABLE 5–9
Price Indices by Maturity[1]

Year	Maturity[2]	Low	High	Diff	Mean	Standard Deviation
1980	Short	98.13	101.26	3.12	99.87	.69
	Medium	96.91	100.32	3.40	99.72	.68
	Long	95.83	100.63	4.80	98.32	.99
1981	Short	98.94	101.57	2.58	100.17	.49
	Medium	98.33	100.61	2.28	99.52	.51
	Long	97.62	100.14	2.52	98.95	.53
1982	Short	99.43	101.04	1.61	100.13	.34
	Medium	98.84	100.68	1.84	99.70	.44
	Long	98.58	100.38	1.80	99.46	.33
1983	Short	99.66	100.54	.87	100.05	.21
	Medium	99.51	101.42	1.90	100.22	.34
	Long	99.58	100.83	1.25	100.21	.27
1984[3]	Short	99.76	100.35	.58	100.11	.15
	Medium	99.89	100.05	1.16	100.53	.39
	Long	99.62	100.53	.58	100.21	.17

[1]Consists of notes issued by banks with redemption taken as maturity date or alternatively to put.
[2]Short: 2.99 years or less.   Medium: 3 to 8.99 years.   Long: over 9 years.
[3]January through July.

sions. This is in contrast to a decreasing rate environment, when the semiannual revisions tend to show greater price appreciation than the quarterly revisions (see Figure 5–3).

4. *Reference Rates.*   There is generally a 1/8 percent point spread between bid and offered rates on the Eurodollar deposit market. Consequently, variations between floating rate notes, with respect to the reference rate, will be accounted for in the price (e.g., 1/4 percent over LIMEAN equals 3/16 percent over LIBOR). In addition, the trend and volatility of reference rates, that is, interbank deposit rates, are similarly reflected in prices of floating rate notes.

TABLE 5-10
Price Volatility of Floating Rate Notes by Sovereign Borrowers

| Borrower | Maturity | Basic Margin* | Interest Period | Pricing Period 1/84 to 6/84 | | | |
				High	Low	Mean	Standard Deviation
Sweden	87/89	1/4	semi	99.73	100.23	100.02	.10
Ireland	88	1/4	semi	99.25	99.88	99.69	.16
Indonesia	88/93	1/4	semi	96.75	98.55	97.73	.56
Spain	88/93	1/4	semi	97.88	99.54	98.29	.46
Malaysia	89/92	1/4	semi	98.30	99.95	98.82	.38
Spain	92/97	1/8	semi	99.50	100.08	99.78	.13

*Reference rate is LIBOR.

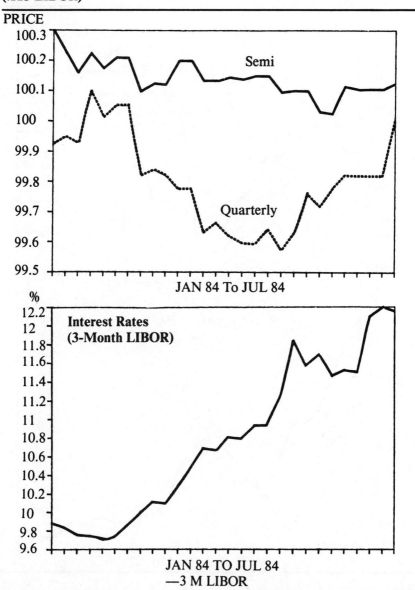

Figure 5–2
**Price Behavior of FRN's
Semi V Quarterly Refix
(.125 LIBOR)**

PRICE

100.3
100.2
100.1
100
99.9
99.8
99.7
99.6
99.5

Semi

Quarterly

JAN 84 To JUL 84

%

12.2
12
11.8
11.6
11.4
11.2
11
10.8
10.6
10.4
10.2
10
9.8
9.6

**Interest Rates
(3-Month LIBOR)**

JAN 84 TO JUL 84
—3 M LIBOR

Figure 5–3
Price Behavior of FRN's
Semi V Quarterly Refix
(.125 LIBOR)

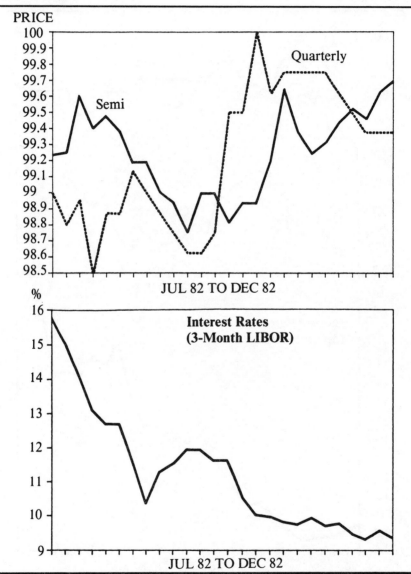

5. *Basic Margin over Reference Rates.*   Average prices on floating rate notes with, for example, premiums of .25 percent over LIBOR, compared to those with premiums of .125 percent over LIBOR, tend to be higher. This is particularly true during periods of declining and low interest rates, when the basic margin contributes a larger percentage to the overall return.

6. *The Borrower.*   With respect to the credit quality of the borrower, in general, prices on floating rate notes of perceived better quality (either objective or subjective) tend to be higher and less volatile (see Table 5–10). Recent offerings by U.S. savings and loans have been collateralized to support a AAA credit rating.

It should be noted that the foregoing demonstrates what is generally true in normal market conditions. However, as these relationships are interrelated and dynamic, there are always exceptions within the marketplace. The skill is recognizing the profitable opportunities that may arise.

TABLE 5–11
Rates of Return (Annualized)

	7/81–12/81	1/82–6/82	7/82–12/82	1/83–6/83	7/83–12/83	1/84–6/84
Floating Rate Notes	17.8	15.8	16.1	10.7	11.4	10.3
Money Market						
Treasury Bill	15.1	13.2	14.0	8.4	9.4	9.7
U.S. Domestic Certificates						
of Deposit	16.7	14.1	15.6	8.8	9.5	9.8
Eurodollar Certificates						
of Deposit	17.1	14.4	16.1	9.0	9.7	10.0
London Interbank Deposit						
(LIBOR)	17.4	14.9	16.2	9.5	10.0	10.1
Capital Market						
U.S. Government	16.0	11.5	44.0	6.9	6.5	−0.9
U.S. Corporates	7.3	11.1	65.1	14.9	3.8	−5.2
Eurodollar Straight	7.4	16.3	52.2	12.5	8.1	0.9

Figure 5-4
3 MO. CD (LINE), 3 MO. T-BILL (DOT), 3 MO. LIBOR (DASH)

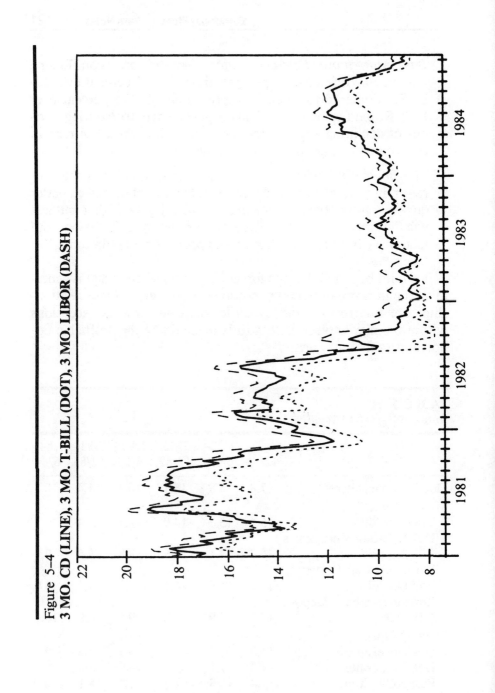

RATES OF RETURN

Typically, Eurodollar floating rate notes are associated with greater rates of return in comparison to money market instruments, as shown in Table 5–11. Several interrelated factors are responsible for this.

First, there is, in general, a tiering in the rate structure of the money market. The reference rate on floating rate notes, that is, interbank deposit rates, normally offers the highest rate (see Figure 5–4). The lowest rates available are typically on Treasury bills. This reflects their high quality and greater liquidity. Rates on U.S. dollar domestic certificates of deposit are higher than Treasury bills primarily due to quality considerations. Eurodollar certificates of deposit rates are typically greater than U.S. domestic certificates of deposit as the absence of Federal Deposit Insurance Corporation fees attached to the latter allow foreign branches to offer higher rates at effectively the same cost to the deposit bank. Also, interbank deposit rates are usually higher than Eurodollar certificates of deposit, which reflects the nonnegotiability of the former.

Second, the difference between returns is directly related to the spread between rates at the start of the measurement periods, that is, the larger (smaller) the spread, the larger (smaller) the expected difference between the respective rates of return. Spreads between Treasury bills and certificates of deposit vary directly with quality, liquidity, and/or tax (state and local) considerations, that is, the spreads widen (narrow) when the latter are of greater (lesser) importance to market participants. In general, bank arbitrage activities keep rates on U.S. domestic and Eurodollar certificates of deposit effectively equal with other Eurodollar funding vehicles (e.g., interbank deposit rates).

Third, it follows that a given spread between rates is of greater (lesser) significance to the respective rates of return when the interest rate level is lower (higher).

Fourth, in most instances, floating rate note coupons are set at a premium to an interbank deposit rate, LIBOR or LIMEAN, mirroring premiums available on the international syndicated credit market, revolving underwriting facilities, and conditions on the capital market.

And last, while rates of return incorporate price changes for respective measurement periods, in general, this is of far less importance than respective coupon payments.

With respect to fixed rate bonds, rates of return on Eurodollar floating rate notes are less variable (refer to Table 5–11) as the frequent resetting of coupons gives rise to greater price stability.

THE ROLE OF FLOATING RATE NOTES IN PORTFOLIO STRATEGY

The recent growth of the floating rate note market is evidence of this instrument's importance in the investment strategies set by portfolio managers. Incorporating favorable features of both money market and fixed coupon instruments, floating rate notes lend themselves to a wide range of investment strategies, some relevant to short-term horizons and others to the long term. In addition, improved returns through active portfolio management are possible, with respect to money market, capital market, and trading strategies.

Money Market

Alternative to Money Market Instruments. The price stability and interest rate structure of floating rate notes combine to make them an attractive alternative investment to other money market instruments. Interest on floating rate notes is tied to the London interbank deposit rate, generally the highest available money market rate (see Figure 5–4), although this alone does not guarantee that they will provide superior returns due to the market risk factor always inherent in such investments. That is, the sale price of floating rate notes in the secondary market is uncertain, whereas the redemption value of money market instruments is known. When consideration is given to both these components of return, however, Table 5–11 shows that floating rate notes have still consistently outperformed money market instruments.

Matching Liability Payments with Higher Yields on Floating Rate Notes. The price stability of floating rate notes at rollover dates provide fund manager the opportunity to match liabilities with higher yielding floating rate notes. This is the traditional role of floating rate notes for banks. A bank will purchase a floating rate note, as a substitute for participation in a syndicated loan, by borrowing in the interbank market. Similarly, money market participants can obtain funds at low rates using government securities as collateral (reverse repo). Investment of these funds in floating rate notes with rollover dates coinciding with the liability payment could lead to arbitrage profit for the duration of the investment, as shown in Table 5–12.

Mismatching the Funding of Floating Rate Notes. It is possible to earn additional yield by mismatching the funding of a floating rate note. When the yield curve slopes upward, borrowing short and buying long will bring in extra return if the long rate exceeds the cost of rolling over the short loan throughout the investment period. Clearly, the risk that an investor takes when mismatching the funding of a floating rate note is that rates will change during the coupon period, eroding the anticipated yield pickup and creating the possibility of a loss.

To minimize this risk, a recent development on the floating rate note market is an instrument with coupons recalculated every month. Like conventional floating rate notes, they have a coupon set at a fixed spread over LIBOR. While the three-month coupon is payable quarterly, it is readjusted every month, and, consequently,

TABLE 5–12
Matching Transaction

	January 3rd	February 3rd
1. Asset: Kingdom of Sweden Floating Rate Note Coupon—11.1875%		
Price—100.32%	– $1,050,436	
Liability: 30-day R.P. at 9.5%	+ $1,050,436	
2. Receipt from sale of asset at 100.38%		+ $1,059,738
Repayment of liability		– $1,058,752
Arbitrage profit		$ 986

the interest the investor receives is a composite rate reflecting the movement of three-month LIBOR during each month of the coupon period.

The frequency of coupon refix and the terms on which it is set make these notes particularly attractive to two types of investors.

1. Investors who, in times of rising interest rates, are primarily concerned with capital preservation.
2. Investors who borrow money in order to purchase floating rate notes. The instrument provides the investor with the opportunity to fund the purchase on a monthly basis while locking in a three-month return. Clearly the key feature influencing the attractiveness of these notes is the spread, current and expected, between one-month and three-month LIBOR. The wider the spread the greater the yield pickup and the more attractive the note. Naturally, the associated risk is that the yield curve will invert or that it will narrow to such an extent that the cost of funding monthly outweighs the extra return.

In August 1984, this concept was taken a step further with a $200 million issue for the Kingdom of Denmark. The coupon is paid twice yearly but is fixed weekly at the higher of LIMEAN for six-month Eurodollar deposits or the one-week offered rate for dollars. These terms mean that the investor is protected if the yield curve inverts.

Anticipation of a Change in Short-Term Interest Rates.   When interest rates are rising, investors tend to acquire floating rate notes with coupons refixed quarterly and sell those with semiannual coupon revisions, thereby supporting the price of the former. Portfolio managers can enhance returns by accurately anticipating changes in the interest rate environment and appropriately structuring their floating rate note portfolio. A recent example occurred in the beginning of 1984, prior to the increase in interest rates. By switching from National Westminster 1990 with semiannual coupon revisions to Chemical Bank 1994 with quarterly coupon refixings, the portfolio would not have experienced the capital depreciation associated with holding the former (see Figure 5–5).

Figure 5–5
Nat West 6/90 (S) v. Chemical 6/94 (Q)

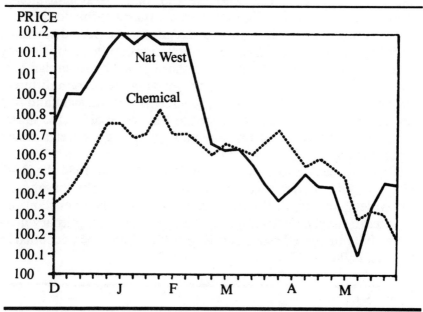

Capital Market

Rate Anticipation Swap. As previously noted, the properties of floating rate notes give rise to a more price-stable instrument than fixed rate securities. The preservation of capital associated with floating rate notes make them an ideal defensive instrument to include in portfolios during periods of uncertain or rising interest rates. The inclusion of these securities clearly reduces the risk of capital erosion, while still maintaining satisfactory income. This is evident from Table 5–11 for the period January through June 1984, when U.S. governments and corporates had a rate of return of − .04 percent and − 2.6 percent respectively, compared to floating rate notes of 10.3 percent.

Intermarket Spread Swap. Swaps can be made between floating rate notes to take advantage of price anomalies between various sectors of the market created by demand and supply. For example, in 1984, changing perceptions with respect to bank borrowers caused by concerns relating to the U.S. banking system altered demand for bank paper. Figure 5–6 tracks the performance of these two sectors measured by adjusted margin for the period spanning July 1982 to July 1984. It shows the relationship between floating rate notes issued by U.S. banks and those issued by sovereign borrowers. Investors believing that the reversal in the margin differential between U.S. bank issues and sovereigns was transient and that the 10–20 basis point spread over the last two years is the norm, would take advantage of this anomaly by selling sovereign issues and investing in U.S. bank names.

Similarly, bank paper traded down when in May 1984 the Bank of England imposed regulations on interbank ownership of subordinated debt, including floating rate notes. Equally important are changes in supply. For example, in the French sector, primary market activity increased significantly in 1982–83 and then declined in the first half of 1984.

Figure 5–6
Sector Analysis
U.S. Banks v. Sovereign Issuers

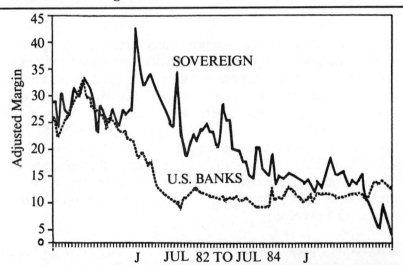

Maturity Swap. Expectations with regard to U.S. interest rates and the value of the dollar on the foreign exchange market causes investors to adjust maturity profiles of portfolios. For example, when rising interest rates are expected, market participants generally prefer short-maturity instruments. In addition, primary market activity concentrated in particular maturity ranges at times can affect market conditions, as it did earlier this year when several long-dated floating rate notes were offered. Consequently, changes in demand and supply, with respect to maturity, reflected in the price of the instruments can give rise to market opportunities.

Substitution Swap. While floating rate notes with exact rollover dates are rare, it is often sufficient to consider swaps between those that have rollover dates within a few days of one another, since their coupons would generally be consistent. For example, on July 12, 1984, the Kingdom of Belgium Floating Rate Note with a redemption of 1994/2004 and coupon refixings semiannually had a current yield of 13.16 percent, compared to a 12.90 percent current yield on the EEC Floating Rate Note due 1990 (also with semiannual coupon revisions). For the former, the last coupon revision was July 9, 1984, and for the latter it was July 5, 1984.

Quality Swap. While most floating rate note borrowers are of a high-quality credit with differences between credits generally small, there are occasions when the credit improvement of a borrower is not fully or adequately recognized. Inclusion of these borrowers notes at the expense of notes with deteriorating credit can lead to enhanced returns in addition to an overall improvement in quality.

In a Trading Environment

The secondary market liquidity for floating rate notes allows for high-turnover debt-trading strategies, particularly for offerings of large size. For example, the $1.8 billion EEC issue typically exhibited high monthly turnover in the secondary market as shown in Table 5–13. This turnover, combined with small price spreads between bid and offered rates, leads to opportunities for profit in various market environments.

TABLE 5–13
Secondary Market Turnover

	Offering Date	Redemption Date	Amount Offered ($ Million)	Annual Turnover
1983				
Sweden	1/83	88–90–93	1,200	5.27
BFCE	1/83	98	500	4.01
Credit Lyonnais	4/83	91–95	300	3.97
CEPME	3/83	88	200	2.66
Denmark	10/83	88–90	500	2.62
BNP	4/82	89	250	2.61
Societe Generale	4/83	90	200	2.30
Sweden	2/82	87–89	650	2.15
EDF	2/83	90–92–95	300	2.14
EEC	6/83	88–90	1,800	2.13
January–October 1984				
EDF	2/84	99	400	5.31
Sweden	10/83	93–03	1,000	5.17
Denmark	1/84	99–04	500	4.99
Denmark	10/83	88–90	500	4.99
CFF	10/83	88–90–93	500	4.88
BNP	8/83	88–91	400	4.56
EEC	6/83	90	1,800	4.40
Sweden	1/83	88–90–93	1,200	4.19
BFCE	1/83	88	500	3.67
Dresdner	10/83	93	400	3.08

Percent Maturity Distribution

	1983	1984
Less than 4.99 years	81%	53%
Greater than 5.00 years	19%	47%

Source: Euroclear.

CHAPTER 6

FLOATING RATE CERTIFICATES OF DEPOSIT

David Muntner
Vice President
Fixed Income Research
The First Boston Corporation

and

Sara Kelly Fields
Assistant Vice President
Fixed Income Research
The First Boston Corporation

In recent years, interest rates have been extraordinarily volatile. Investors have consequently looked for securities that preserve the market value of principal while providing incremental yield to alternative money market investments. Investors have been using floating rate securities to address this problem, causing issuance of these securities to increase dramatically. Over $100 billion of domestic and Euro floaters have been issued in the past six years, and forecasts point toward continued growth.

The floating rate note (FRN) market, with its well-chronicled and marketed issues, has dominated the floating rate securities market.

The floating rate certificate of deposit (FRCD), however, offers an investment opportunity that is often higher yielding. The FRCD market has depth and offers a great diversity of issuers and structures. As measured by transaction size and costs, the liquidity of the FRCD market rivals that of the FRN market.

This chapter describes the structure, the history, and the market of FRCDs; it outlines several valuation and portfolio management techniques that will provide an investor with returns greater than those achieved by traditional money market portfolio management; and it analyzes the use of FRCDs in conjunction with interest rate swaps. The net result of the latter transaction—a synthetic fixed rate instrument—may yield more than either a term CD or a corporate note of the same issuer. Floating rate CDs can be an integral part of a fixed income portfolio because of their high quality, liquidity, and range of maturity and payment structures.

FLOATING RATE CERTIFICATES OF DEPOSIT

Floating rate certificates of deposit are bank liabilities on which the coupon changes periodically in accordance with a specified formula. FRCDs typically have intermediate-term maturities, most often ranging between 18 months and 5 years. They can be issued by money center, regional, or foreign banks domiciled in the U.S. (Yankee banks) in either domestic or European markets. As a bank deposit, an FRCD is an obligation that is senior to holding company notes, and thereby offers investors greater credit protection.

The attributes used to describe an FRCD are illustrated below.

Issuer	Index	Margin	Maturity	Frequency of Pay/Reflex	Current Coupon	Next Coupon Change	Market Price
Toronto Dominion	3 mo. CD	+ 35	11/3/86	Q/Q	9.20	5/3	99.95

Additional features that will affect the value of selected FRCDs are call provisions at the issuer's option and caps or ceilings on future coupons. A few FRCDs in the marketplace also use optional index-coupon formulas, whereby the investor is given the option of choosing one of several pricing formulas on a given refix date.

The origination and underwriting of an FRCD are generally undertaken in response to specific inquiries, frequently allowing an investor to help determine the structure of the security. Issues range in size from $5 million to over $100 million. While an individual CD may not be rated, the underlying bank and/or holding company frequently does have a rating from both Standard & Poor's and Moody's.

Despite the specific nature of the issue, the secondary market for FRCDs is quite liquid. A group of primary dealers maintains an active secondary market in FRCDs, with several street brokers assisting in the process. A par amount of $5 million is the typical trading size, with $1 million denominations being good delivery. Securities are delivered physically and must be put into registered or nominee names.

Although the security structure can vary widely, the coupon payment calculations are quite uniform. Nearly all FRCDs calculate interest on a money market basis (the actual number of days in the period/360 day year).

Finally, each FRCD of FDIC member institutions is currently entitled to insurance up to $100,000 principal amount. In the case of pension- and profit-sharing plans, each plan participant's interest in an FRCD is insured up to $100,000.

HISTORY OF FLOATING RATE CERTIFICATES OF DEPOSIT

FRCDs have been issued in the U.S. since 1977. The initial issuers were primarily Japanese banks who offered one- to three-year CDs indexed to LIBOR. Domestic banks then entered the market with FRCDs indexed to the CD composite. As volatility in the credit markets increased, the limited structure of the existing floaters could no longer provide the principal protection that investors sought. To lessen interest rate risk, issuers began increasing the frequency of coupon adjustments and employing a variety of index rates that are more sensitive to the issuer's credit in the coupon formulas. These structural alterations not only enabled FRCDs to preserve principal to a greater degree but also encouraged more active portfolio management by investors.

In addition, the gradual deregulation of the financial markets has encouraged a more diversified group of investors to participate in the FRCD market. The introduction of Money Market Deposit Accounts encouraged banks and savings and loans to purchase FRCDs as an asset to offset MMDAs. Money market funds, state and local governments, corporations, insurance companies, and money managers have increased their participation in the market as well. These investors have substantially expanded the size and sophistication of the FRCD market.

More recently, interest rate swaps have contributed to the development of the floating rate securities market. With this vehicle, an investor or liability manager can convert one floating rate cash flow to another floating rate basis or to a fixed rate. FRCDs are particularly applicable to interest rate swaps because they are generally not callable.

THE STRUCTURE OF THE FRCD

In addition to credit quality and maturity, there are three additional structural variables which have a major impact on value and price volatility of FRCDs. These additional variables are the index and margin, the frequency of interest payments, and the frequency of the coupon refix.

Index and Margin

The selection of an index (the base rate for determining future coupons) when choosing a floating rate asset is a critical decision. Whether the investor uses an FRCD as an asset to offset floating rate liabilities, as the base of an interest rate swap, or as part of multi-sector, total return portfolio management, the selection of the index rate requires a judgment on the future spreads among alternative indices. Greater sensitivity of the index rate to the issuer's industry fundamentals, cost of funds, and credit quality dampens the principal fluctuation of the FRCD.

Issuers of floating rate certificates of deposit have used a broad range of indices in FRCD coupon-refix formulas. Currently, FRCDs are indexed to *market rates* such as LIBOR and Treasury bills; Federal Reserve *composite rates* such as those for domestic bank CDs, Aa/AA industrial commercial paper, and the Federal funds effective rate; and *administered rates* such as the prime rate, the rate at which commercial banks lend to their most creditworthy customers. FRCDs also have optional index schemes whereby under certain circumstances the investor may change the index underlying the coupon.

Index Description

The *London Interbank Offered Rate* (LIBOR) is the predominant refix index. It was introduced to the FRS market by Yankee banks. LIBOR is a sensitive and efficient index rate in determining floating rate coupons because it represents the global banking system's costs for gathering deposit liabilities. As such it reflects the supply and demand for bank credit and reflects perceived changes in the creditworthiness of the banking system. As a result, an FRCD indexed to LIBOR can be expected to have less price volatility than those with other indices.

LIBOR rates are quoted by the major London banks when offering Eurodollar deposits to one another. While LIBOR reflects the costs of Eurodollar deposits for terms ranging from overnight through five years, the most popular LIBOR rates used for coupon resets are the one-, three-, and six-month rates.

The internationalization of the bank deposit market has caused foreign (LIBOR) and domestic (CD composite) yields to trade on an arbitrage basis. At any given time, the LIBOR rate for a given maturity will be higher than the CD rate because Federal Reserve policy generally allows Eurodollar deposits to be free from reserve requirements. In the absence of any sovereign risk, the difference between the CD rate and LIBOR of the same maturity will be largely explained by the cost of reserves.

In practice most LIBOR-based coupons are set by referring either to the "LIBOR" page of Reuters' News Service or to the rate set by a specific reference bank. Reuters posts LIBOR levels of several major London banks at approximately 11:00 A.M. London time. Alternatively, an FRCD may specify a basket of reference banks and determine the coupon with an averaging formula.

The *Treasury bill* bond equivalent yield is another frequently used index for FRCDs. Typically, banks have used the bond equivalent yield of the three- or six-month T-bill as determined in the weekly auctions and announced by the Treasury. The investor will receive the bill rate plus a margin—a positive yield spread—which represents the credit risk premium. The bond equivalent yield of the Treasury bill (actual/365) plus the margin typically determines the coupon, but interest is still paid on a CD basis (actual/360).

U.S. Treasury bills are considered to be a riskless security. By virtue of their high quality, short maturity, and liquidity, Treasury bills provide the lowest money market rate. The quality spreads between Treasury bills and other rates have been very volatile and can be affected by the supply and demand for bank credit as well as by investor perception of the risks inherent in the worldwide banking system. For this reason, the market prices of floating rate securities indexed to Treasury bills are more volatile than those indexed to either LIBOR or other credit sensitive rates.

Three additional indices employed in coupon calculations for FRCDs are the *CD composite rate,* the *CP composite rate* (money market yield adjusted), and the *Federal funds effective rate.* As alternative funding methods for the subset of domestic banks, these rates share some of the credit sensitivity and pricing efficiency of the LIBOR index. An FRCD indexed to Federal Reserve-related indices should therefore be expected to be more volatile than a LIBOR-indexed floater. Its yield should fall between FRCDs indexed to LIBOR and those indexed to Treasury bills.

These rates are determined daily by a survey of major market participants conducted by the Federal Reserve Bank of New York. The results of the survey are released daily on the Federal Reserve tape (212-791-6693) and published weekly in the Federal Reserve Statistical Release H-15.

Prime rate indexed certificates of deposit are a more recent innovation in the market. In this case, the coupon payments are indexed to the posted prime rate of a specified bank or a group of reference banks. Since prime is an output rate, coupons on prime-indexed FRCDs refix at a spread below prime. The administered nature of the rate and the resultant lagging nature can create volatile spreads between prime and other rates, since banks tend to change the prime rate up or down in discrete steps while market rates move more continuously. Since it is a controlled lending rate, prime has almost always had a positive spread to bank funding rates. Because of the less predictable behavior of the changes in the prime rate and its spread relationship to other market rates, careful analysis is required prior to purchasing prime-indexed FRCDs, but returns can be the highest of all FRCDs.

Index Relationships

Understanding the historical relationship among these indices helps in selecting the appropriate FRCD. The yield spread relationship between three-month LIBOR versus the three-month CD rate and the bond equivalent rate of three-month Treasury bills from January 1984 to November 1985 is displayed in Exhibit 6–1. The yield spread of LIBOR to Treasury bills is wider and more volatile than the spread of LIBOR to the CD rate, since CDs and LIBOR are both affected, although not equally, by actual or perceived changes in bank credit quality.

The second method of reviewing yield spreads and the volatility of the spread is shown in Table 6–1. The average yield spread of three-month LIBOR to three-month CDs, three-month Treasury bills, the Federal funds rate, and the prime rate, as well as the standard deviation of each yield spread, have been calculated for the same 23-month period. The average spread of LIBOR to Treasury bills was + 92 basis points. The LIBOR to prime spread was – 125 basis points; that is, the prime rate averaged 134 basis points above LIBOR.

The standard deviation of the yield spread indicates how volatile the spread to LIBOR is for each index. The least volatile spread relationship is that between LIBOR and CDs with a standard deviation of 13.0 basis points. This means that statistically for the 23-

TABLE 6–1
**Summary of Yield Spreads Between 3–month LIBOR and Other Indices
January 1984–November 1985**

	Average Yield Spread to LIBOR (BP)	Standard Deviation of Yield Spread (BP)
3–Month CD	+ 35	13.0
3–Month Commercial Paper	+ 28	18.7
3–Month T-Bill	+ 92	35.9
Federal Funds	+ 48	46.2
Prime Rate	– 134	49.1
(All yield calculations are done on a money market equivalent basis)		

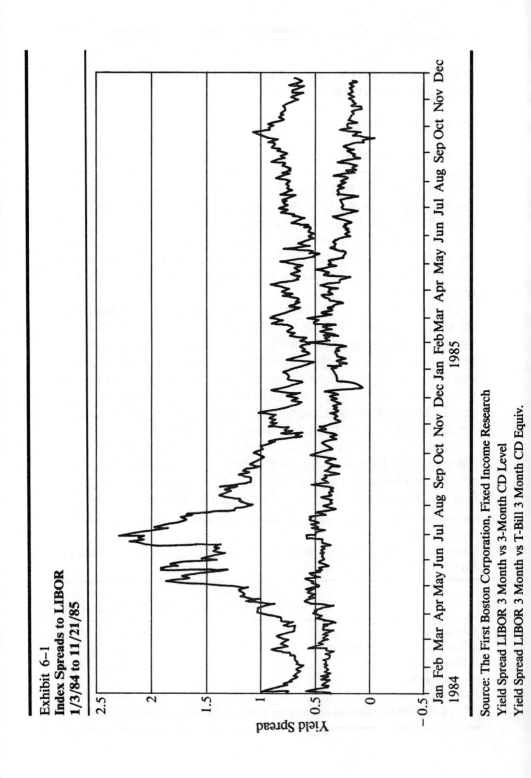

Exhibit 6–1
Index Spreads to LIBOR
1/3/84 to 11/21/85

Source: The First Boston Corporation, Fixed Income Research
Yield Spread LIBOR 3 Month vs 3-Month CD Level
Yield Spread LIBOR 3 Month vs T-Bill 3 Month CD Equiv.

month period under review, two-thirds of the spread observations were within 9.6 basis points of the 35 basis point average. By contrast, the LIBOR to prime-spread relationship was the most volatile. Over the 23-month period, the standard deviation of the average 134 basis point spread between the two indices was 49.1 basis points. Two-thirds of the observations fell above or below the 134 basis point average by 49.1 basis points, establishing a much wider 98.2 basis point range between LIBOR and the prime rate.

Frequency of Interest Payment

The timing of the cash flows from FRCDs has an impact upon the yield: for the same nominal coupon rate, the more frequent the coupon payment, the higher the yield. FRCDs tend to pay interest on either a monthly, quarterly, or semiannual basis. Table 6–2 demonstrates the yield advantage of more frequent payments of a nominal rate of interest. All rates are expressed as semiannual equivalents. For example, at 12 percent, monthly payments produce a 12.30 percent equivalent rate, or return 30 basis points more than semiannually paying securities.

Frequency of the Coupon Refix

The frequency of the coupon refix is the final structural variable of an FRCD. In general, the refix schedule tends to parallel the matu-

TABLE 6–2
The Value of Compounding (Bond Equivalents Basis)

Nominal Rate	Frequency of Payments				
	Daily*	Monthly	Quarterly	Semiannually	Annually
8%	8.16%	8.13%	8.08%	8.00%	7.85%
10%	10.25%	10.21%	10.13%	10.00%	9.76%
12%	12.37%	12.30%	12.18%	12.00%	11.66%
14%	14.50%	14.41%	14.25%	14.00%	13.54%
16%	16.65%	16.54%	16.32%	16.00%	15.41%

*FRCDs are not paid on a daily basis. Daily payments are included here only for comparison to overnight repo rates or Federal funds.

rity of the index underlying the coupon. Since LIBOR, CDs, and Treasury bills tend to be weekly, monthly, quarterly, or semiannual instruments, FRCDs indexed to these rates tend to refix on a similar basis. For example, Treasury bill indexed FRCDs often refix weekly according to the weekly Treasury bill auction results. FRCDs indexed to Federal funds tend to refix either daily or weekly. The daily refix uses the Fed fund's effective rate of the prior day; the weekly refix uses a simple average of the prior week's daily rates. Most prime-indexed FRCDs refix randomly on each date that the reference bank changes its prime rate.

The refix frequency of an FRCD can have a significant effect on its price fluctuation during a given holding period. Frequent refixes serve to keep the FRCD coupon current with market rates, thereby decreasing interim principal fluctuation. FRCDs with less frequent refixes resemble fixed rate securities, an attribute preferable in a period of falling rates.

FLOATING RATE CERTIFICATES OF DEPOSIT: ANALYTICAL METHODS

The growth of FRN and FRCD markets in the U.S. has caused an evolution in security analysis techniques. Since the two products are hybrids of money market and fixed rate instruments, the investor must use a form of analysis that can compare these sectors.

A two-step process is required in order to analyze FRCDs. First, yield to maturity should be calculated, which will allow the analyst to compare floating rate securities to other investments, either fixed or floating rate. Second, a spread analysis should be performed to calculate the incremental return afforded by the FRCD over rolling the underlying index security to the maturity of the FRCD. An investor can evaluate FRCDs of similar indices to determine the adequacy of compensation for credit, liquidity, and other aspects of the security structure.

Yield to Maturity (YTM)

The yield to maturity for a fixed coupon security measures the rate of return on an initial investment (price plus accrued interest) based upon regular coupon payments and principal returned at maturity. The same measure can be calculated for a floating rate security based on an assumed index to project the coupon payment stream. This method of analysis enables an investor to measure the value of any floating rate security.

The YTM of a floating rate security is the semiannually adjusted, bond equivalent, internal rate of return and is calculated from four components: the initial investment at settlement, the current coupon on the FRCD, the principal returned at maturity, and the assumed future coupon payments. Since future rate levels are uncertain, to simplify the analysis future coupons can be set initially assuming current market levels prevail until maturity. Later adjustments to current rates can be analyzed to test the sensitivity of returns to interest rate movements.

The YTM can be used to compare an FRCD to investment alternatives whether they be money market securities, fixed rate, or floating rate notes. A sample of the YTM calculation is illustrated in Exhibit 6–2.

Methods of Spread Analysis

A comparison of the YTM to the return that could be achieved by rolling the underlying money market index until the maturity of the FRCD will allow an investor to gauge if he is adequately compensated for holding the FRCD. The additional yield or the difference between the returns is payment for the credit risk and the structural features associated with the FRCD.

The two predominant methods by which to calculate this spread are *YTM spread* and *spread for life*. YTM spread is a consistently more accurate analysis because it measures the differential between two internal rates of return, while spread for life uses a straight line-accounting treatment of gains and losses. Because the market is slowly evolving to YTM spread from spread for life, both methods will be outlined.[1]

---

[1] Spread for life is discussed in Chapter 9. A more detailed discussion of YTM spread is given in Chapter 10.

Exhibit 6–2
Toronto Dominion FRCD

Maturity:	November 3,1986	Frequency of Refix:	Quarterly
Current Coupon:	9.20	Frequency of Payment:	Quarterly
Index:	3-Month CD composite	Type of Payment:	Actual/360
Refix Spread:	+35	Current 3-mo. CD comp. rate:	8.25
Settlement:	April 1,1985	Next Coupon Date:	May 3,1985
Market Price:	99.95	Next Coupon:	8.60

Coupon Payments*

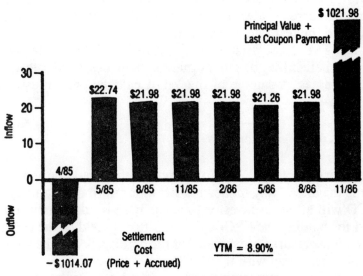

* Different interest payment amounts result from the different number of days in the payment periods.

YTM Spread

As mentioned, YTM spread is the difference between the YTM of the floating rate securities and the bond equivalent IRR of the index roll. It is illustrated in Exhibit 6–3.

Exhibit 6–3
Return from Rolling 3-Month CDs

Time Period:	4/1/85 to 11/3/86
1-Month CD Rate:	8.40%
Assumed 3-Month CD Rate:	8.75% (Bond Equivalent)
Market Price:	100.00

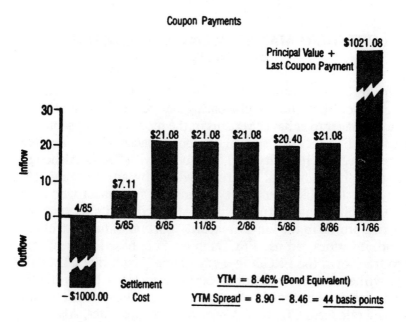

Coupon Payments

Spread for Life

Spread for life (SFL) was developed in the early stages of the floating rate securities market. It is easy to calculate and is widely accepted in Europe where LIBOR is virtually the only index in the market.

The SFL is composed of three elements: the spread between the current FRCD coupon and short-term rates, the refix spread, and the gain or loss amortized to maturity.

Spread for life can be a useful method for measuring the incremental return of an FRCD, but investors must note its limitations. First, it assumes straight line treatment of any discount or premium, a method that can give misleading results when the price of the security diverges from par. Second, SFL does not adjust for different payment frequencies, which makes it more difficult to compare dissimilar investment alternatives. The spread for life calculation for the same data used in the YTM spread example generates a spread of 42 basis points.

PORTFOLIO MANAGEMENT AND THE USE OF FRCDs

There are three major applications for FRCDs within a fixed income portfolio. First, the use of floating rate securities can allow a portfolio manager to enhance returns in the money market sector of his portfolio. FRCDs are a significant tool because of their flexible structures, excellent liquidity, and fungibility with FRNs. Although a portion of the additional return provided by any floating rate security is attributable to maturity extension, a manager who uses FRCDs to attain greater returns will be afforded flexibility to readjust the risk profile in the longer maturity portion of his portfolio.

Second, investors can use FRCDs in an asset-based interest rate swap to transform the FRCD to a "synthetic" fixed rate CD. This strategy will enable the investor to obtain a yield on the synthetic fixed rate instrument that is often higher than those available on either fixed rate term CDs or short-term corporate notes. Also, one can create an asset with a maturity that was otherwise unavailable. To accomplish this, the investor purchases an FRCD and then enters into an interest rate swap whereby he pays a floating rate and receives a fixed rate.

The implications of the asset-based swap are powerful—the universe of investment alternatives has doubled for portfolio managers. An investor seeking fixed rate assets is now able to consider the entire universe of floating rate assets and use the interest rate swap to transform the yield to a fixed rate basis.

In Exhibit 6–4, the investor owns a floating rate CD which pays 6-month LIBOR + 1/8 percent. The investor enters into a swap

Exhibit 6–4
Interest Rate Swap with a Floating Rate CD

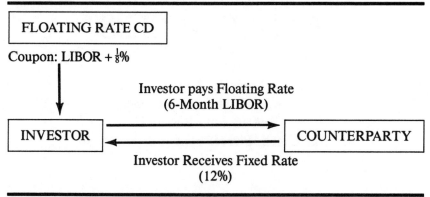

whereby he agrees to pay a floating rate, six-month LIBOR in return for a fixed rate payment of 12 percent. Through the swap transaction he has created a synthetic fixed rate CD yielding 12.125 percent

$$(LIBOR + 1/8\% - LIBOR + 12\%).$$

Finally, an arbitrageur can use FRCDs to match against a floating rate liability and lock in a spread. For example, if funds could be borrowed at the CD Composite Rate and an FRCD offered a coupon of that rate + 30 basis points, the transaction would be executed if costs plus expected return amounted to less than 30 basis points. The selection process is simplified because the maturity, index, and frequency of payment of the FRCD are determined by the liability side of the match.

CONCLUSION

Interest in FRCDs continues to grow. In an environment of volatile interest rates, FRCDs enable the investor to reduce interest rate risk and principal fluctuation. FRCDs can also allow portfolio managers to create synthetic securities that can achieve higher fixed rates than are otherwise available. Finally, in a period of rising interest rates, FRCDs will result in higher returns than those of long-term fixed rate alternatives.

CHAPTER 7

SHORT-TERM TAX-EXEMPT FLOATING RATE VEHICLES

James L. Kochan
Vice President and Manager
Fixed Income Research
Merrill, Lynch, Pierce, Fenner & Smith, Inc.

Serial bonds have traditionally been the primary vehicle for municipal borrowing because this structure was consistent with the revenue stream of most borrowing units. In addition, serials fit nicely the investment needs of the primary institutional buyers of municipals—the banks and the casualty insurance companies. The banks were major buyers of the short-to-intermediate maturities while the insurance companies would prefer the longer maturities, including the long-term issues that typically comprised the bulk of the revenue issues.

The very short end of the market (issues maturing in less than one year) was, until recently, a relatively quiet place. Borrowing activity here consisted primarily of the twice-monthly auctions of Federally-guaranteed housing project notes, the annual Spring borrowing by New York State and an occasional sale of notes by governments faced with a temporary revenue shortfall. Since most investors did not regard their tax-exempt portfolios as a source of liquidity, underwriters and public finance officials saw little reason to develop additional short-term financing vehicles.

However, the short-term market began to change dramatically at the beginning of this decade, as the banks and insurance companies were displaced by individual investors as the major buyers of tax-exempt securities. The growth of the tax-exempt mutual funds greatly enhanced the demand for more liquid securities. In addition, with casualty company demand very weak, the municipal yield curve became unusually steep. This, in turn, implies far greater differentials between the cost of issuing long- and short-term debt. As a result, borrowers began searching for financing techniques that would take advantage of the considerable cost savings available in the short-term sector of the market. Before discussing floating rate vehicles, and why they have become a popular financing vehicle, tax-exempt commercial paper will be discussed.

TAX-EXEMPT COMMERCIAL PAPER

Municipal underwriters, learning from the taxable markets, introduced tax-exempt commercial paper (TECP) as a new financing technique. TECP maturities range from one to 270 days, averaging 30 to 60 days. These securities are especially popular with the tax-exempt money market funds whose average maturity will rarely exceed one or two months. TECP is an unusually flexible financing technique that is often the least expensive in terms of both issuance and debt service costs. Maturities can be scheduled to match the issuer's financing needs and the borrower can "roll over" or reissue new commercial paper to replace outstanding paper on its maturity date. Thus, once an issuer's name is accepted in the market, TECP can become an ongoing financing vehicle. It is not unusual for a TECP program to be authorized to continue for several years. Also, within the authorization period, all or any portion of the program may be retired without penalty to the issuer.

In order to assure broad investor acceptance, TECP is supported by a formal credit facility—a letter of credit or a line of credit from a commercial bank or other financial institutions. This credit facility assures investors of safety and liquidity in the event a TECP issuance cannot be rolled over. While these credit facilities involve additional cost to the borrower, this is a small price to pay for access to cheaper, short-term funds.

One disadvantage to the borrower of this type of financing is the short-term nature of the investors' commitment. Corporations, tax-exempt money market funds, bank trust departments and individual investors are ongoing buyers of TECP. However, funds allocated to this product are, by their very nature, somewhat uncertain. They could be withdrawn from the tax-exempt market for a variety of reasons. Consequently, there was a need for a financing vehicle that promised a more stable supply of investor funds at borrowing costs close to those for TECP.

VARIABLE RATE DEMAND OBLIGATIONS

Variable rate demand obligations (VRDOs) combine long-term and short-term financing techniques and benefits. While they carry a nominal maturity ranging from 1 to 40 years, they also include a "put" feature that permits investors to request payment of the principal well before the maturity date. Because yields on VRDOs are adjusted quite frequently, investors are protected against the capital losses that attend longer-dated fixed-rate assets when market yields rise. To be sure, owners of VRDOs do not capture the price gains that attend longer, fixed-rate bonds when market yields fall. But portfolio managers seeking liquidity are willing to forego those potential price gains in exchange for the relative safety of securities whose behavior mirrors that of money market instruments.

Yields on VRDO's are typically set to float with yields on taxable money market instruments such as Treasury bills or with an index of yields on short-term, tax-exempt issues such as notes or commercial paper. The yields are adjusted in accordance with the schedule set when the issue is brought to market. There are issues for which the yield is adjusted daily, weekly, monthly, quarterly, semiannually, and annually. At each yield adjustment date, the investor has the option to "put" or redeem the issue.

A major advantage to the borrower is that a VRDO can be converted to a fixed-rate, long-term bond. When developing a VRDO program, an issuer can build in an option to convert the obligations to fixed-rate, long-term securities without issuing new securities. Conversion can take place at any time during the life of the issue, triggered, for example, by a predetermined date or by market rates reaching some pre-specified level. Because the put feature is removed and the credit-support facility is usually terminated at conversion, many investors in the original VRDO put the obligations back to the issuer at the conversion date. The issuer, in turn, has the debt remarketed to other buyers through a remarketing agent. Remarketing at conversion requires a revised Official Statement and involves additional compensation to the remarketing agent.

Thus, while the VRDO investor enjoys liquidity, the issuer benefits from low interest costs; the flexibility to convert the debt to fixed-rate, long-term securities; and the option to call the securities without premium before conversion. In addition, by adding various other financing techniques to the structure of a VRDO issue, issuers can establish interest rate ceilings to protect against upturns in interest rates.

Interest on VRDOs is set at a specified percentage of a common money market instrument or a short-term, tax-exempt index. Adjusted daily, weekly, monthly, quarterly, semiannually, or annually, the interest rate should be synchronized with the "put" interval to achieve the widest possible acceptance.

A bank letter of credit or line of credit is usually required as liquidity backup for VRDOs. In the event of a put by an investor, a remarketing agent would attempt to resell the VRDOs in the secondary market. If placement were not possible, however, the issuer would draw upon the credit facility to repay the obligation.

Because VRDOs float at a rate lower than the long-term borrowing rate, they can be an economical means of financing capital needs. During periods of high long-term rates, they permit borrowing without commitment to those rates. At the same time, the option to convert the obligations to fixed rate securities permits the issuer to time entry into the long-term marketplace, based on market factors as well as internal needs. Finally, depending on market conditions, VRDOs can be a cost-effective means to fund interim operating cash flow requirements.

On the surface, the put feature of a VRDO would appear to saddle the issuer with all the headaches associated with a short-term borrowing program. Experience has shown, however, that most buyers of VRDOs are attracted more by the variable rate feature than the put feature. If the formula used to calculate the interest rate accurately reflects changing market conditions, the amount of bonds put to the issuer is generally small. Thus, VRDOs can be used to fund all or part of a borrowing program. The major advantages of VRDOs to issuers are the flexibility afforded by their long nominal maturity, the option to convert to fixed-rate, long-term bonds, and the comparatively minimal administrative requirements.

A NEW HYBRID PROGRAM

The latest financing innovation is a hybrid vehicle that combines many of the advantages of VRDOs and TECP. One version of this new vehicle is called UPDATES[1] (Unit Priced Demand Adjustable Tax-Exempt Securities).

An UPDATES program allows a borrower to offer pieces of an issue at various interest rates for different interest rate periods much like commercial paper. However, UPDATES are issued for interest periods ranging from one day to final maturity. At the end of each interest rate period, each piece is remarketed with a new interest period and a new interest rate. The flexibility of UPDATES is enhanced by a system that allows the issuer to choose, on a continuous basis, among three different pricing modes: (1) unit pricing, (2) VRDO pricing, and (3) fixed-rate, longer term pricing.

In the unit pricing mode, the remarketing agent, typically a dealer firm, establishes a new interest rate scale each day. The investor can then choose the maturities, ranging from 1 to 180 days, that exactly match his cash flow requirements. This mode is similar to a TECP program.

The issuer may also select a VRDO option such as a weekly or monthly repricing schedule with put options at the repricing dates. This mode generally requires higher interest rates than unit pricing.

An UPDATES financing may also be converted to a fixed-rate, long-term security at any time during the life of the program. However, unlike a standard VRDO program, these fixed-rate periods may be set at periods less than the stated nominal maturity date.

[1] UPDATES is a service mark of Merrill Lynch and Co., Inc.

For example, an issuer may choose a two-year, fixed-rate period and at the end of that period switch to a five-year period or even to the Unit Pricing or to the VRDO mode. A conversion to a fixed-rate mode is not irreversible as it would be in a standard VRDO program.

Advantages of the Hybrid Products

Programs such as UPDATES provide the issuer with maximum flexibility in selecting short-, intermediate-, or long-term pricing mechanisms in order to take advantage of the outlook for interest rates at any time. Putting portions of an issue into different pricing modes minimizes the risks associated with committing an entire issue to a single interest rate mechanism. The recent volatility of interest rates has emphasized the difficulty of selecting interest rate "windows" to minimize borrowing costs. An averaging strategy is easily accomplished with an UPDATES structure.

Unlike commercial paper programs in which issuers must authorize each new piece sold, issuers need not be involved with the ongoing remarketing of a hybrid program. An issuer may choose to leave the remarketing and repricing tasks to a dealer. Moreover, in a hybrid program, documentation and authorization for all the different pricing options is accomplished at the outset of the program. The mechanism for changing modes is always in place. This allows an issuer to take advantage of financing "windows" through the use of a quicker and more efficient process.

PRECAUTIONS

All financing vehicles involve some risks and these new programs are no exception. Though interest costs are lower for the unit pricing and VRDO modes than for fixed rate pricing, they are variable over time. Floating rates could, in the future, exceed those of securities whose rates are initially fixed. Budgeting for interest expense is more difficult in a variable rate mode than in a fixed-rate borrowing.

Access to the secondary market is crucial to the success of a hybrid program. A remarketing agent, typically a dealer, usually pledges to resell UPDATES that have matured in the unit pricing mode or have been put back to the issuer in a VRDO mode. Should

TABLE 7–1
Representative Yields for September 1985 in Percent

Maturity	TECP	Updates	VRDOS	General Market Notes and Bonds
1–7 Days	$4\frac{5}{8}$%	$4\frac{7}{8}$%	$5\frac{1}{4}$ %	–
30–44 Days	$4\frac{3}{4}$	$5\frac{1}{8}$	5.30	4.90
90–119 Days	5	$5\frac{1}{8}$	5.40	5.20
6 Months	$5\frac{1}{2}$	$5\frac{5}{8}$	$5\frac{3}{4}$	5.35
1 Year	–	–	6.00	5.60
2 Year	–	–	$6\frac{7}{8}$	$6\frac{3}{4}$
3 Year	–	–	$7\frac{1}{4}$	7
10 Year	–	–	–	8.10
20 Year	–	–	–	8.90

the remarketing agent experience difficulty in selling the notes in the secondary market, the issuer would be required to repurchase the obligations. A credit facility is usually arranged with a lender to guard against this eventuality. The remarketing agent is critical when multiple interest rate modes are utilized. The success of the total program depends on the agent's ability to sell securities in the short- and long-term segments of the market.

Table 7–1 indicates that fixed-term issues generally offer lower yields than the variable maturity issues such as VRDOs and UP-DATES. Borrowers must provide investors with additional interest income in order to capture the flexibility inherent in the variable maturity instruments. However, when the municipal yield curve is very steep, borrowers can achieve substantial savings in interest costs by using such products as VRDOs instead of selling a serial issue that would include maturities as long as 20 to 30 years. In September 1985, the average interest cost of a serial issue would have been approximately 8 percent, compared with costs in the 6–7 percent range for one- or two-year variable rate bonds. These savings are a major reason why the variable rate instruments have proven very popular with a variety of state and local borrowing authorities.

CHAPTER 8

ADJUSTABLE RATE MORTGAGES

Kenneth H. Sullivan
Managing Director
Drexel Burnham Lambert Incorporated

and

Andrew D. Langerman
Associate
Drexel Burnham Lambert Incorporated

INTRODUCTION

The primary mortgage market in 1984 was dominated by adjustable rate mortgages (ARMs), accounting for more than one-half of all mortgage originations. In the past three years alone over $100 billion of ARM loans have been made, creating a market which already totals nearly 20 percent the size of the entire market in long-term corporate debt.

Despite the size of this market, there has been relatively little secondary market activity. There are a number of reasons for this, including the diversity of ARM products and the desire of many lenders to retain floating rate assets. Furthermore, market participants have not felt comfortable pricing this relatively new instrument.

ARMs have been treated as a single instrument or class of

product in much the same way that fixed rate mortgages (FRMs) have been grouped and classified. ARMs are really a number of different products. The common feature among ARMs is that they do not have a fixed interest rate: the mortgage interest rate and payment are reset periodically on the basis of a predetermined formula. In simple terms, when market interest rates go up, the mortgage rates will go up, and vice versa. In practice, originators have designed a wide variety of specific programs both to stimulate consumer demand and to satisfy their own needs for interest-rate-sensitive assets of a particular type. Because of this, ARMs seem difficult to evaluate not only compared to FRMs, but also compared to each other.

After a brief discussion of the history and size of the ARM market, we will focus on the structural components of ARMs and on ARM pricing. We will also have much to say about the option-like features of ARMs and the question of credit quality and associated costs. The central issue in valuing ARMs, as in valuing any investment, is to compare the instrument to other capital market alternatives. Most mortgage market investors are unfamiliar with floating rate instruments; yet this is precisely what an ARM is. When the fancy features are stripped away, the pure floater accounts for more than 90 percent of the value of the ARM. We have used the terms currently available in the interest rate swap market to convert the ARM to the equivalent of a fixed-rate medium-maturity instrument. This allows comparison to the Treasury yield curve and gives a solid basis for answering the question, "How much should an ARM yield?"

SIZE OF THE ARM MARKET

California thrifts began issuing ARMs in 1979, followed by the Federally-charted thrifts in 1981, but it was a combination of market forces that ultimately caused the explosion of ARMs in 1983 and 1984. The deregulation of financial markets and the birth of money market funds as competition for deposits combined to alter the cost and floating rate nature of thrift liabilities. Floating rate assets such as ARMs immediately became more attractive to lenders than ever before, because their repricing frequencies could be designed to match the maturities of the newly deregulated liabilities. Demand on the part of borrowers, however, languished until the persistent high level of interest rates was accompanied by a steep upward-sloping yield curve. The substantially lower short-term costs allowed lenders to offer initial rates on ARMs that were sufficiently attractive to lure a large proportion of borrowers away from the 30-year fixed rate mortgage.[1]

ARM originations have followed the pattern shown in Figure 8–1. ARMs are not a temporary phenomenon, as can be seen from the consistency of the originations; nor are they popular only in thrift lending programs. Substantial percentages of overall originations by mortgage bankers (70 percent of their total) and commercial banks (35 percent of their total) were ARMs in the first half of 1984. Despite their short history, ARM originations already amount to 25 percent of the mortgage pass-through securities outstanding and 20 percent of the corporate bonds outstanding.[2]

STRUCTURAL ELEMENTS OF ARMs

Market participants—originators, traders, and investors—have been intimidated by the number of features that have been built into ARMs. Liquid markets for some floating-rate corporate securities have developed with seeming ease, while confusion has dominated the ARM market. Corporate floaters have the advantage of simplicity (their rates are generally a calculated constant spread over some well-known index) and certainly as to holding period, either through

---

[1] Much discussion in the industry has focused on whether credit quality has been compromised by qualifying too many borrowers at low initial rates, leaving to the future the potential problem of payment shock—the inability to make higher payments resulting from adjustment upward.

[2] A pass-through security is a security which derives its cash flow from underlying mortgages where the issuer passes through to the investor the principal and interest payments made on the mortgages on a monthly basis. For a further discussion, see: Kenneth H. Sullivan, Bruce Collins, and David Smilow, "Mortgage Pass-Throughs," Chapter 6 in *The Handbook of Mortgage-Backed Securities,* Frank J. Fabozzi, editor (Probus Publishing, Chicago, IL: 1985).

Figure 8–1
Originations of Arms
(Percentage of all Originations)

Percent Arms

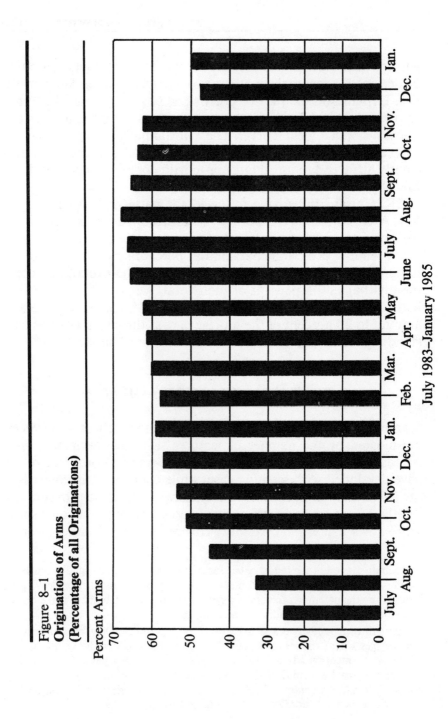

July 1983–January 1985

specific maturities or through puts. This combination allows investors with access to term funds denominated in the index to lock in a spread or rate of return. The index and the spread over the index are similarly the most important features of the ARM. The mortgage rate on essentially all ARMs issued today is set on a periodic basis by adding a fixed spread, called the margin, to an interest rate index. As an example, many ARMs are set once a year at 200 basis points (2 percent) over the one-year Treasury rate (currently about 9.7 percent). The mortgage payments are also reset on a periodic basis (usually, but not necessarily, the same as the frequency for resetting the index) to amortize the loan fully over the remaining term at the then-current rate. These features are discussed below.

Index

The index represents the base or beginning point for calculating the periodic interest rate. Some indices are higher than others, and some are more volatile than others. Additionally, some are based on rates that are determined in the public securities markets, while others are based on derived rates such as the cost of funds for thrifts.

The most popular current indices are the Treasury constant maturity yields. Each day the Federal Reserve gathers the yields of all Treasury securities which traded during the day and constructs a yield curve. The Treasury yields are then taken from this yield curve. Values are compiled daily for 1-, 2-, 3-, 5-, 7-, 10-, 20-, and 30-year maturities. These numbers are published weekly by the Fed. Many ARMs are priced from the weekly average of the one-, three-, or five-year Treasury constant maturity yields. A survey by the National Association of Realtors in October, 1984 showed that almost 70 percent of all new ARMs were tied to Treasury indices with 49 percent using the one-year index.

The second most popular indices are the FHLBB cost of funds. The Federal Home Loan Bank maintains indices on the average cost of funds for each of its 12 districts. These indices are popular among "portfolio" lenders, particularly on the West Coast, who may perceive that they will have no need to sell the loans, and only desire to lock in a spread over their costs. A pricing question arises with the use of cost-of-funds indices since the composition of the liabilities can change over time due to maturity restructuring by lenders.

Repricing Period

Continuously floating rate mortgages would be impractical, which makes the selection of a repricing period (also commonly known as the adjustment frequency) a very important economic term of an ARM. The existence of a yield curve measuring the relative costs of money at different maturities means that in a competitive capital market the return required on the mortgage instrument will always be a function of the repricing period. In an environment with an upward-sloping yield curve, reducing the term exposure by reducing the repricing period will cost a lender in terms of yield received. It should be noted that there need not be any connection between the index and the repricing period. For example, an ARM could have an index equal to the one-year Treasury and a repricing period of six months. When we examine the composition of the ARM market, we will see that the one-year repricing period has been the overwhelming choice in the marketplace (see Figure 8–2, p. 164).

Net Margin

The net margin, also known as reset margin, is an amount which is added to the index to determine the total interest payment to the investor. Net margin differs from the total margin or gross margin stated in a mortgage contract by the amount of servicing retained by the originator. Obviously a higher net margin is more valuable than a lower net margin, but in an absolute sense, the question of value is more complicated and depends on the index selected, the repricing period, and credit and other considerations. The net margin can be important in other ways, such as its effect on prepayment rates. Given two mortgages that have the same index and repricing period, the one with the higher net margin should be more valuable; however, since the likelihood of refinancing by the mortgagor could be presumed to be higher for the mortgage with the higher net margin, the two mortgages will not have the same expected average life. An investor who determines value on the basis of a "locked-in" spread for a certain term will experience some difficulty in paying up for the incremental net margin, to the extent that the higher margin increases the uncertainty of the duration or holding period.

The index, repricing period, and net margin are by far the most important structural elements of an ARM. In the section covering the modeling of ARM prices it can be seen that these three terms generally account for well over 90 percent of the value of an ARM. The balance is, of course, determined by the other features of an ARM, the most important of which are discussed below.

Teasers

We define the teaser to be the difference between the initial mortgage rate (net) and the rate that would have prevailed on the basis of summing the index and the net margin. The teaser is equivalent to a rate that has been brought down by the borrower or the seller of the ARM. Ignoring for the moment the effect that this buydown or teaser has on the credit quality of a loan, the incremental effect on the price that would otherwise prevail is the aggregate present value of all interest payment reductions below the formula rate. This sounds simple; however, the use of teasers in combination with the caps discussed below can produce effects that last well beyond the initial teaser period.

Periodic Interest Rate Caps

Usually annual, periodic interest rate caps (and sometimes floors) are restrictions specifying the maximum adjustment in the interest rate and may, at times, prevent the ARM from adjusting to its formula rate. As an example, the current most common interest rate cap is a 2 percent annual cap. This means that the mortgage interest rate can rise no more than 2 percent per year regardless of changes in the formula rate. Any interest required by the formula rate but over the cap rate is simply lost to the investor. The caps, therefore, have the characteristics of an option written to the mortgagor by the investor. Specifically, the mortgagor has the right to put at par to the investor a mortgage with interest at the cap rate and then must repurchase it at par at the end of the repricing period. If the formula rate is 13 3/4 percent and the mortgage is capped at 13 percent, one can imagine the mortgagor putting a 13 percent one-year note to the investor for the remaining principal, and using the proceeds to purchase a 13 3/4 percent one-year note. Of course, if the formula rate is less than 13 percent, the put expires worthless. Each year the game continues; if the formula rate exceeds the cap, the borrower is subsidized by the investor.

Lifetime Interest Rate Caps

Like annual caps, lifetime caps represent a restriction on the ability to adjust the interest rate on the loan. The most common example in today's market is a 5 percent lifetime cap over the initial mortgage rate. Again, this cap is properly viewed as a series of puts written to the mortgagor by the investor. At each interest-adjustment period, the mortgagor has the right to put at par to the investor a mortgage at the life cap rate.

Key to the consideration and valuation of a lifetime cap is the spread between the formula rate and the lifetime cap, not the quoted lifetime cap which is usually the difference between the initial rate and the maximum rate. For example, a mortgage with a 5 percent lifetime cap, a formula rate of 12 percent, and a teaser rate of 10 percent will have a maximum interest rate of 15 percent. The lifetime cap is only 3 percent over the current formula rate. Programs with low teaser rates and lifetime caps will trade at a greater discount to comparable mortgages with nominal teasers than is implied by the initial interest *give-up*. This is because the lifetime cap is "closer to the money" and thus more valuable to the mortgagor (i.e., a greater *give-up* by the investor). Teasers, in general, bring all caps closer to the money, thus increasing the value of the puts and lowering the value of the ARM. An extreme but not uncommon example is a mortgage with a 2 percent annual cap, a formula rate of 12 3/4 percent, and an initial rate of 9 percent. The first annual put with its "strike rate" of 11 percent is already deep in the money compared to the 12 3/4 percent formula rate.

The value of the caps to the mortgagor is also strongly dependent on interest rate volatility. This will come as no surprise to those familiar with option valuation. For loans without teasers (or where the teaser period has lapsed) stable interest rates cause the value of the caps to decline to zero. This is because the caps are unlikely ever to be hit. A major flaw in many of the valuation models currently in use is that they are blind to changes in market volatility. To the extent that markets become more volatile, a good pricing model should produce a lower valuation for ARMs with caps even if market yields remain unchanged, since the probability and the severity of losses due to the caps increase as volatility increases.

Payment Caps and Negative Amortization Limits

Payment caps represent a periodic restriction on the adjustment of the mortgage payment. A typical ARM calls for annual payment adjustments where the payment is set to fully amortize the loan over the remaining term at the then-current formula rate. A payment cap subjects this adjustment to a percentage limit such as 7.5 percent. If the fully amortizing payment exceeds the cap, the unpaid interest is added to the loan balance. It is important to note that interest is not lost, but simply deferred. It is possible that in a rising interest rate environment the loan would never positively amortize, leaving a balloon payment larger than the original loan on the loan maturity date. In practice, almost all payment-capped loans have additional provisions which prevent this. First among these is a negative amortization limit. Most "neg am" limits allow the loan balance to increase to 125 percent of the original loan amount before negative amortization must cease. After this, any interest shortfall caused by the payment cap is lost to the investor. Additionally, many payment-capped ARMs include a lifetime interest rate cap. It is a fact that under reasonable interest rate volatility assumptions (less than 300 basis points change per year on average), a payment-capped ARM with a lifetime cap of 5 percent to 6 percent will not reach 125 percent of the original balance. Thus the neg am limit is valueless when accompanied by a lifetime rate cap and the valuation problem reduces to valuing the rate cap. This is slightly more difficult in the presence of negative amortization because the volatility assumption may affect the principal balance at any time and thus the amount of principal being "invested" in the cap. For example, a 5 percent life cap on a $100 loan is worth $1.30 under certain volatility and prepayment assumptions, but will be worth $1.43 on a $110 loan.

Some ARMs have a payment adjustment period different than

the interest rate adjustment period. A typical example here is a loan with monthly interest rate adjustments but annual payment adjustments. This type of loan is also subject to negative amortization.

The question of credit quality arises in evaluating loans with negative amortization because the traditional, anticipated improvement with seasoning in loan-to-market value ratios might not occur. To the extent that negative amortization erodes the borrower's realized equity, the probability of losses from defaults and foreclosures increases.

Summary

These are the kinds of structural features commonly found in ARMs. In assessing ARMs it is useful to segment these features according to their overall contribution to the value of the ARM, as we have done below.

Principal Elements

- Index
- Repricing Period
- Net Margin

Incremental Features

- Teaser Rates (buydowns)
- Periodic Rate Caps
- Lifetime Rate Caps
- Periodic Payment Caps

The many combinations of features have resulted in the creation of thousands of ARMs. This proliferation of structures has been the principal obstacle to participation in the secondary market by nonthrift investors. To sustain the growth of ARMs, capital from outside the thrift industry will have to be attracted, but to do so will require the reduction of the many ARM structures to a small number of basic parameters which allow the effective comparison of ARMs to all interest-bearing capital market alternatives, not just to other ARMs.

COMPOSITION OF THE ARM MARKET

From a wide-open market with no predominant ARM structures, a smaller number of generic ARM types has begun to emerge. ARMs with indices based on Treasury yields, which benefit from the ready availability of Treasury data, have experienced rapid growth, and a few basic cap features have accounted for most of those offered with ARMs. In Figure 8–2 we break down the ARM market as it exists today into major segments by the types of ARM features.

Several current developments should serve to exert pressure for Treasury indices and standardized cap features. The importance of maintaining liquidity, either through securitization or standardization of terms to enhance marketability, will increase as the loanable funds, which surged following deregulation of deposit account rates, become fully employed in less liquid loans. Many institutions may be forced to sell ARMs in the secondary market or to borrow against them. Valuation is important in either event and market participants will feel most comfortable with Treasury-indexed ARMs.

A second impetus toward Treasury indices and uniform caps is the agencies' preference for Treasury-indexed ARMs.[3] The credit support of Government National Mortgage Association, Federal Home Loan Mortgage Corporation, or Federal National Mortgage

---

[3] Several Federal programs have contributed to the establishment and growth of the secondary market, Government National Mortgage Association (GNMA), Federal Home Loan Mortgage Corporation (FHLMC), and Federal National Mortgage Association (FNMA), which are known as the "agencies" because of their varying degrees of Federal support. These three agencies have important roles in the following secondary market functions:

- The purchase of mortgages from originators. These purchases are financed by agency borrowings or mortgage pass-through sales.

- The exchange of pass-through securities for mortgages supplied by originators.

- The sale of securities to portfolio investors by originators providing permanent financing for mortgage loans.

- The use of agency securities as collateral for long-term borrowing by the originator, which provides permanent financing for mortgage loans.

- The use of securities to facilitate short-term borrowing by an originator under a reverse repurchase agreement, which provides interim financing or replenishes funds lost to disintermediation.

Figure 8-2
Arm Characteristics

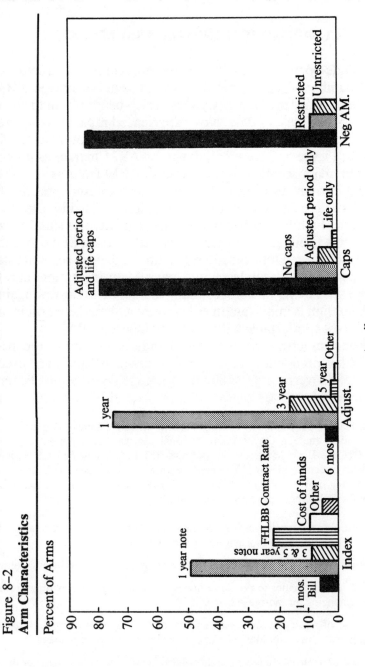

Association backing obviates the need for investor review of underwriting standards. These agencies, however, require conformity to their standards in lenders' programs.

Another factor is the growing controversy within the private mortgage insurance industry. To enhance the ability of borrowers to keep up with payment increases, the insurers have pressured for protective devices like caps. Even legislators have proposed such requirements. Caps have become an increasingly common feature of ARMs.

Finally, portfolio investors outside the thrift industry, who will be important for continued growth and liquidity, have historically exhibited a decided preference for market-oriented investment indices (Treasury-indexed) as opposed to indices based on thrift industry costs of funds. They also prefer to avoid direct involvement with underwriting guidelines and collections, a preference which should give ARM-backed securities an advantage over packages of whole loans.

All of these factors should cause a growing share of ARMs to have Treasury indices and standardized cap features. Even with standardized features, the valuation of an ARM is not simple. Two years into the ARM-era market, participants still lack assurance where the determination of ARM values is involved.

EARLY EVALUATION TECHNIQUES

Most techniques in use today dodge the principal question: "What should be the price or value?" Instead, they assume a price, an interest rate scenario and a prepaid life, and then calculate a yield or an adjusted margin. If you can identify your cost of funds under the same assumptions and are sure of your scenario or scenarios (a big "if"), then a yield (or margin) calculation may suffice. For those who trade or hedge ARMs, scenario-based yield calculations are insufficient, especially in light of the losses experienced by some major players. This type of approach cannot be right even if some sort of "privileged" scenario is assumed because the scenario approach does not account for the option-like nature of ARMs. It does not make any allowance for volatility. One way of analyzing volatility using scenarios is to evaluate tens of thousands of randomly generated scenarios and then take the average price. This is fine if your traders can wait 30 minutes for a single price.

The agencies have all announced purchase and/or guarantor programs for ARMs. These are summarized in Table 8–1. FNMA pricing is fairly typical. FNMA makes quotes of a yield and margin at which it is willing to buy ARMs. Both the yield and the margin are net of servicing that is required to be at least 0.5 percent. The required margin is adjusted upward to accommodate teasers, in effect paying for the teaser on the installment plan. Any interest in the first period above the required yield, or any margin above the adjusted margin, is retained by the seller. If there is no interest or margin shortfall, FNMA pays par. If there is a shortfall, the price is determined as the present value of the ARM cash flows discounted at the required rate with an assumed life of 12 years. The ARM cash flows are calculated at the initial rate until the first rate adjustment, and at the required rate less the difference between the adjusted required margin and the mortgage margin for all subsequent periods. In addition, there is an upfront rate differential fee of 75 percent of the initial rate shortfall for a 1 percent annual cap, and 50 percent of the shortfall for a 2 percent annual cap. FHLMC has a similar pricing scheme. The quoted required yields are changed every Tuesday and are equal to the required net margin (1 percent, 1.2 percent and 1.4 percent on the one-, three- and five-year programs, respectively) plus the weekly average of the relevant index for the past week (Monday–Friday).

ARM UNCERTAINTY—BAD NEWS AND GOOD NEWS

Before we discuss the specifics of ARM pricing, it seems logical to ask the question, "Why would anyone want to buy these things?" Upon initial examination they seem extremely complicated and totally uncertain. All the time-honored techniques for analyzing fixed income securities seem irrelevant when future cash flows are totally uncertain. A question even more to the point may be, "Why should anyone invest money when he doesn't know what he is getting?"

These questions raise some interesting points about holding fixed income securities. What kind of certainty forms the investor's real interest? Investors holding low coupon bonds during the last ten years had almost total certainty about future cash flows as they watched the value of their investment fall from 100 to 60. Pure floating rate instruments such as uncapped ARMs offer a high degree of price certainty. The interest rate will be set to the market rate on a periodic basis. If the price was par at issue, it should be near par on every rate reset date. The only uncertainty in this case is basis risk; that is, a year ago the market thought a given type of security was fairly priced at 150 basis points off the Treasury curve, but this year the required yield is only 130 points. Price certainty (asset value certainty) has additional benefits in the universe of mortgage-backed securities because it alleviates concerns about call protection. ARMs can generally be prepaid without penalty, but since the interest rate on the ARM is near the market rate, the prepayment neither helps nor harms the investor. If he wishes to be long in ARMs, he simply buys more. For capped ARMs that are currently below market (i.e., rates have approached or risen above the caps) there is at least the consolation that the ARM outperformed a fixed rate security for some period of time before it hit the caps, and that prepayments in this circumstance are of great benefit to the investor.

With any coupon instrument there is always uncertainty as to total return over a given holding period. Yield to maturity is certainly the wrong way to compare different instruments since it implies different reinvestment assumptions for different instruments over the same period. Horizon analysis has been developed as a way of equalizing assumptions. In this context ARMs can be analyzed on a footing totally equal with that of other investments. The reinvestment assumption needed to run the horizon analysis serves as a future interest rate which allows computation of the ARM cash flows with certainty. The same probability models which allow us to value the option features of ARMs can be used in probability-driven horizon analyses providing a comparison of two investment alternatives. Such horizon analyses take account of all future interest rate scenarios, giving each its proper weight.

Imagine a security backed by uncapped ARMs, each of which has conservative underwriting standards. Suppose further that the

TABLE 8–1
Summary of Agency ARM Program Characteristics

	FNMA		FHLMC	
	Treasury Indexed ARMs	Cost of Funds Indexed ARMs	Treasury Indexed ARMs	Cost of Funds Indexed ARMs
Indices				
One-Year Treasury	X		X	
Three-Year Treasury	X		X	
Five-Year Treasury	X		X	
11th Dist. FHLB		X		X
Repricing Period (Interest reset)	Same as maturity of index	Monthly	Same as maturity of index	Monthly, after first six months
Payment Changes	Annually	Annually	Annually	Annually
Interest Rate Caps (Annual/Life)				
One-Year Treasury	0%A/5%L 1%A/5%L 2%A/5%L		0%A/5%L 1%A/5%L 2%A/5%L	

	Column 1	Column 2	Column 3
Three-Year Treasury	None	None	None
Five-Year Treasury	None	None	None
11th Dist. FHLB	0%A/5%L	0%A/5%L	0%A/5%L
Payment Caps (Annual Increase/ Maximum Negative Amortization)			
One-Year Treasury	$7\frac{1}{2}$%/125% (0%/5% program only)	$7\frac{1}{2}$%/125% (0%/5% program only)	$7\frac{1}{2}$%/125% (0%/5% program only)
11th Dist. FHLB	$7\frac{1}{2}$%/125%	$7\frac{1}{2}$%/125%	$7\frac{1}{2}$%/125%
Maximum Loan-to-Value	95%	95%	95%
Borrower Interest Coverage	28%/36%	28%/36%	28%/36%
Rate Used for Qualification	Initital Rate	Initial Rate	Initial rate if loan-to-value ratio is 90% or less. Otherwise index plus margin is used.

security is a fully modified pass-through with the backing of one of the agencies.[4] Lastly, suppose that the initial issue were big enough to support active secondary market trading. If this ARM security were set at 300 basis points over the one-year Treasury and priced at par, then you could not print the certificates fast enough. There is clearly no reason why an instrument with so little risk should yield so much. There are active capital markets in interest rate swaps in which this security could be arbitraged, and there is clearly some number less than 300 basis points above Treasuries at which par is the market price. Once we price such a relatively risk-free floating rate instrument, we should be able to price any capped ARM similar to it. In the next section, we will discuss the important considerations in pricing ARMs, including the trade-offs between caps, teasers, and index margins given volatility assumptions and active capital markets.

PRICING ARMs

Given a base index and a repricing period (or adjustment frequency) and assuming that the ARM being analyzed is a pure floater (no caps or teasers), there should be one net margin that will currently produce a price of par and maintain an equilibrium with other capital market alternatives. Of course, as market conditions change, the equilibrium net margin will change to maintain the position of the ARM in terms of expected return and risk relative to comparable securities. The principal factors that contribute to risk, and will therefore require incremental margin over the index, are:

- Basis risk (ARMs repriced each year are not one-year investments),

- Credit risk (The credit risk of all ARMs is not uniform and it differs from other mortgage market alternatives),

- Liquidity risk (The spreads required to transact in ARMs are higher than the spreads for FRMs).

[4] A fully modified pass-through is a pass-through security for which the timely payment of principal and interest is guaranteed by the issuer. A GNMA is an example of a fully modified pass-through.

Basis Risk

If one-year ARMs had a put at par each year, there would be little to discuss about basis risk. In the event that the initial net margin over the one-year Treasury is insufficient in view of market conditions in the second year, the investor simply puts the ARM back to the borrower at par and reinvests at the new net margin over the one-year Treasury. Because they do not have a put, investors should demand a premium over the one-year Treasury to compensate for the commitment to buy ten consecutive one-year instruments (assuming the expected average life of the ARM is ten years).

Quantifying basis risk is difficult for any floating rate instrument, but in most cases the magnitude of the spread risk will be similar to that of comparable maturity fixed-rate instruments in the mortgage sector. This should be true due to the existence of interest rate swaps and other devices that allow investors or borrowers to shift their exposure to the longer end of the maturity structure. The purchase of an ARM that has an agency guaranty but no caps, combined with a position in a ten-year interest rate swap (in which the investor receives the current ten-year Treasury yield less a fixed spread for ten years and pays a floating rate each year equal to the then-current one-year constant maturity Treasury rate) creates the same economic effect as the purchase of a discount agency with a duration of about five and one-half to six years. The cash flows are not identical, but the total return to a six-year horizon and the interim sensitivity to yield changes should be quite close. If the total return is not similar, then an "arbitrage" exists and one strategy will be favored over the other. Table 8–2 derives a minimum net margin required for an ARM to be competitive with a longer term mortgage market alternative.

The required margin for equilibrium seems quite stable and will remain stable as long as the terms in the interest rate swap market follow the yield differentials in the Treasury market at the different maturities.

The foregoing analysis indicates required margins of 125 to 150 basis points for uncapped, essentially risk-free ARMs. The premise, of course, is that the buyer of the ARMs is a capital markets participant who monitors the alternatives and acts accordingly. At this

TABLE 8-2
Derivation of Required Net Margin for a One-Year ARM
(Agency Backed—No Caps)

	Mean for Last 12 Mos.	Mean for Last 3 Mos.	Current
1. Discount MBS Yield (GNMA-9 bond equivalent)	13.46%	12.58%	12.92%
2. Differential Between Fixed Rate Paid and Floating Rate Received in an Interest Rate Swap:			
Received (1-Year Treasury)	10.78	9.38	9.89
Paid (10-Year Treasury)	(12.40)	(11.58)	(11.88)
(Swap Spread)	.50	.75	.55
Net Swap Differential	(1.12)	(1.45)	(1.44)
3. Realizable Floating Rate Yield/Required Initial ARM Yield[a] (bond equivalent) (1) plus (2)	12.34%	11.13%	11.48%
4. Required Initial ARM Yield[b] (monthly cash flow yield)	12.03	10.88	11.21
5. One-Year Constant Maturity Treasury Yield	10.78	9.38	9.89
6. Required Margin for Equilibrium (4) minus (5)	125 b.p.	150 b.p.	132 b.p.

[a] The realizable floating rate yield, that which is obtainable by purchasing a fixed rate investment and then swapping a fixed for a floating rate, must equal the required ARM yield for investors to be indifferent between the two alternatives, all other things being equal.

[b] The formula for converting a semiannual bond equivalent yield to a monthly cash flow yield is:

$$MY = 1,200 \times [(1 + \tfrac{BEY}{200})^{(1/16)} - 1]$$

point the market has not become liquid enough for this premise to hold.

Another factor to consider is the purchasing practice of FHLMC and FNMA which, for example, will purchase, subject to certain conditions, one-year Treasury-indexed ARMs with a net margin of 100 basis points. Does this imply that their purchase standards represent the market? This is true only if you desire to and are able to sell into their programs. Otherwise, market-oriented standards of equilibrium, such as those described above, may apply. The spread between the two standards should narrow as the market becomes more liquid.

Credit Risk

This component is by far the most difficult to quantify once we leave behind the assumption that the ARM is backed by an agency. A large number of factors relating to underwriting standards, private mortgage insurance, initial terms designed to accommodate marginal borrowers, protective features like interest rate and payment caps and, finally, potential risks such as negative amortization all contribute to the necessity of a premium return over the agency-backed case where credit is not a critical concern.

The problem of quantifying the credit risk of specific ARMs lies in the lack of data. Most one-year adjustable loans were made in 1983 or 1984 so there is very little default or delinquency experience from which to draw. Furthermore, there was a general rate decline during the period, which makes the limited existing data practically useless. Some have tried to extrapolate the experience with GPMs to the ARM market. This may be fruitful, but it must be remembered that GPMs have known and increasing payments while ARMs have the potential for unexpected increases.

The point of this section is not to identify actuarial relationships between pricing terms and defaults, because no one can do that as yet, but to highlight the spread/net margin implications of higher default and delinquency rates. The qualitative judgment can then be expressed as an incremental component of required net margin.

The base case from which we make default and delinquency adjustments is the data for conventional loans published by the Mortgage Bankers Association of America. This aggregate data showing

TABLE 8-3
Delinquency Rates for Conventional Loans
(Fourth Quarter, 1984)

Total Past Due	30 Days Late	60 Days Late	90 Days or More	Foreclosures Commenced in Quarter
4.11%	2.83%	.68%	.60%	.15%

seasonally adjusted delinquency rates is presented in Table 8–3.

This data can be interpreted to produce an economic penalty relative to GNMA mortgage pass-throughs as set forth in Table 8–4. When payments are received late, for whatever reason, the investor loses the time value of the use of the money. For all conventional loans, the delay penalty attributable to delinquencies, expressed in terms of required additional yield, is only one basis point over the entire portfolio. Each 30 days of delay in receipt of payments costs the investor approximately 15 basis points in yield on the delinquent portion. Since most loans are paid on time, the overall effect of delinquencies is small, perhaps surprisingly so given the amount of discussion focused on delinquencies.

Defaults resulting in foreclosures are more difficult to evaluate. Converting a quarterly default rate of .15 percent of loans outstanding into a yield penalty requires that we factor loss severity, including unreimbursed foreclosure costs, into the analysis. The law con-

TABLE 8–4
Economic Penalty for Delinquencies
(Conventional Loans)

Delinquency Category	Penalty (Basis Points)	Portfolio Weighting (Table 5–3)	Required Adjustments
Past Due 30 Days	15 b.p.	.0283	.4 b.p.
Past Due 60 Days	30	.0068	.2
90 Days or More	45	.0060	.3
All Delinquencies			.9 b.p.

cerning foreclosure varies considerably from state to state, thereby introducing a demographic variable into the analysis. The range of default rates by state is from half to nearly twice the national average. Thus, any penalty we derive could err significantly unless it is adjusted to reflect specific state demographics.

The yield penalty for foreclosures results from delay in recouping the investment and from failure to recoup it in full. Table 8–5 demonstrates the effect of these variables given a large pool of 30-year conventional mortgages. The penalty in terms of required additional yield becomes most substantial when the loss severity rises. For example, even if foreclosure rates on very low loan-to-value properties reached very high levels, for example, .5 percent per quarter, or more than triple the national average, the lost yield would be only about 15 basis points as long as the average loss could be kept at 5 percent of the loan balance.

Table 8–5 sensitizes investors to the risk of negative amortization in a rising rate environment. Default rates should rise, and the loan balance will grow while market values stagnate or shrink. This is the economic scenario that has maximum risk. Very bad underwriting practices or a localized depression could also produce large loan losses in combination with negative amortization. Contrary to current opinion, however, it takes an extremely bad pool of ARMs to require a 50 basis point (or more) credit premium.

Historical experience with instruments specially designed to make it easier to qualify for a loan indicates that high loan-to-value ARMs will default three to four times more frequently than conventionals, while moderate loan-to-value ARMs should experience

TABLE 8–5
Economics of Foreclosures
(Conventional Loans: 180-Day Delay)

Quarterly Foreclosure Rate	Required Yield Penalty in Basis Points for Foreclosures Percentage of Loan Lost (Average)			
	0%	5%	10%	15%
.15%	1 b.p.	5 b.p.	10 b.p.	13 b.p.
.30	1	10	17	25
.45	2	14	26	39

only one-third more defaults than conventionals. When high loan-to-value ratios are combined with negative amortization, the effects could be compounded, if not on delinquencies, then certainly on foreclosures.

More statistical evidence is needed, particularly in a rising rate environment, before definitive positions can be taken; however, the implied credit spreads in the market today reflect compensation for extremely severe losses due to defaults.

Liquidity Risk

The secondary market for ARMs is clearly not yet as liquid as the MBS markets, or even the fixed rate whole loan market. For this reason, participants should require a discount, in effect a prepaid yield spread, probably on the order of one-half point or eight basis points. As the market evolves, this spread should diminish to some degree, but in any event, it is not a major determinant of relative value.

PRICING THE OPTION-LIKE
FEATURES OF ARMs

Our ARM pricing model uses standard-option pricing techniques to value the puts associated with rate-capped ARMs. In simple terms, option pricing models work by assigning a probability distribution to the value of the underlying asset on the option maturity date. This distribution is characterized in part by its standard deviation or volatility. The value of the option is just the expected value of the option on its maturity date discounted back to the present. We have assumed that future interest rates are normally distributed with a mean equal to the current rate.[5] A volatility or standard

---

[5] Others have assumed that the distribution of future rates has a mean equal to the implied forward rate. We are not persuaded that this assumption is an improvement, since we are not persuaded that implied forward rates represent a forecast of future rates that is better than simply using the current rate. However, we do implicitly incorporate forward rates into our pricing to the extent that the interest rate swap spreads used to establish term structure equilibrium are the result of forward arbitrage.

Figure 8–3
**Volatility of Some Popular ARM Indices
(Basis Points of Yield Per Year)**

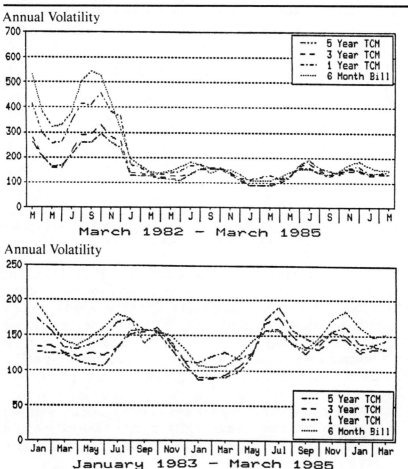

deviation assumption such as 125 basis points a year means that
approximately 66 percent of the time the year-to-year change in
rates is less than 125 points, and that 95 percent of the time the
change is less than 250 basis points. Figure 8–3 illustrates some
measures of recent volatility of instruments commonly encountered
as the base index for ARMs.

Figure 8–4
Effect of Volatility on ARM Prices
(ARM Priced to Yield 175 over Treasury)

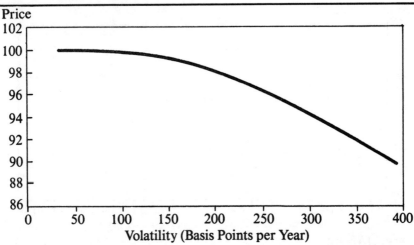

It should be understood that we are not trying to predict interest rates. We are simply trying to get a measure of the probability of hitting the caps. Knowing the current ARM rate and the value of the index, we can assign a probability to any interest rate/mortgage rate combination at any point in the future. In technical terms, we use a binomial model to measure probabilities in the next period, allowing the value of the periodic caps in the next period to be determined by the mortgage rate in the current period. If it seems complicated, remember that yield and duration calculations were beyond the reach of most investors 15 years ago. We have produced several graphs to illustrate the incremental effects of certain structural features.

In Figure 8–4 we show the price of a rate-capped ARM as a function of interest rate volatility. This ARM has a 2 percent annual cap and a 5 percent life cap. It adjusts annually and is set at 175 basis points over the one-year Treasury. There is no teaser; it is priced to yield 175 basis points over Treasuries to a 12-year life. We observe that at low volatility (less than 80 basis points a year) the ARM is priced at par. This is to be expected since there is little likelihood that a cap will ever be hit. For volatility less than 160 basis points a year the total value of the puts is less than $1 (per

Figure 8–5
Effect of Volatility on Initial Margin
(ARM Priced at Par)

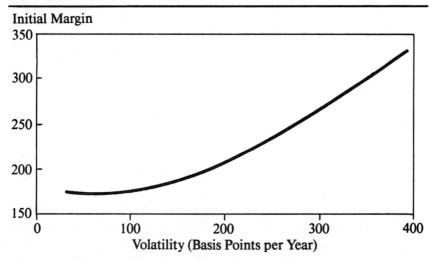

Initial Margin

Volatility (Basis Points per Year)

$100). This confirms our earlier claim that ARM values depend mainly on the index, the margin, and the repricing period; that is, on capital market valuation of the underlying floater.

Figure 8–5 examines the same type of security as Figure 8–4. In this case, however, we turn the pricing question on its head. To maintain the price at par and keep an "expected" yield of 175 basis points over Treasuries, by what amount do we have to raise the periodic reset margin? Said another way, as volatility increases, the value of the caps increases, and the value of the ARM decreases. The investor can be compensated either by being charged less initially or by being paid on the installment plan, that is, by increasing the margin. It should come as no surprise that the additional required margin can be computed "on the back of an envelope" by solving the problem of how much the yield on the pure floater must be increased to cover the cost of the option. One subtle point that is easily missed is that the initial rate on this ARM goes up as the index margin goes up. For the price graph, the initial mortgage rate was always 11.36 percent. Here, however, the initial rate goes from 11.36 percent (very low volatility) to a high of 13 percent.

In Figure 8–6 we show the price effect of an initial period discount or teaser. The top curve has no teaser, the next has a 100 basis point initial period teaser, and the bottom curve has a 200 basis point initial period teaser. For low volatility, the effect of the teaser is simply to lower the price enough to cover the interest lost in the first year (again, we are pricing to yield 175 basis point₃ over Treasuries for a 12-year life). Each 100 basis points costs a little less than $1. Note that as volatility increases, however, the spread between the curve increases. This is the effect of the discount on the value of the caps. An initial period discount has the effect of bringing the caps "closer to the money" and thus raising their value. If the contract rate (index plus margin) is 11.36 percent, and the mortgage rate is discounted to 9.36 percent, the 2 percent cap is "at the money." The mortgage rate in the next year can go no higher than 11.36 percent. The magnitude of this effect is clearer when we look at the effect on the index margin required to keep the ARM price at par, as illustrated in Figure 8–7.

For very low volatility the margin required to compensate for a 200 basis point discount is about 207 basis points over the index, or 32 basis points above a non-discounted (unteased) loan. Thus there is a moderate chance that the borrower will refinance after the discount expires. This is particularly true on some newer ARMs where the 5 percent life cap is set from the initial contract rate and not from the discount rate. For slightly higher volatility (140–160 basis points per year) the margin required on a 200 basis point discount is about 238 basis points. Thus, the cost of increased volatility is 30–35 basis points. This compares to a 10–15 point cost for increased volatility when there is no teaser. Again, it is hard to bank on recovering the discount with a loan that will end at over 50 basis points above the market. In studying this figure, it is important to remember that, as shown above, the initial mortgage rate increases as the margin increases. Without this linkage, the discount would increase above the 100 or 200 point level. Thus the mortgages in the above two figures are not entirely comparable.

Finally, we look briefly at the price sensitivity of ARMs to changes in yields. Figures 8–8 and 8–9 show the price of an ARM which is priced to yield 175 basis points over Treasuries for Treasury rates from 5 percent to 17 percent. These are 2/5 ARMs as

Figure 8–6
**Effect of Volatility on ARM Prices
(Examination of Teaser Rates and Prices)**

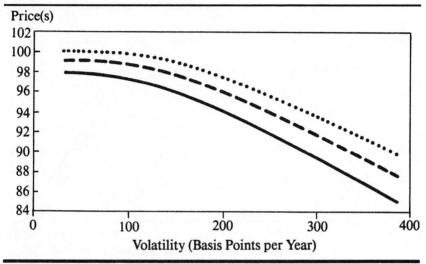

Volatility (Basis Points per Year)

Figure 8–7
**Effect of Volatility on Initial Margin
(Examination of Teaser Rates)**

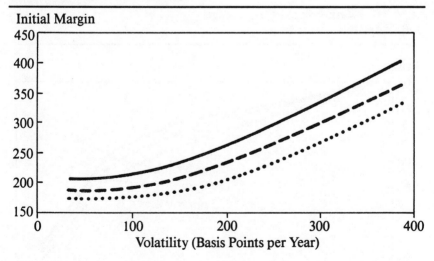

Volatility (Basis Points per Year)

Figure 8–8
**ARM Price Response to Index Change
(Rate Adjustment Imminent)**

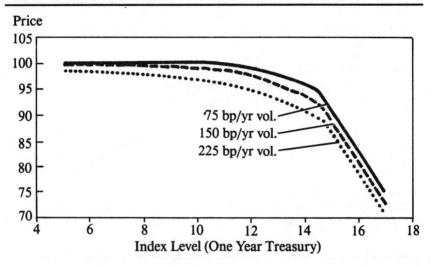

Figure 8–9
**ARM Price Response to Index Change
(Rate Adjustment Just Past)**

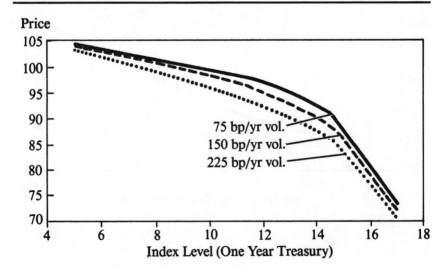

before with an initial interest rate of 11.36 percent. In Figure 8-8, we assume that a mortgage rate adjustment will occur later in the same day, that is, that the current rate has prevailed for 364 days. In Figure 8-9, we assume that the mortgage rate has just adjusted to its level of 11.36 percent and that it won't adjust again for a year. Curves are plotted for three different volatility levels—75, 150, and 225 basis points per year.

When the rate adjustment will occur later in the same day, the price is flat, as expected, across a wide range of yields. The price is very slightly under par because of the caps, with the discount from par increasing as volatility increases. As the index rate increases, the life cap gets closer to the money, until the index rate passes 14.6 percent, at that point, the option is in the money. This effect is magnified at higher volatilities. For these high yields, the ARM performs like a fixed-rate long-duration instrument and the price is very sensitive to changes in yields. At the low yield end of the graph, the duration is essentially zero given the impending rate adjustment, which imparts a near-cash quality to the ARM.

In Figure 8-9, the ARM has a full year until the next adjustment, and so performs like a one-year security for low yields and volatility. Note that both these graphs can be reinterpreted as showing the effects of buydowns. For market levels greater than the current mortgage rate of 11.36 percent, the graph looks like an ARM with a teaser.

Two important points can be made by examining Figures 8-8 and 8-9. The first is that the value of the call associated with the borrower's right to prepay is very small when compared to a fixed rate mortgage, for even when rates drop, ARMs trade at relatively small premiums to par. The worst case associated with this point comes when there is a full year until the next repricing period. Even here, however, the call has very little value. One reason for this is that the ARM responds to changes in yield like a one-year instrument so that the price at low yields is low compared to a fixed rate security. A second reason is that the caps lower the price of the ARM, again lowering the value of the call. Mortgage-backed securities, even those with full government guarantees, often trade over 100 basis points (bond equivalent) off the Treasury yield curve. This yield advantage is due in part to the risk of prepayment. With ARMs, prepayment hurts the investor very little even in the worst case and in most cases is a benefit.

We will mention the second issue only briefly here. This is the question of hedging ARMs. To successfully hedge any interest-rate-sensitive instrument, it is necessary to compute the price sensitivity to changes in yield (this is the role of modified duration). As we have seen, this sensitivity increases as we move toward higher yields and as rate volatility increases, but sensitivity decreases as we approach rate adjustments. A complex strategy combining several instruments is required to hedge the characteristics of ARMs because they do have a volatility-sensitive option component, and because they are sensitive to changes in either or both of short- and long-term rates.

To sum up the pricing considerations for ARMs, we have seen that the most important variables for an ARM with a given net margin over a specified index are:

- Basis to Treasuries—Recently 100 to 150 basis points over Treasuries depending on the index selected, market conditions and the yield curve.
- Credit Risk Relative to Agencies—Usually less than 10 to 15 basis points unless loan-to-values exceed 80 percent, and probably not more than 40 to 50 basis points unless the ARMs are heavily teased as well as combined with negative amortization.
- Liquidity—Probably a 5 to 10 basis point penalty, depending on the investor horizon.

- Caps/Option Feature—Depending on the combinations, significant adjustments to market value may be required.

- Volatility—For most ARMs with 2/5 caps, a change in volatility of 25 basis points per year results in a 3/4 point change in ARM value.

A sample ARM is priced in Figure 8–10. The left-hand column indicates a range of cash flow margins over the one-year Treasury required by investors; the higher the required margin, the lower the price. In determining the price, we distinguish between the pure floater, "float value," which includes the teaser effect, and the imbedded option-like caps "option value." Purchase at the indicated price results in the expected yields to investors (designated "cash flow yield" and "bond equivalent yield"). An alternate assessment of rela-

Figure 8–10
Drexel Burnham Lambert: Mortgage Backed Securities Analytics

Rate Capped ARM Price Calculator

Net Mortgage Rate (%):	10.5	Months to Maturity	360
Months to Rate Adj:	12	Months bet. Rate Adj:	12
Periodic Rate Cap (bp):	200	Life Rate Cap (bp):	500
Service Fee (%):	.375	Payment Delay:	54
Index Value (%):	9.89	Net Margin (bp):	187.5
Fixed Rate (%):	11.83	Floating Receives (bp):	− 75
Horizon (months):	84	Mon. CPR (%):	
Index Volatility (bp/yr):	175		

Cash Flow Mar.	Bond Eq. Mar.	Price	Float Value	Option Value	Cash Flow Yield	Bond Equiv Yield	Term Equiv Yield	Term Treas. Spread
150	177	98.71	99.83	1.12	11.39	11.66	12.85	102
160	188	98.23	99.35	1.12	11.49	11.77	12.96	113
170	198	97.76	98.87	1.11	11.59	11.87	13.06	123
180	209	97.29	98.40	1.11	11.69	11.98	13.17	134
190	219	96.82	97.93	1.11	11.79	12.08	13.27	144
200	230	96.36	97.46	1.10	11.89	12.19	13.38	155
210	240	95.90	96.99	1.10	11.99	12.29	13.48	165
220	251	95.44	96.53	1.09	12.09	12.40	13.59	176
230	261	94.98	96.07	1.09	12.19	12.50	13.69	186
240	272	94.53	95.61	1.08	12.29	12.61	13.80	197
250	282	94.08	95.16	1.08	12.39	12.71	13.90	207
260	293	93.63	94.71	1.08	12.49	12.82	14.01	218
270	303	93.19	94.26	1.07	12.59	12.92	14.11	228
280	314	92.74	93.81	1.07	12.69	13.03	14.22	239
290	325	92.30	93.37	1.06	12.79	13.14	14.33	250
300	335	91.87	92.92	1.06	12.89	13.24	14.43	260

tive value is the "term equivalent yield," which represents the total fixed-rate expected yield that results from combining purchase of the ARM at the price indicated with a position in an interest rate swap on current terms. The "term equivalent yield" represents a spread over the long-term Treasury indicated in "term treasury spread."

CONCLUSION

At the time of this writing the secondary market in ARMs has certainly not yet arrived. Even though ARMs are new and therefore unfamiliar they are comprised of components that can be understood and priced. Key elements that make ARMs seem so complicated include the proliferation of many different types of ARMs with different features, and the option-like component of ARMs. The first issue is slowly working itself out as the market selects a smaller number of ARMs that are both attractive to borrowers and lenders and that have a large enough origination volume to support secondary market trading. The agencies have currently settled on three general rate-capped programs and three payment-capped programs, which should help homogenize the market.

To facilitate the trading of ARMs and the use of ARMs as collateral in financing arrangements, a more sophisticated approach to valuation must become commonplace. While most written research focuses on the valuation of caps (option-like features), the principal determinants of value are term structure equilibrium and credit quality. Concerning the option-like features, we have tried to show that they are not as mysterious as they seem, and that for low to medium volatility markets, they have a secondary rather than a primary effect on the price.

ARMs offer investors a high level of asset protection which, given the experience of the past five years, should be a valuable commodity. Further, ARMs can often provide arbitrage or swap opportunities against their fixed rate cousins farther out along the yield curve and substantial yield pick-ups relative to corporate floaters.

CHAPTER 9

EVALUATING FLOATING RATE NOTES

Kenneth E. Jaques
Vice President and Senior Product Manager
for Domestic Floating Rate Notes
PaineWebber Inc.

In the financial community, there are literally hundreds upon hundreds of investment portfolios, and for each one a fairly standard number of investment parameters. Each individual portfolio manager has his own aims and goals, whether they are set down by management or by the individual investor. Day after day, the same securities are offered to almost all investors, and inevitably, what looks expensive to one looks relatively attractive for the price to another. Different parameters breed different methods of evaluating securities.

This element is most prevalent in the floating rate note market. Since floating rate notes have numerous coupons over their life, it is virtually impossible to calculate a yield to maturity as in the fixed rate market. Since this long-standing tool of measurement is not applicable to floaters, development of evaluation techniques for floating rate notes has resulted in various schools of thought on the best method to be used in determining the real value of the floater.

What is "real value"? As previously mentioned, a real value to one investor may make no sense to another. Real value can only be determined by the individual. Real value is better termed "unique value" or that value which best allows an individual investor to meet those parameters he has set forth for that security.

The absence of a uniform method of measuring the value of a security, such as yield to maturity, necessitates an alternative means of appraising variable rate securities. Wall Street, in its own inimitable fashion, has done this many times over. Through careful research into the investment needs of various types of portfolios, a number of evaluation methods for floaters have been developed. The purpose of this chapter is to describe these methods and to illustrate their application in one's portfolio.

CURRENT YIELD EVALUATION

Current yield is determined by dividing the current interest rate by the dollar price of the security. This results in a measurement of the per diem return on one's investment.

In the world of floaters, a large group of investors—namely trust departments, investment advisors, and other actively traded portfolios—utilize floating rate notes (FRNs) as money market surrogates. Taking capital earmarked for short-term investment and comparing the prevailing rates of money market instruments to the current returns offered by floating rate notes (whose interest rates are tied to these same securities, usually at a nominal premium) will determine if the time is right to use FRNs for short-term investment. For instance, assume that a particular portfolio has recently acquired a sum of investment capital but has no real conviction about the direction of the long-term market. One would most likely consider parking these funds in short-term instruments as a "pit stop" for these funds until the market develops a trend. The alternatives are Treasury bills and Certificates of Deposit (CDs).

For example, suppose that the six-month Treasury bill is yielding 9.15 percent (CD equivalent yield) and six-month CDs are yielding 9.35 percent. At the same time, suppose that Citicorp FRNs due May 1, 2004, which float at 1 percent above the six-month Treasury bill and whose coupon refixes every May 1 and November 1, are yielding approximately 12.15 percent with the coupon refixed at 11.75 percent one month ago. Since the 11.75 percent coupon will be in effect for the next five months, it is extremely attractive in comparison to the rates available in the money market. It would seem to be advantageous to use this security as an alternative to the Treasury bill or the CD market. The opportunity to purchase Citicorp FRNs at 11.75 percent due May 1, 2004 at a price of 96.00 provides an excellent temporary investment while outyielding other short-term instruments by 275–300 basis points.

Now, let us consider the comparison of two floating rate notes with different coupon refixing dates under the current yield method of evaluation. In this scenario, assume that one has decided to purchase FRNs as an alternative to the money market. The only question that remains is which floater should be purchased. In order to compare two different refix floaters, we must analyze both over the same investment period. This method for comparing floaters is based on a comparison of the weighted average rate (WAR) of the securities under consideration. Underlying the WAR approach to comparing variable rate securities is the assumption that all floating rate notes using the same base rate (Treasury bill, LIBOR, etc.) and having the same frequency of coupon refixing (weekly, quarterly, semiannually, etc.), regardless of maturity, should produce the same current yield.

WAR is simply the weighted average coupon rate for the number of days in the interest period under consideration. It is computed by first weighting the present coupon rate and the assumed coupon rate at the refixing by the number of days to refixing and the number of days remaining in the interest period after refixing, respectively. The result is then divided by the number of days in the interest period.

The formula for the weighted average rate is:

$$\text{WAR} = \frac{(C \times D) + (AC) \times (D' - D)}{D'}$$

where C = Present coupon
       D = Number of days to refix
       AC = Assumed new coupon
       D' = Number of days in interest period

The current yield (CY) is then found by dividing the weighted average rate by the price as a percentage of par (P).[1]

$$\text{CY} = \frac{\text{WAR}}{P}$$

---

[1] In this chapter, price will mean the price as a percentage of par rather than dollar price.

To illustrate how to use the weighted average rate approach to compare two floating rate notes, suppose that on December 1, 1984 an investor was considering the acquisition for 180 days of one of two Citicorp floating rate issues—Citicorp 04s at 96 or Citicorp 98s at 96 1/4. The fixing spread for both issues is 100 basis points above the six-month Treasury bill rate. On December 1, 1984, the present coupon is 11.75 percent for the Citicorp 04s and 12.15 percent for the Citicorp 98s. The Citicorp 04s refix in 150 days and the Citicorp 98s refix in 90 days. Making the assumption that, based upon the prevailing Treasury bill rate, the new coupon for both securities, since their fixing spreads are identical, will be 10.15 percent, the weighted average rate for the Citicorp 04s is 11.48 percent and the current yield is 11.96 percent, as shown below:

Citicorp 04:

Number of days in interest period	$= D'$	$= 180$ days
Number of days to refix period	$= D$	$= 150$ days
Present coupon	$= C$	$= 11.75\%$
Assumed new coupon	$= AC$	$= 10.15\%$
Price	$= P$	$= 96.00$

$$WAR = \frac{(11.75) \times (150) + (10.15) \times (180 - 150)}{180} = 11.48\%$$

$$\text{current yield} = \frac{11.48}{96.00} = 11.96\%$$

The weighted average rate for the Citicorp 98s is 11.15 percent and the current yield is 11.58 percent, as shown below:

Citicorp 98:

Number of days in interest period	$= D'$	$= 180$ days
Number of days to refix period	$= D$	$= 90$ days
Present coupon	$= C$	$= 12.15\%$
Assumed new coupon	$= AC$	$= 10.15\%$
Price	$= P$	$= 96.25$

$$WAR = \frac{(12.15) \times (90) + (10.15) \times (180 - 90)}{180}$$

$$= 11.15\%$$

$$\text{current yield} = \frac{11.15}{96.25} = 11.58\%$$

Even though, on the surface, Citicorp 98s (12.15s at 96.25) out-yield Citicorp 04s (11.75s at 96.00) 12.62 percent to 12.24 percent, the fact that the Citicorp 04s will carry the 11.75 percent coupon for 60 days longer than the Citicorp 98s will carry the 12.15 percent coupon must be taken into consideration.

SPREAD FOR LIFE

There are obviously a number of ways to evaluate floaters. Adding to the confusion is the fact that, depending upon whom one is speaking to, the same calculations may frequently be called by different names. Throughout this chapter, I will attempt to refer to each method by its several alternative names.

Spread for life (SFL), or, as it is sometimes called, *simple margin,* or *positive margin,* originated in the Eurofloater market as a means for banks, historically the largest issuers as well as buyers of floating rate notes, to calculate the relative value of a floater in comparison to the syndicated loan market. The calculation itself is a "simple" amortization calculation which measures the value of the discount (or negative value of the premium) coupled with the constant fixing spread, over the life of the floater.

Spread for life is extremely useful to those investors who are interested in a conservative approach to matching their assets to their outstanding liabilities. Taking into consideration the length of an outstanding liability and matching the maturity to that of a floater with a premium fixing spread over a common base rate provides an opportunity to create a positive index hedge in one's portfolio.

The most prominent users of this particular method of evaluation are thrift institutions and commercial banks. In 1982, the domestic floater market witnessed the birth of the "weekly" floater. This floating rate note was created solely for the purpose of attracting the enormous amount of capital being created by the introduction of the deregulated Money Market Demand Accounts (MMDA) by the thrift institutions around the country.

Taking in deposits, payable on demand, at variable interest rates that are based upon Treasury bills or some other money market index, and reinvesting in floating rate notes that refix weekly at a wider spread over a similar security, guarantees the institution a positive index hedge, providing the floater is held to maturity. For example, suppose a thrift institution is offering to pay interest at .50 percent over the weekly 91-day Treasury bill auction to its depositors. By taking these deposits and investing them in a weekly floater which floats off the same auction results but refixes at 1 percent over that rate, one would guarantee the institution a .50 percent positive margin over the amount that it is paying out. If the floater is trading at a discount to par, the positive margin would be even greater; if it is trading at a premium, the margin would be less.

In essence, this method measures the amortization of the discount or the depreciation of the premium, as the case may be. Coupled with the constant refixing spread, this results in a guaranteed, locked-in spread over the base rate for the life of the floater. If the floater is held to maturity, one is assured of this margin over the base rate regardless of the movement of interest rates.

The formula for the spread for life (simple margin/positive margin) is:

$$\text{SFL} = \frac{\dfrac{(100-P)}{BY} + \dfrac{F}{100}}{\dfrac{P}{100}} \times 100$$

where BY = bond years
F = fixing spread in basis points

For example, suppose that on December 1, 1984 the Citicorp floating rate notes due on March 1, 1985 are selling for 99.90. The coupon rate on this floater is refixed weekly at 100 basis points over the three month Treasury bill auction rate. The current coupon is 9.90 percent. The spread for life is 140.14, as shown below:

Citicorp 9.90 3/1/85 at 99.90:
    Price   = P = 99.90
    Bond years   = BY = .25
    Fixing spread = F   = 100 basis points

$$\text{SFL} = \frac{\dfrac{(100-99.9)}{.25} + \dfrac{100}{100}}{\dfrac{99.9}{100}} \times 100$$

$$= 140.14$$

Keep in mind that this particular method of evaluation does not take into consideration interest rates (coupon rate and base rate). If the present coupon of the floater and the base rate are about the same, this method should suffice as an accurate evaluation method.[2]

EFFECTIVE MARGIN

As previously mentioned, the spread for life method of evaluation does not take interest rates into consideration. It is simply a calculation of the amortization of a premium or discount over the life of that security. The *effective margin* or *total margin* or *adjusted simple margin* technique, however, takes the spread for life computation one step further in that it factors in the affect of the current coupon and the prevailing interest rates to achieve a more accurate evaluation of the floater.

After measuring the value of the discount or premium of the floater, the effective margin approach includes the impact of the spread between the coupon and the base rate over the period of time until the next coupon refixing. It is the most effective way of evaluating a floater if the coupon and the base rate are substantially different. In simplified terms, the effective margin (total margin/ adjusted simple margin) method, like the spread for life method, measures the amortization or depreciation of the discount or premium of the floater, coupled with the fixing spread, but also takes into consideration the positive or negative spread between the coupon and the base rate and weights it over the number of days until the next coupon fixing. The result of such a calculation is a measurement of the locked-in spread (SFL), plus or minus the bonus or penalty associated with the positive or negative "carry" over the base rate, over the coupon period. The "carry" is defined as the spread between the base rate and the coupon. If the coupon is higher than the base rate, the carry is positive. If the base rate is higher than the coupon, the carry is negative.

---

[2] Virtually the same results can be obtained on a bond calculator by using 0 percent as the coupon and calculating a yield to maturity. Coupled with the fixing spread, it produces an approximate spread for life.

The positive or negative spread is a direct adjustment of the purchase price of the floater. If the carry is positive, the purchase price is adjusted downward. If the carry is negative, the purchase price is adjusted upward. The formula to compute the effective margin follows. First, compute the adjusted price (AP) as shown below:

$$AP = P - \frac{\left(\frac{C-B}{100}\right) \times (P+AI) \times \left(\frac{D}{360}\right)}{1 + \left(\frac{B}{100} \times \frac{D}{360}\right)} \times .01$$

where B = base rate
    AI = accrued interest
and P, D and C are as defined earlier.

The effective margin (EM) is then found by:

$$EM = \frac{\frac{(100-AP)}{BY} + \frac{F}{100}}{\frac{AP}{100}} \times 100$$

where F and BY are as defined earlier.

To illustrate how to compute the effective margin, suppose that on September 15, 1984 Chase Manhattan floating rate notes due on May 28, 1996 were selling for 99.40 with a present coupon rate of 12 percent. For this floater, the fixing spread is 1/8 of 1 percent (12.5 basis points) over three-month LIBOR. The base rate (three-month LIBOR) is 11.8125 percent. The coupon rate refixes quarterly on November 3, 1984 (49 days). The adjusted price for this floater is 99.3997 as shown below:

Chase 12% 5/28/96 at 99.40
    Price   = P   = 99.40
    Present coupon   = C   = 12.00%
    Base rate   = B   = 11.8125%
    Accrued interest   = AI = .144
    Number of days to refixing   = D   = 49

$$AP = 99.40 - \frac{\frac{(12.00-11.8125)}{100} \times (99.40+.144) \times \left(\frac{49}{360}\right)}{1 + \left(\frac{11.8125}{100} \times \frac{49}{360}\right)} \times (.01)$$

$$= 99.3997$$

Given the adjusted price of 99.3997, the effective margin is 17.79 percent as shown below:

Adjusted price = AP = 99.3997
Bond years   = BY = 11.6
Fixing spread = F   = 12.5

$$EM = \frac{\dfrac{(100 - 99.3997)}{11.6} + \dfrac{12.5}{100}}{\dfrac{99.3997}{100}} \times 100$$

$$= 17.79\%$$

As previously mentioned, when the current coupon and the base rate are relatively close, the spread for life (simple margin/positive margin) method should suffice. But, when there is a wide disparity between these two rates, the effective margin (total margin/adjusted simple margin) method is more accurate. Also, remember, the spread for life method measures the value over the life of the security. The effective margin approach measures relative value until the next coupon change. The major difference is that the effective margin method takes the effect of the current yield over the short term into consideration.

Since this method involves all aspects of the security and its relative position in the marketplace, I believe that this is the most accurate of all methods in evaluating floating rate notes. I will expand upon this later in this chapter.

TOTAL ADJUSTED MARGIN

Total adjusted margin or *adjusted total margin,* as it is also called, is basically an enhancement of the effective margin method. Whereas the effective margin approach takes into account the positive or negative spread between the base rate and the current coupon rate over the period until the next coupon refixing, the total adjusted margin reflects that spread relationship over the entire life of the floater.

Unfortunately, in order to utilize this evaluation one must make some dramatic long-term assumptions. Since no one is capable of predicting the future movement of interest rates over long periods of time with any assurance, one must assume an average rate of both the base rate (Treasury bill or LIBOR) and the interest rate of the floater. Based upon prevailing economic data, the level of interest rates, and the educated forecasts of experts, one can ascertain some historical data on the interest rates in question and their relationship in order to arrive at an estimated average rate to use in the calculation of the total adjusted margin.

It is my opinion that the projection of an estimated average base rate over long periods of time would be quite a feat, given the gyrations of interest rates in recent years. Most investment managers find it difficult enough to establish an interest rate scenario over the very near term, let alone a period of five to ten years. Furthermore, the total adjusted margin approach does not represent, in my opinion, the most accurate indication of the relative value of a floater, unless one assumes an unchanging estimate for the base rate, regardless of the maturity of the floater in question. Nevertheless, this practice, no matter how accurate or deceptive, is commonly utilized and relatively widely accepted in the investment community. One reason for this could be the lack of a better alternative for evaluating a floating rate note over long periods of time.

It is true that, according to the nature of the beast, the evaluation of floaters over any length of time requires an assumption or projection of the future. This may lead us to the conclusion, held by many all along, that floating rates are in fact short-term, money market instruments.

The first step in computing the total adjusted margin is to compute the adjusted price. The formula for the adjusted price is the same as that given earlier to compute effective margin. Given the adjusted price, the total adjusted margin (TAM) is then found using the following formula:

$$TAM = \frac{\left(\frac{100-AP}{BY}\right) + F + \frac{(B)\times(100-AP)}{100}}{\frac{AP}{100}} \times 100$$

where all the variables were defined earlier.

To illustrate how to compute the total adjusted margin, suppose that on November 15, 1984 Bank of Boston floaters due February 15, 1996 were selling for 99.40 with a current coupon rate of 9.5625 percent. The coupon rate is refixed quarterly at the three-month LIBOR rate. The next refix is February 15, 1985 (90 days). The next base rate (three-month LIBOR) is assumed to be 9.50 percent. The adjusted price for this floater issue is 99.3866, as shown below:

Bank of Boston: 9.5625% 2/15/96 at 99.40:

Price	= P	= 99.40
Present coupon	= C	= 9.5625%
Assumed base rate	= B	= 9.50%
Accrued interest	= AI	= 0
Number of days to refixing	= D	= 90

$$AP = 99.40 - \frac{\left(\frac{9.5625 - 9.50}{100}\right) \times (99.40 + 0) \times \left(\frac{90}{360}\right)}{1 + \left(\frac{9.50}{100} \times \frac{90}{360}\right)} \times .01$$

$$= 99.3866$$

The total adjusted margin is then 11.37 percent as shown below:

$$TAM = \frac{\left(\frac{100 - 99.3866}{11.21}\right) + 0 + \frac{9.50 \times (100 - 9.3866)}{100}}{\frac{99.3866}{100}} \times 100$$

$$= 11.37\%$$

DISCOUNTED CASH FLOW MARGIN/YIELD TO MATURITY MARGIN

Since floating rate notes will have numerous coupons throughout their life, it is impossible to calculate a yield to maturity in the same manner as it is calculated in the fixed-rate market. However, if one makes, as in the total adjusted margin (adjusted total margin) method, a long-term assumption on the estimated average coupon for the individual interest payment periods over the life of the bond, a "hypothetical" yield to maturity can be computed.

This can be accomplished by using a discounted cash flow calculation, which measures each cash flow for each interest period over the life of the security. That is, one uses the prevailing base rate to determine if the floater were to adjust its coupon today, an assumed coupon rate for the life of the floater. Armed with this information (assumed coupon rate, maturity and price), a stream of margin calculations can be constructed to arrive at a margin over the base rate.

Using the same information described above (assumed coupon rate, maturity and price), a traditional yield to maturity can be calculated. The result is a "hypothetical" yield at best, but in order to evaluate floaters over long periods of time, estimates—realistic and intelligent one hopes—must be made. Once the yield to maturity is calculated, subtract the assumed base rate from the result to attain the discounted cash flow margin (DCFM) or yield to maturity margin. A more sensible alternative to this method might be to subtract the yield of a comparable maturity U.S. Treasury security from the yield to maturity of the floater. This method is more in line with the traditional method of measuring the relative value of a fixed-rate security. The discounted cash flow margin (yield to maturity margin) is discussed further in the next chapter.

Remember that when employing all calculations, with one or two exceptions, an actual days/360 basis must be used. Another point worth remembering is that unless the current base rate is used as the assumed average rate and the present coupon is used as the assumed average coupon, there is little chance that any two individuals will arrive at the same total adjusted margin or discounted cash flow margin for a particular floater. If all floaters are compared on the basis of the same assumptions, a ranking according to their margins will accurately show relative attractiveness among issues.

THE FORS SYSTEM

As we have seen, the question of evaluating floating rate notes can become quite confusing. Not only may two investors appraise the same floater in completely different ways, but even if they are using the same method, they may be using different base rates and different time horizons.

A ranking of floating rate notes in order of their current yield would be of little use to the investor who evaluates floating rate notes according to a positive index hedge. On the other hand, ranking floating rate notes by means of discounted cash flow would not satisfy the needs of the "cash equivalent" investor. Therefore, it seems obvious that a more broadly based evaluation method would satisfy the investment needs of almost all types of investors and create a certain amount of uniformity in the sometimes uncertain world of floater evaluation.

In January 1984 an experimental system was developed by the author in collaboration with the Ryan Financial Strategy Group. This system, "FORS" (Floater Overall Ranking System), is an equally weighted combined calculation of the most widely accepted evaluation techniques in the floater market today. The result is a more precise measurement of the value of each floating rate note relative to the entire floater universe.

Each security is evaluated and ranked numerically in eight categories. The sum of these results equals the FORS raw score. The final FORS ranking is arrived at by tallying all the categories and dividing the result by the sum of the highest scores in each category.

Since floating rate notes have varying coupon fixing dates, the WAR is used for all floaters in all calculations. The only calculation that uses the current coupon of each floater is the yield to maturity category.

The eight categories of the FORS system are: (1) current yield, (2) spread for life (simple margin/positive margin), (3) effective margin (total margin/adjusted simple margin), (4) total adjusted margin (adjusted total margin), (5) discounted cash flow margin (yield to maturity margin), (6) a numerical matrix of Moody's and S & P ratings,[3] (7) a numerical value based on the size of the issue (a proxy for liquidity), (8) the total score minus the length of maturity (a proxy for risk/reward).

Some special factors are taken into consideration in the FORS system. If a floater has a sinking fund, the average life of the floater is used as the maturity date. If the floater is putable prior to maturity, the put date is used as the maturity date. If the coupon fixing spread declines over the life of the floater, the weighted average fixing spread is used to the maturity date, put date, or the average life.

It is the contention of the creators of the FORS system that by investing in the top five FORS ranked securities at all times, one is

---

[3] Recently the numerical matrix of Moody's and S & P ratings has been replaced by the PaineWebber numerical ratings.

virtually assured of obtaining the best possible returns in the market. This is not to say that the lesser ranked floaters are not of some value in various interest rate environments.

Numerous FORS ranking calculations also revealed how it is possible to evaluate the floater universe, as a whole, versus the fixed rate market. When the highest possible ranking score was comparatively low in relation to the previous month's results and the spread between the highest ranked floater and the lowest ranked floater was relatively narrow, the floater segment of the market appeared to be less attractive in relation to the fixed rate market index performance.

To demonstrate the performance results of the FORS system, a model portfolio was created utilizing the following constraints: (1) a starting date of January 1, 1983, (2) an initial capital base of $10 million, (3) capital invested equally (par value) at all times in only the top five ranked floaters, (4) if a held bond dropped from the top five rankings it was liquidated and replaced with its successor, (5) portfolio reviewed and turned over on the first business day of each month, (6) present positions not able to be added to or reduced, (7) all excess cash invested at the lowest of three comparable indices' returns being used for comparison, and (8) portfolio measured against: (a) the cash index[4], (b) the Ryan Index (U.S. Treasury Index), and (c) the floater index.

In the case of the yield to maturity category, the hypothetical yield is compared to a comparable U.S. Treasury maturity yield. One of the features of the FORS system is that it can be customized to utilize any rate desired by the portfolio manager as the comparison rate.

The performance of the FORS portfolio from January 1, 1983 to December 31, 1983 in comparison to the indices cited earlier was as indicated in Table 9–1. As can be seen, the FORS portfolio outperformed the other indices for the one-year period.

TECHNOLOGY

In the past two years, a number of programs have been written for evaluating floating rate notes. Most of these products have been

---

[4] The cash index is based on six-month certificate of deposits.

TABLE 9–1
Comparison of the Performance of the FORS Portfolio, 1983

Month	"FORS"	Floater Index	Cash Index	Ryan Index
January	+ 2.83%	+ 4.12%	+ 0.66%	− 1.22%
February	+ 2.63	+ 1.40	+ 0.91	+ 3.48
March	+ 2.61	+ 2.54	+ 0.31	− 0.58
April	+ 2.59	+ 1.03	+ 1.03	+ 2.99
May	+ 0.26	+ 1.60	+ 0.41	− 2.42
June	+ 0.13	− 0.24	+ 0.66	+ 0.58
July	+ 0.51	+ 0.24	+ 0.54	− 3.03
August	+ 1.49	+ 2.20	+ 0.91	+ 0.49
September	+ 1.15	+ 1.01	+ 1.12	+ 3.79
October	+ 1.48	+ 1.17	+ 0.73	− 0.41
November	+ 0.63	+ 0.62	+ 0.69	+ 1.58
December	+ 0.58	+ 0.12	+ 0.74	+ 0.03
Totals (non-annualized)	+ 18.19%*	+ 16.92%	+ 9.06%	+ 5.08%

developed for "in-house" use by professional banking houses, but a few are available to investors. Below is a list of those that are available along with a brief description of the pros and cons of the product.

PRODUCT	DESCRIPTION
Floater Brain (Decision Programming Corporation)	–Desktop calculator –Calculates adjusted total margin for quarterly and semi-annual floaters –European format (day, month, year) –cumbersome input process –single issue format

PRODUCT	DESCRIPTION
Floating Rate Note Calculator (Randolph Stuart Associates)	–IBM computer program –built in data base (400 issues) –designed for Eurofloater market –European format (day, month, year) –calculates simple and total margins –swap programs (by price or by margin) –coupon fixing monitor –price/margin limit monitor –ease of input and updating –print capabilities –single/multiple issue format
Floating Rate Note Calculator (Ryan Financial Strategy Group)	–APPLE computer program –built in data base (100 issues) –designed for domestic market –calculates simple, total, adjusted margins to put, call, and maturity dates –automatic FORS calculation –print capabilities –user friendly –in final stages of experimentation –single issue format
Floating Rate Calculator (PaineWebber Inc.)	–APPLE computer program –built in data base –calculates simple and total margins –calculates current yield and spreads to CDs –automatic FORS calculation –designed for either domestic or Eurofloater market –print capabilities –single/multiple issue format
DCFM Calculator (First Boston Corporation)	–IBM computer program –user friendly –built in data base –domestics and Euros –single issue format –calculations center on DCFM

CHAPTER 10

EVALUATING FLOATING RATE NOTES: II

David Muntner
Vice President
Fixed Income Research
The First Boston Corporation

In an environment of volatile interest rates, floating rate securities are important to investors who want to reduce interest rate risk and principal fluctuation. Moreover, they are becoming increasingly important in portfolio management.

Structurally, the floating rate security market has matured significantly since its inception in 1970 in London. Issuers and investors can select the index, maturity, and coupon reset and payment frequency. Indices include Treasury bills, CDs, commercial paper, prime rate, Federal funds, and LIBOR. The maturity of these indices typically ranges from one month to one year. The maturity of the issues typically ranges from six months to 20 years (with perpetual floaters having no maturity). Coupon reset frequency ranges from daily to annually, and coupon payment frequency ranges from monthly to annually.

This market, however, is still quite primitive analytically. The uncertainty of the size of future coupon payments renders traditional bond mathematics (e.g., yield to maturity, realized yield, duration) inappropriate. Trying to compare floating rate securities keyed to different index rates with changing refix spreads adds to the complexity. Furthermore, standard bond yield calculators cannot accommodate the specific terms of floating rate securities.

Virtually all market participants use yield spread calculations in their floating rate security strategies. Cash investors who normally invest part of their short-term portfolio in one of the index rates and execute a "roll" program have used the spread formula to calculate expected incremental return from floaters. For example, a one-year floating rate security with a + 65 basis point spread over the three-month Treasury bill provides 65 basis points of additional yield compared to rolling over the three-month Treasury bill for one year. Funded investors have used the floating rate market to lock in a positive spread. A bank that can borrow funds at a cost of "LIBOR" and invest in a floating rate security to receive the equivalent of "LIBOR + 20" would receive an annualized investment profit of 20 basis points.

Unfortunately, there is no one standard method for computing yields and spreads on floaters. Results from the various methods in use can be quite disparate, and the unwary investor can be misled. For example, the standard accounting used by most U.S. investors uses corporate bond mathematics (30/360). By contrast, the majority of European investors analyzes securities using money market standards (actual/360). Therefore, stating that the yield spread is 20 basis points without mentioning the type of accounting used does not provide sufficient information for comparison.

The purpose of this chapter is to present yield to maturity (YTM) as the standard index for valuing floating rate securities (these securities include floating rate notes and floating rate certificates of deposit). YTM can analyze the terms of any security available in the market. More importantly, the results of this technique enable investors to quickly compare one floating rate security to another or to any fixed rate security.

The chapter is divided into three sections. The first section discusses the inadequacies of two of the most widely used methods of determining the return on a floating rate security. In the second section, the recommended method, YTM, is advanced as the most accurate method and the most consistent with the methodology used in all other aspects of fixed income analysis. Two methods of computing incremental return to an index, YTM spread and discounted margin, are then presented. Finally, the application of these formulas in portfolio management is illustrated.

EXISTING FORMULATIONS

Issuers and investors in the floating rate market initially used formulas designed solely to calculate yield spreads. The cost or value of a security was judged by its relationship to its index rate (e.g., Treasury bills or LIBOR). The resulting spread measured the yield advantage offered by the floating rate instrument. These measures are described and illustrated in the previous chapter. Two of the most commonly used measures are reviewed below.

The first generally accepted yield spread formulation for floaters was *spread for life*. As the name indicates, the spread represents the size of the basis point differential between the return of the index rate and that of the floating rate security from the settlement date until the maturity date. The calculation involves simple mathematics and requires no forecasting of interest rates. Call dates and prices are generally substituted for maturity dates and par prices for securities trading at a premium; put dates and prices are used for issues trading at a discount.

The spread for life calculation is a reasonable estimate of value when the price of the security is near par. When the security is selling at either a premium or a discount, however, the use of straight-line amortization distorts the value. In the case of a discount security, the capital gain is not received until the maturity (or put) date, while straight-line amortization erroneously assumes an equal share of the gain is given to the investor each year. The assumed extra income biases the resulting spread upward and thereby overstates the spread. The converse is true with premium issues, where the measure undervalues the return of the floating rate security.

The spread for life calculation incorporates the entire coupon refix spread without comparing it to the market price. Spread for life values equally a 50 basis point refix spread, whether the security was purchased at a discount, at par, or at a premium. This measure needs an adjustment to reduce the impact of the margin for premium securities and increase the benefit for discount issues. This error is most evident when analyzing securities carrying large margins and trading at prices more than two points from par.

Several formulas incorporating adjustments to the basic spread for life calculation are used in the market to reduce the magnitude of these errors. In Europe, where almost all floating rate securities reset coupons to a LIBOR index and trade at prices near par, the simple spread formula has been modified to include adjustments for the accrued interest of the security. The refined measure is known as *simple margin*. It includes the total settlement price (market price plus accrued interest), and values the investment on the next coupon payment date using the short-term index rate. After subtracting the next coupon payment, the amortized gain or loss is computed and added to the refix spread. While this formulation provides a more accurate measure of yield spread than does spread for life, the simple margin method does not solve the problem inherent in using straight-line amortization to evaluate capital gains or losses.

To summarize, the spread for life approach is easy to use and generates adequate results on floating rate securities trading at or close to par. The simple margin approach produces a more refined yield spread, but does not eliminate the problem of straight-line amortization of discount or premium.

Two additional problems with the spread for life and simple margin formulations should be noted. First, they incorporate neither the coupon payment frequency nor the maturity of the index. Consequently, the yield spreads for floating rate securities can be compared only when the alternative floating rate issues refix to the same index and have the same coupon payment frequency.

Second, these measures do not have provisions to analyze some terms of the more recent floating rate securities. The floating rate market has added several new features, including percentage refix spreads, refix spreads that change over time, conditional or optional refix formulas using different indices, coupon payment delays, coupon payment calculations, and frequent coupon refixings. These features will be discussed in more detail in the next section.

VALUATION BASED ON YIELD TO MATURITY FOR FLOATING RATE SECURITIES

The basic goal of floating rate security analysis is to facilitate the comparison of a floating rate security to either a fixed rate security or another floating rate security. In order to directly compare these securities, the formula must properly generate the projected cash flows of any floating rate security, and must calculate a standard value.

Except in magnitude, the cash flows of a floating rate security resemble those of a fixed rate bond having the same coupon payment frequency and maturity date. The standard bond market method of quantifying the cash flows is the yield to maturity. Yield to maturity is the rate which, when used to discount the future coupon and principal payments back to the settlement date, produces the settlement cost, including any accrued interest.

The cash flow of a floating rate security differs from that of a fixed rate security of the same maturity only in its future coupon payments, which are unknown. At best only the first coupon payment of a floating rate security is known, because it is the current coupon of the security. Sometimes no coupons are known, as is the case when the coupon rate of the security refixes between payment dates. Therefore, to calculate the yield to maturity for a floating rate security, an estimate of the security's index rate must be made for future coupon dates. A single rate is normally selected as the average expected rate for the index. Using this assumption, the future coupon payments can be determined and the YTM can be calculated. The only difference between the two cash flow formulations is that the accrued interest and first coupon payment for the floating rate security will be determined by one coupon rate (the current coupon) and all of the subsequent coupon payments will be computed using a second coupon rate (the average expected index rate plus the quoted margin).

In order to generalize the yield to maturity formula for all existing floating rate securities, one must provide for the different features found in the market. The resulting formula, given below, enables the investor to compare floating rate and fixed rate investments.

YTM for floating rate securities:[1]

$$P + A = \sum_{i=1}^{N} \frac{C_i}{\left(1 + \dfrac{YTM}{200}\right)^{2 \times T_i}} + \frac{100}{\left(1 + \dfrac{YTM}{200}\right)^{2 \times T_N}}$$

[1] The YTM for floating rate securities, as in the case of fixed rate securities, is solved by using an iterative process.

where A = accrued interest, in %

C_i = coupon payment in period i, in %

C_1 = next coupon payment, in %

$C_{2...N}$ = estimated coupon payment (index rate + margin), in %

N = number of coupon payments

P = market price, in %

T_i = time to the ith coupon payment, in years

YTM = yield of floating rate security (assuming semiannual compounding), in %

The yield to maturity for a floating rate security is the same as the calculation used in the fixed rate market. YTM *is the most accurate and consistent measure of the value of a floating rate security.*

To illustrate how to compute the YTM for floating rate securities, consider the following hypothetical security:

Market price = 98.00

Maturity = 2 years, 2 months (2.1667 years)

Current coupon rate = 10.50%

Assumed future index rate = 9.00%

Quoted Margin = .50%

Semiannual coupon payments

The YTM for this hypothetical floating rate security is found as follows:

$$98 + 3.50 = \frac{5.25}{\left(1 + \frac{YTM}{200}\right)^{2 \times .1667}} + \frac{4.75}{\left(1 + \frac{YTM}{200}\right)^{2 \times .6667}}$$

$$+ \frac{4.75}{\left(1 + \frac{YTM}{200}\right)^{2 \times 1.1667}} + \frac{4.75}{\left(1 + \frac{YTM}{200}\right)^{2 \times 1.6667}} + \frac{104.75}{\left(1 + \frac{YTM}{200}\right)^{2 \times 2.1667}}$$

Using an iterative process, the YTM is found to be 10.63 percent.[2]

---

[2] If the hypothetical had been a fixed rate security with a coupon rate of 10.50 percent, its YTM would be

$$98 + 3.5 = \frac{5.25}{\left(1 + \frac{Y}{200}\right)^{2 \times .1667}} + \frac{5.25}{\left(1 + \frac{Y}{200}\right)^{2 \times .6667}} + \frac{5.25}{\left(1 + \frac{Y}{200}\right)^{2 \times 1.1667}} + \frac{5.25}{\left(1 + \frac{Y}{200}\right)^{2 \times 1.6667}}$$

$$+ \frac{5.25}{\left(1 + \frac{Y}{200}\right)^{2 \times 2.1667}}$$

Using an iterative process, the yield to maturity (Y) is found to equal 11.55%

In the general yield to maturity formula, the cash flows of a floating rate security are calculated according to their payment dates. Then the dollar amounts are discounted to the settlement date using semiannual compounding. The resulting yield, YTM, is the rate that equates the sum of the discounted future payments with the settlement cost (i.e., price plus accrued interest).

The domestic corporate bond market assumes semiannual compounding of interest and uses 30/360 accounting. The general formula enables the investor to compare the yield to maturity of a fixed rate bond to that of a floating rate investment, or to compare two floating rate securities even when they refix to different index rates. This requires adjustments for the compounding effect of monthly, quarterly, and annually paying securities and for issues that compute payments using money market (actual/360) accounting standards.

The features of floating rate securities that affect the cash flows and therefore the yield are discussed next.

Coupon Payment Frequency

Floating rate securities offer monthly, quarterly, semiannual, and annual payments. If the cash flows are computed on the correct basis, then the YTM formula will evaluate the returns accordingly. For instance, the yield to maturity of a monthly paying floating rate security is increased to obtain its equivalent bond yield in the same manner as monthly-pay mortgage security yields are increased. Exhibit 10–1 displays the value of frequent coupon payments for nomi-

Exhibit 10–1
Bond Equivalent Yields

Nominal Yield	Frequency of Coupon Payments				
	Daily*	Monthly	Quarterly	Semiannually	Annually
8%	8.16%	8.13%	8.08%	8.00%	7.85%
10%	10.25%	10.21%	10.13%	10.00%	9.76%
12%	12.37%	12.30%	12.18%	12.00%	11.66%
14%	14.50%	14.41%	14.25%	14.00%	13.54%
16%	16.65%	16.54%	16.32%	16.00%	15.41%

*Daily payments are included here only for comparison to overnight repo rates or Federal funds rates.

nal yields from 8 to 16 percent. For example, a monthly paying security with a yield to maturity of 12 percent would have a bond equivalent yield of 12.30 percent.

Coupon Delay Days

The end of the coupon period does not necessarily correspond to the coupon payment date. Payment frequency and payment delay schedule are stated in the prospectus (or on the face of the certificate). For example, most weekly refixing coupon securities have quarterly payments with a delay period. If the coupon period ends May 31, the payment would be expected on June 1 but might not be paid until June 10. This nine-day delay reduces the yield of the security. The YTM formula accounts for payment delays.

Refix Spread Formulas

Changing refix spreads complicates the cash flow calculation. Several domestic floating rate securities have coupon refix spreads that change over time. An issue that currently resets at 100 basis points over six-month Treasury bills might drop to 75 basis points and again to 50 basis points before maturity. These terms are stated in the prospectus (or on the face of the certificate) and must be incorporated into the analysis.

In addition, many floating rate securities issued after 1982 have multiple coupon refix formulas involving more than one index rate and more than one spread. On the refix date each formula must be valued, at which time the selection criterion (i.e., the highest or the lowest) stated in the prospectus (or on the face of the certificate) is applied to determine the new coupon rate. For example, the new coupon rate may be defined as three-month Treasury bills plus 150 basis points or three-month LIBOR plus 25 basis points, whichever is higher at the time of refix.

Coupon Payment Calculation

Coupon payments and accrued interest are usually determined by one of three types of accounting methods: corporate bond (30/360), government bond (actual/365) and money market (actual/360). Assuming the same coupon rate the largest coupon payment is derived using money market accounting.

The benefit of presenting YTM on a bond equivalent basis is that it facilitates comparisons to most fixed rate securities. If the alternative investment makes interest payments on a monthly, quarterly, or annual basis, the formula is adjusted to provide a yield on the same basis. This is accomplished by changing the yield compounding calculation used in discounting future cash flows.

Many floating rate securities include redemption features which are important to issuers and investors. Call dates and prices or put dates and prices can be included in the yield to maturity formulation. The analysis is modified to end at the call date or put date and the corresponding price is substituted when it is not par. Investors usually assume that premium securities will be called by the issuer, while discount securities will be put back to the company on the put date. Issuers, on the other hand, usually consider the yield to maturity for par and premium securities, and the yield to put for discount securities.

YTM is an internal rate of return. This implies that the coupon payments received are (or can be) reinvested at the same yield level. When this assumption seems inappropriate a separate reinvestment rate can be substituted in the formula; the resulting yield will be a realized yield or realized compound yield or total rate of return.[3]

Spread Analysis

The spread for life and simple margin approaches to analyze floating rate securities sought to compare the return of the floater to the return of the index. These methods make the most sense when all of the securities being considered use the same index for establishing new coupon rates (e.g., three-month LIBOR or six-month Treasury bills). As the floater market has grown, frequent issuers have been using both the domestic and European markets, a variety of indices, and a variety of coupon refix formulas. Consequently, yield spread

---

[3] For an explanation of this yield measure see: Frank J. Fabozzi, "Bond Yield Measures and Price Volatility Properties," Chapter 4 in F. J. Fabozzi and I. M. Pollack, *The Handbook of Fixed Income Securities* (Dow Jones-Irwin: Homewood, IL., 1983).

calculations in floating rate security analysis have become less valuable. To address the difficulties in the early formulations of yield spreads, two formulas have been developed—YTM spread, used in the United States, and discounted margin, used in Europe. A summary of each method follows.

YTM Spread

The YTM spread is the difference between the YTM of the floating rate security and that of the index rate. The return of the index rate is the expected return obtained by rolling over investments in the index rate, and can be computed using the YTM formula. It uses the short-term index rate as the first coupon and the assumed index rate in place of future coupon rates. Coupon payments are based upon the proper accounting basis (i.e., actual/360, 30/360, actual/365) so that the yield to maturity of the index rate is the internal rate of return for these cash flows. This yield is expressed on the same compounded basis as the floating rate security.

Using the yield to maturity calculation, given below, the investor can now accurately calculate the yield spread (or the expected incremental return) of the floating rate security over the expected return of the index rate.

$$\text{YTM SPREAD} = (\text{YTM}_{FRS} - \text{YTM}_{INDEX}) \times 100$$

where YTM_{INDEX} is found from the following equation:

$$100 = \sum_{i=1}^{N} \frac{I_i}{\left(1 + \frac{\text{YTM}_{INDEX}}{200}\right)^{2 \times T_i}} + \frac{100}{\left(1 + \frac{\text{YTM}_{INDEX}}{200}\right)^{2 \times T_N}}$$

where I_i = index rate, in %
I_1 = short term index rate, in %
$I_{2 \ldots N}$ = estimated index rate, in %
N = number of coupon payments
T_i = time to the ith coupon payment, in years
YTM_{INDEX} = yield of the index (assuming semiannual compounding), in %

Using the hypothetical floating rate security used to illustrate the calculation of the YTM, the YTM spread can be found as follows:

YTM of the index rate (assuming an 8.00% short-term index rate)

$$100 = \frac{1.3333}{\left(1 + \frac{YTM_{INDEX}}{200}\right)^{2 \times 1.1667}} + \frac{4.50}{\left(+ \frac{YTM_{INDEX}}{200}\right)^{2 \times 1.6667}}$$

$$+ \frac{4.50}{\left(1 + \frac{YTM_{INDEX}}{200}\right)^{2 \times 1.1667}} + \frac{4.50}{\left(1 + \frac{YTM_{INDEX}}{200}\right)^{2 \times 1.6667}}$$

$$+ \frac{104.50}{\left(1 + \frac{YTM_{INDEX}}{200}\right)^{2 \times 2.1667}}$$

Using an iterative process, the YTM_{INDEX} is found to be 8.93%.

$$\text{YTM Spread} = (10.63 - 8.93) \times 100 = 170 \text{ basis points}$$

Discounted Margin (DM)

The current standard for measuring the value of a floating rate security in the European market is discounted margin. It represents the increment over the index rate (e.g., LIBOR) that is returned by an investment in the floating rate issue.

Discounted margin requires values for the short-term index rate and an assumed index rate. The formula discounts the future cash flows and solves for the value of DM that causes the present value of the cash flows to equal the settlement cost of the security, as shown below:

DM (ORIGINAL):

$$\left(P + CR_1 \times \frac{d_{LS}}{360}\right) \times \left(1 + \frac{I_S + DM}{100} \times \frac{d_{S1}}{360}\right) = CR_1 \times \frac{d_1}{360}$$

$$+ \frac{(CR_2) \times \left(\frac{d_2}{360}\right)}{\left(1 + \frac{I_E + DM}{100} \times \frac{d_2}{360}\right)} + \frac{CR_3 \times \left(\frac{d_3}{360}\right)}{\left(1 + \frac{I_E + DM}{100} \times \frac{d_2}{360}\right) \times \left(1 + \frac{I_E + DM}{100} \times \frac{d_3}{360}\right)}$$

$$+ \ldots + \frac{100 + (CR_N) \times \left(\frac{d_N}{360}\right)}{\left(1 + \frac{I_E + DM}{100} \times \frac{d_2}{360}\right) \times \ldots \times \left(1 + \frac{I_E + DM}{100} \times \frac{d_N}{360}\right)}$$

where CR_i = coupon rate in the ith period, in %

CR_1 = current coupon rate, in %

$CR_{2 \ldots N}$ = estimated index rate + quoted margin, in %

DM = discounted margin

d_{LS} = number of days from last coupon payment date to settlement date

d_{S1} = number of days from settlement date to first coupon date

d_i = number of days in coupon period i

I_E = expected index rate, in %

I_S = short-term index rate to next coupon payment date, in %

N = number of coupon payments

P = market price, in %

Discounted margin was originally used to analyze European issues, which use LIBOR as an index. It assumes that coupon payments are calculated on a money market basis, which affects the coupon payments and the present value of the cash flow. It also assumes that the yield compounding frequency is the same as the coupon payment frequency. As a result, yields for issues with different payment frequencies cannot be compared. First Boston has refined the original formula to accept accounting standards other than money market as follows:

DM (REFINED):

$$(P + A) \times \left(1 + \frac{I_s}{100} \times T_{iA} + \frac{DM}{100} \times T_{iB}\right) = C_1 + \frac{C_2}{\left(1 + \frac{I_E}{100} \times T_{2A} + \frac{DM}{100} \times T_{2B}\right)}$$

$$+ \frac{C_3}{\left(1 + \frac{I_E}{100} \times T_{2A} + \frac{DM}{100} \times T_{2B}\right)\left(1 + \frac{I_E}{100} \times T_{3A} + \frac{DM}{100} \times T_{3B}\right)} + \ldots$$

$$+ \frac{100 + C_N}{\left(1 + \frac{I_E}{100} \times T_{2A} + \frac{DM}{100} \times T_{2B}\right) \times \ldots \times \left(1 + \frac{I_E}{100} \times T_{NA} + \frac{DM}{100} \times T_{NB}\right)}$$

where A = accrued interest, in %

C_i = coupon payment in the ith period

DM = discounted margin, in %

I_E = expected index rate in %

I_S = short term index rate to next coupon payment date, in %

P = market price, in %

T_{iA} = time in the ith coupon payment period, using index rate accounting, in years

T_{iB} = time in the ith coupon payment period, using discounted margin accounting, in years

In most cases, YTM spread and the refined discounted margin differ by less than two basis points.

For our hypothetical floating rate security, DM is calculated as follows:

$$(98 + 3.50)\left(1 + \left(\frac{8 + DM}{100}\right) \times .1667\right) = 5.25 + \frac{4.75}{\left(1 + \frac{9 + DM}{100} \times .5\right)}$$

$$+ \frac{4.75}{\left(1 + \frac{9 + DM}{100} \times .5\right)^2} + \frac{4.75}{\left(1 + \frac{9 + DM}{100} \times .5\right)^3} + \frac{104.75}{\left(1 + \frac{9 + DM}{100} \times .5\right)^4}$$

Using an iterative process, the DM is found to equal 169.9 basis points.

Exhibit 10–2 is a matrix displaying the values for YTM and the four spread calculations for six floating rate securities. YTM spread and discounted margin differ by at most four basis points. Simple margin and spread for life, however, differ from YTM spread by as much as 26 basis points.

BREAKEVEN ANALYSIS

Floating Rate vs. Fixed Rate

The most difficult part of the YTM analysis is selecting an expected yield level for the index. An alternative approach to measuring the expected return of a floating rate security is to calculate the breakeven index rate needed to produce a specified return. The breakeven rate will indicate the required future coupon payments for the internal rate of return of the floating rate security to equal the targeted return.

Exhibit 10–2
Comparison of Results from Floating Rate Security Analysis
Settlement Date August 15, 1985

	YTM	YTM Spread	Discounted Margin (Refined)	Simple Margin	Spread for Life
Issue 1—Index: 6-month T bill Maturity: Oct. 15, 1987					
Refix Freq: Semiannual Payment Freq: Semiannual					
Current Coupon: 10.50% Margin: 50 bp					
Short-Term Rate: 8.00% Future Index Rate: 9.00%					
Price: 98.000	10.63%	170.1 bp	169.9 bp	157.7 bp	157.7 bp
Issue 2—Index: 6-month LIBOR Maturity: July 15, 2008					
Refix Freq: Semiannual Payment Freq: Semiannual					
Current Coupon: 11.50% Margin: 12.5 bp					
Short Term Rate: 8.00% Future Index Rate: 10.00%					
Price: 99.875	10.20%	28.8 bp	29.2 bp	19.2 bp	19.2 bp

Issue 3—Index: 3-month CD
Maturity: July 15, 1990
Refix Freq: Quarterly
Payment Freq: Quarterly
Current Coupon: 9.45% Margin: 65 bp
Short-Term Rate: 8.00% Future Index Rate: 10.00%
Price: 97.000

11.39%   147.5 bp   147.8 bp   127.9 bp   128.7 bp

Issue 4—Index: 6-month T bill
Maturity: July 15, 1998
Refix Freq: Semiannual
Payment Freq: Semiannual
Current Coupon: 11.00% Margin: 175 bp
Short-Term Rate: 8.00% Future Index Rate: 10.00%
Price: 104.000

11.11%   122.1 bp   123.0 bp   148.1 bp   148.1 bp

Issue 5—Index: 6-month LIBOR
Maturity: Jan. 15, 1987
Refix Freq: Semiannual
Payment Freq: Semiannual
Current Coupon: 9.00% Margin: 25 bp
Short-Term rate: 15.00% Future Index Rate: 9.00%
Price: 99.750

9.34%   − 153.4 bp   − 151.0 bp   − 142.2 bp   − 141.2 bp

Issue 6—Index: 6-month LIBOR
Maturity: Sept. 15, 1986
Refix Freq: Semiannual
Payment Freq: Semiannual
Current Coupon: 15.00% Margin: 25 bp
Short-Term Rate: 8.00% Future Index Rate: 15.00%
Price: 99.875

15.27%   87.5 bp   91.5 bp   89.2 bp   88.3 bp

One of the primary benefits of this type of analysis is its simplicity. The selected target return is usually taken from current market yields. The calculation outlined to find the YTM yield is modified to solve for the breakeven rate as follows:

BREAKEVEN INDEX RATE:

$$P + A - \frac{C_1}{\left(1 + \frac{Y}{200}\right)^{2 \times T_1}} - \frac{100}{\left(1 + \frac{Y}{200}\right)^{2 \times T_N}} = \sum_{i=1}^{N} \frac{(BR + M) \times TP_i}{\left(1 + \frac{Y}{200}\right)^{2 \times T_1}}$$

where A = accrued interest, in %
    BR = breakeven index rate, in %
    C_1 = next coupon payment, in %
    N = number of coupon payments
    P = market price, in %
    M = margin, in %
    T_i = time to the ith coupon payment, in years
    TP_i = time in the ith coupon period, in years
    Y = targeted YTM (assuming semiannual compounding), in %

For example, assume a targeted YTM of 10.0% has been selected for our hypothetical security. Then,

$$100 + 3.50 - \frac{5.25}{\left(1 + \frac{10}{200}\right)^{2 \times .1667}} - \frac{100}{\left(1 + \frac{10}{200}\right)^{2 \times 2.1667}} = \frac{(BR + .5) \times .5}{\left(1 + \frac{10}{200}\right)^{2.6667}}$$

$$+ \frac{(BR + .5) \times .5}{\left(1 + \frac{10}{200}\right)^{2 \times 1.1667}} + \frac{(BR + .5) \times .5}{\left(1 + \frac{10}{200}\right)^{2 \times 1.6667}} + \frac{(BR + .5) \times .5}{\left(1 + \frac{10}{200}\right)^{2 \times 2.1667}}$$

Using an iterative process, BR is found to equal 8.73%.

All of the future coupon payments have the same value and are equal to the coupon refix margin plus the breakeven rate. The yield used for discounting is the targeted rate. In this way the required coupon level can be computed; the breakeven index rate can then be calculated by subtracting the refix spread from the coupon.

If the index rate is expected to be higher than the breakeven rate, the floating rate security will generate more income than will the fixed rate alternative. If the index rate is expected to be lower than the breakeven rate, then the alternative market investment should be selected.

Floating Rate vs. Floating Rate

A second use of breakeven rates is to compare two floating rate securities that use different index rates when resetting coupons. The unknown in this analysis is the spread between the index rates of the floating rate securities. Therefore, a breakeven yield spread is required to help identify the better investment.

First, select two securities with different index rates but with similar quality and maturity (e.g., three-month Treasury bills and three-month LIBOR). Second, decide on several hypothetical rates of return on which you want to base the YTM and spread calculations (e.g., 9 percent, 12 percent, and 15 percent). Third, calculate the YTM for one of the floating rate securities given the assumed index rates (e.g., given a 9 percent Treasury bill rate, the floating rate YTM might be 10.64 percent). Then, calculate the breakeven index rates of the second security that would result in the same floating rate yield to maturity (e.g., a floating rate yield of 10.64 percent would be generated by a LIBOR index rate of 10.26 percent). Finally, calculate the breakeven yield spread as the difference between the two index rates (e.g., 10.26 percent minus 9 percent is a breakeven spread of 126 basis points). If the expected yield spread between the two index rates is less than the calculated breakeven spread, 126 basis points in this example, the security reset to the lower yielding index rate (i.e., Treasury bills) will generate a higher return.

The breakeven yield spread will change slightly as interest ratesmove. Exhibit 10–3 displays the yield spread results for the two securities at three interest rate levels. A 600 basis point range in Treasury bill rates has changed the breakeven yield spread only 21 basis points (i.e., from 126 to 147 basis points). This technique is used to evaluate floating rate alternatives, both assets and liabilities, available in the market.

Exhibit 10–3
Breakeven Yield Spread Analysis

Selected 3-Month Treasury Bill Rates (Security 1)	FRS YTM (Both Issues)	Breakeven 3-Month LIBOR (Security 2)	Breakeven Yield Spread
9%	10.64%	10.26%	126 bp
12%	13.75%	13.35%	135 bp
15%	16.88%	16.47%	147 bp

CONCLUSION

The analysis of floating rate securities has so far been relatively crude. Spread for life and simple margin are unable both to incorporate all of the features of floaters and to compare yields of securities using different indices. The YTM formula corrects these weaknesses, providing a more accurate measure of a security's value. YTM spread, which uses YTM in its calculation, is consequently the most accurate yield spread formula (along with the refined formula for discounted margin).

YTM requires an index rate forecast to build the future cash flow stream and solve for the return. Breakeven analysis allows for floating rate security valuation when there is no forecast for the index rate. Breakeven analysis calculates the yield level of the index rate that produces an equal return for two investment alternatives.

These methods should become market standards, resulting in fast and accurate investor analysis, and consequently in improved market liquidity for floating rate securities.

CHAPTER 11

THE CHOICE OF INTEREST RATE INDEX ON PERFORMANCE

Neal M. Soss, Ph.D.
Economist Department
The First Boston Corporation

The relationships among interest rates are not constant. For example, the relationships between longer- and shorter-term rates vary; the relationships between rates on riskless and risky obligations vary; and the relationships between domestic and Euromarket interest rates vary. Therefore, the choice of interest rate index is a critical element in the performance of a floating rate security (FRS). This chapter discusses the trade-offs among interest rate risks and analyzes some of the elements to consider in choosing an interest rate index from which to set a floating yield.

ILLUSTRATION OF HOW CHOICE OF INDEX IMPACTS PERFORMANCE

Consider a floating rate security originated at the end of 1983 with an interest payment due in July 1984 based on the average June value of the index plus some specified spread. Suppose that in creating the FRS the choice of index is either three-month U.S. Treasury bills or three-month domestic bank CDs, both measured on an annualized bond equivalent yield basis.[1] If the assumption were made that the relationship between these two yields would remain the same in 1984 as its average in 1983—CDs yielded about $\frac{1}{4}$ percent more than bills—then issuer and investor would have been indifferent to the choice of pricing formulas: Pricing alternatives such as (T-bills + 100 basis points) or (CDs + 75 basis points) both would have been expected to result in the same flow of payments.

Interest rates on both bills and CDs had risen by mid-1984, but not equally, and the CD-to-bill spread had widened from 1983's $\frac{1}{4}$ percent average to $1\frac{1}{4}$ percent. Thus, the July 1984 interest payment under the CD-indexed formula would be 1 percent higher, or $10,000 per $1 million of principal, than under the bill-indexed formula. If the bill-indexed formula had been chosen, the issuer would be "1 percent better off;" if the CD-indexed formula had been chosen, the investor would be "1 percent better off."

The analysis applies equally to the trading of existing floaters in the market. Suppose an investor considered two otherwise equivalent floating rate investments—one promising to pay (T-bills + 100 basis points) and the other (CDs + 75 basis points). If the two FRS had the same price at the end of 1983, the interpretation would be an implicit market assumption that the 1983 CD-bill spread would persist. All other things being equal, by mid-1984 the CD-indexed FRS would command a higher market price due to its higher interest payment.

Unanticipated changes in the relationships among interest rates thus substantially affect investment performance. Setting the FRS rate off the highest of several indexes removes the investor's market risk by putting the joint risk of rising interest rates and changing

---

[1] The measurement of interest rates for FRS purposes is more complicated than it might at first appear. Interest rates on some instruments may be quoted on a discount or bond equivalent-yield basis; on a 360-day or 365-day basis; and on a bid, asked, or average basis. The index for periodic repricing may be computed as of a specific date or as an average over some period of time. Official statistical sources such as the U.S. Treasury or Federal Reserve, individual financial institutions, and commercial data services may report different interest rate quotations on the same instrument due to market imperfection or differences in definition or sample coverage, although the variances are usually slight. Market conventions have come into existence to resolve these problems. Careful definition of the basis and source of data for FRS periodic repricing is an important component of the transaction.

spreads entirely on the issuer. Setting the FRS rate off the lowest of several indexes has the opposite effect. Features such as collars, caps, and put options similarly affect the degree to which the issuer and the investor bear the burden of changes in interest rates, thus influencing the investment performance of floating rate securities.

SOME SPECIFIC INTEREST RATE COMPARISONS

While many different interest rates could be chosen as the index off which to set the yield on a floating rate security, the most suitable choice depends on the expected relative patterns of different interest rates in the future. Comparable FRS will fluctuate in price relative to one another depending upon movements in the spreads between the interest rate indexes chosen. Thus, analysis of the factors affecting the spreads is a key aspect of understanding FRS. The following sections discuss the spreads between three pairs of interest rates often used in floating rate financings.

T-Bills vs. CDs

Like all prices, the interest rates on U.S. Treasury bills and prime commercial bank certificates of deposit—and hence the spread between them—result from the balance of supply and demand.

The Treasury auctions three-month and six-month bills each week as part of the overall program to meet its cash needs. Except in the most general sense, the supply of bills is not sensitive to interest rates. In the short run, the supply of bills does vary from time to time when federal debt ceiling limitations are approached and the Treasury adjusts the volume of bills auctioned until Congress acts to raise the debt limit. At such times, bill yields may be lower than they would be otherwise, reflecting their scarcity value. These effects, however, are short-lived and usually small. Because of their large volume, highly liquid secondary market, short maturity and high quality, Treasury bills are a premier store of liquidity. Thus, at times of heightened economic or financial fear and uncertainty, bill yields may be lower than otherwise, reflecting increased demand for safe assets. This phenomenon is known as "flight to quality."

Negotiable certificates of deposit are issued by commercial banks and thrift institutions in minimum denominations of $100,000 and for a minimum period of seven days. CDs are part of the banks' managed liabilities and vary in supply according to their funding needs (basically the strength of loan demand) and the alternative funding sources available to them (federal funds, consumer deposits, etc.).

Funding alternatives available to U.S. banks are determined, in part, by government regulation. In 1982, for example, when regulatory change authorized the introduction of Money Market Deposit Accounts (a more attractive consumer deposit instrument than previously allowed), banks cut back their issuance of CDs, tapping the consumer funds market instead. More generally, Federal Reserve administration of reserve requirements, reserve availability and discount rate policy can affect funding alternatives and the supply of CDs issued by banks.

As the obligations of private entities issued in denominations at or above the limits of FDIC deposit insurance coverage, CDs carry a credit risk premium in their yields relative to T-bills. The general soundness of the U.S. banking system and the safety net of governmental support (including the Federal Reserve and FDIC) usually restrain this premium. Thus, CDs are generally regarded as a relatively safe and liquid money market investment. Occasionally, an individual bank's standing is called into question and its CDs and other obligations are treated accordingly. Also, economic or financial shocks that have direct impact on the banking system may reduce overall demand for CDs and boost their yields above what they would be otherwise. In such circumstances, the resulting "flight to quality" widens the spread of CD rates over bill rates as demand for CDs shrinks and demand for bills expands.

The patterns in Exhibit 11–1 reflect the influences on the spread of three-month prime domestic bank CDs over three-month Treasury bills. For example, in mid-1974 the spread reached 450 basis points at a time when public confidence in the banking system was at a low ebb (it was the era of Franklin National Bank and Herstatt). CD rates rose sharply, reaching $12\frac{1}{2}$ percent over the summer, while bill yields were relatively stable in the vicinity of $8\frac{1}{2}$ percent.

The mid-1970s saw a return of confidence in the U.S. banking system and correspondingly narrower spreads. This lasted until the

Exhibit 11-1
Basis Point Spread—Three-Month CD over Three-Month T-Bill

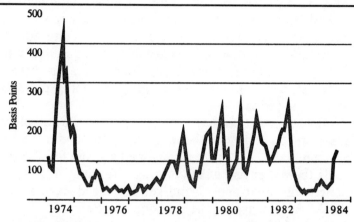

Iranian crisis erupted in 1978, leading to the fall of the Shah, a huge run-up in oil prices, and fears of disorder in the international banking system. The widening of CD-bill spreads reached a high-water mark late in the year as the U.S. countered a foreign exchange crisis with a dollar defense program that included a supplementary reserve requirement on CDs.

The next spike occurred in the Fall of 1979, when the banking system suffered the triple blows of dramatic changes in Federal Reserve operating procedure in support of a tighter monetary policy and the twin Iranian crises of the hostages and the asset freeze. From August to November, even a hefty $2\frac{1}{2}$ percentage point rise in three-month bill yields didn't keep pace with the $3\frac{1}{4}$ percentage point explosion in comparable CD rates. This widened the spread between them by a distinct 75 basis points to $1\frac{3}{4}$ percent.

In March 1980, the U.S. invoked credit controls and the Federal Reserve slapped a 3 percent surcharge on discount window borrowings by large banks. These actions changed the relative costs of the banks' funding alternatives. The CD-bill spread widened by 150 basis points over a two-month period (reaching $2\frac{1}{2}$ percent), mirroring a 2 percentage point jump in CD yields. The economy sank promptly into recession, interest rates plummeted across the board with the CD-bill spread narrowing sharply, and the credit controls program was dismantled.

Late in 1980 and continuing for about a year, the Federal Reserve reimposed discount window surcharges, sometimes as stiff as 4 percent, and the CD-bill spread remained wide. Although the surcharges had been removed in late 1981, the nearly simultaneous eruption of financial crises involving Drysdale, Penn Square, and Mexico in mid-1982 provoked a sharp "flight to quality," widening the spread. Between April and September, yields on three-month bills collapsed over 500 basis points, far outpacing the 380 basis point fall in CD yields.

A dramatic contraction in the spread began in the Fall of 1982, as confidence in the ability of the authorities to handle the banking situation stabilized. The spread remained narrow for about a year and a half thereafter as banks got ample funding from the newly deregulated consumer deposit market and faced sluggish loan demand in the early phases of the economic recovery.

In October 1983 and again in April and May 1984, the Treasury had to reduce the size of weekly bill auctions because of debt ceiling problems. The slight widening of CD-bill spreads at these times seems to reflect the resulting relative scarcity of bills. In the Spring of 1984 the CD-bill spread opened up as the problems of Continental Illinois and some money center banks with large Latin American exposure shook confidence in the banking system yet again.

LIBOR vs. CDs

As noted, regulations affect the funding alternatives available to commercial banks. Indeed, U.S. bank regulations lie at the heart of banks' choice between raising funds in the U.S. market or its offshore Eurodollar counterpart.

LIBOR—the London InterBank Offered Rate—is the posted rate at which prime banks offer to make Eurodollar deposits available to other prime banks. Since these banks usually operate in both the U.S. and offshore markets, domestic and Eurodollar funding are available as competing alternatives. Thus, LIBOR and domestic CD rates are related to each other through market arbitrage (although the instruments are not identical)—banks will raise funds in the cheaper market until the net interest costs of domestic funds and Eurodollar funds are equal.

Domestic CD liabilities are subject to (non-interest earning) reserve requirements imposed by the Federal Reserve, whereas Eurodollar deposits are not (unless used to support domestic assets). In addition, domestic liabilities are subject to FDIC insurance premiums. These differences are factored into net interest costs. This is analogous to the taxable, tax-exempt calculation in the municipal bond area.

All other things being equal, LIBOR will exceed the CD rate by a spread that rises along with increases in reserve requirements or FDIC insurance premiums. In addition, as the burden of reserves is greater at higher interest rates, the LIBOR-CD spread will rise as interest rates rise.

An additional component of the LIBOR-CD spread is the so-called "sovereign risk premium"—by definition, Eurodollars are U.S. dollar obligations payable in a foreign jurisdiction. This risk premium generally is restrained by several factors: the global standing of the prime banks; sanguine perceptions of the freedom from relevant capital controls in London and other Euromarket centers; and reliance on central bank support of the banks active in the Euromarket. However, when confidence in the international banking system is shaken, the LIBOR-CD spread tends to widen.

Following the removal of the U.S. interest equalization tax, the LIBOR-CD spread was rather tight through the first half of 1974, as shown in Exhibit 11–2. Then at the end of June, Germany's Bankhaus I. D. Herstatt suddenly failed, casting doubt on the status of hundreds of millions of dollars of international transactions. There was great uncertainty as to the attitude of the central banks toward the Euromarket, and the LIBOR-CD spread exploded to 100 basis points over the next few months. The spread remained relatively wide for about a year as Franklin National Bank in New York followed Herstatt into insolvency in the Fall and the financial effects of the OPEC price shock were digested.

Thereafter, as U.S. interest rates settled down and the market perceived the attitude of the authorities toward Eurodollars with greater equanimity, the LIBOR-CD spread stabilized at around 25–30 basis points through the mid-1970s.

The spread spiked in 1978 and again in 1979 in response to combinations of Federal Reserve tightening of reserve requirements, rising U.S. interest rates, and financial uncertainty provoked by the successive Iranian crises.

Exhibit 11–2
Basis Point Spread—LIBOR over Three-Month CD

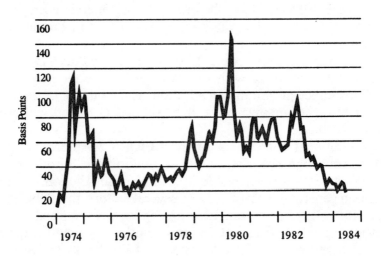

In March 1980, the Federal Reserve imposed a 3 percent surcharge on discount window borrowings of large banks, and in April it raised the marginal reserve requirement on "managed liabilities" to 10 percent. The LIBOR-CD spread instantly opened up to 150 basis points, the highest level recorded in the last decade.

The marginal reserve requirements were eliminated later in 1980, but discount rate surcharges were used for another year and a half. Gyrations in the spread during this period reflect the Federal Reserve's moves to tighten or ease conditions, but the spread remained wider than during the mid-1970s (averaging about twice its earlier level), reflecting much higher U.S. interest rates. Again in mid-1982, the spread widened significantly, this time in response to the threat to the world banking system posed by the Latin American debt crisis and the heightened perception of "country risk" that it engendered. As confidence in the management of the "international debt crisis" was restored, the LIBOR-CD spread narrowed and later was held down by relatively lower U.S. interest rates.

Prime vs. LIBOR

LIBOR and the CD rate represent input costs to banks—that is, banks' costs for gathering deposit liabilities. While many floating rate securities are indexed to banks' input costs, some are indexed to banks' output price—that is, a rate banks charge for loans, such as the prime rate.

The definition of the prime rate has been the subject of litigation in recent years. A working definition is that the prime rate is whatever a bank announces as its prime rate, although a connotation lingers that the prime relates to the interest rate a commercial bank charges on loans to its most creditworthy customers. In any event, the prime is an administered (rather than a market) rate, and most major U.S. commercial banks' prime rates move closely together.

Over time, bank output prices must exceed input costs, and therefore, the prime rate typically is higher than deposit rates such as LIBOR. However, as an administered rate, prime tends to lag LIBOR, with the spread between them narrowing when LIBOR is rising and widening when deposit costs such as LIBOR decline. Moreover, banks may be slow to change their prime rate at times because of the political climate, although this effect is naturally episodic. The prime-LIBOR spread can also be affected by trends in the forms of paying banks for lending. These trends—such as changing reliance on loan origination and syndication fees and compensating balances—are rather gradual. Finally, the prime-LIBOR spread can reflect money and credit policy developments, particularly those that actively discourage bank loan growth. In contrast to the spreads illustrated earlier, this spread is occasionally negative. But if banks are to find lending a profitable activity, it must, on average, be positive.

The period of negative prime-LIBOR spreads in late 1978, shown in Exhibit 11–3, illustrates the lag in prime rate hikes when deposit costs rise rapidly. Because of the U.S. program to defend the foreign exchange value of the dollar and other world events, LIBOR jumped by 240 basis points between September and November 1978, reaching $11\frac{1}{2}$ percent. The prime rose from $9\frac{1}{2}$ percent to 11 percent in a series of steps, allowing the spread to swing from + 34 basis points to − 54 basis points. Thereafter, of course, the prime caught up and

Exhibit 11–3
Basis Point Spread—Prime Rate over LIBOR

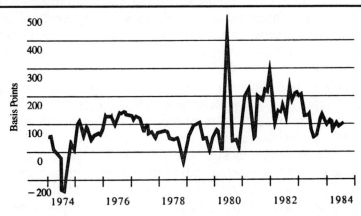

the spread turned positive and widened. The reverse phenomenon occurred in the latter half of 1981 as the economy sank into recession: LIBOR receded from peaks above 19 percent in May to around 13½ percent in December while the prime stepped down (only) from 19½ percent to 15¾ percent, spiking the prime-LIBOR spread to around 325 basis points.

The 1980 spike in the prime-LIBOR spread shows the strong effects of monetary and credit policies. The Spring credit-controls program in the U.S. included a component aimed directly at restraining the growth of bank credit. This forced the banks to find a mechanism to ration lending, resulting in a sharp run-up in the prime rate. The economy promptly went into a tailspin, and banks' funding costs sank. The combination of the bank credit restraint policy and the prime's usual lag in following LIBOR downward created a 500 basis point spike in the prime-LIBOR spread in May 1980, the widest in the last ten years.

WHAT THE SPREADS TELL US

This abbreviated financial history of the last decade, as told from the vantage point of interest rate spreads, leads to a fuller understanding of the factors that determine floating rate security performance:

- Interest rates on different instruments are highly correlated—they tend to move in the same direction at the same time. But they are not perfectly correlated—they do not move together to the same degree at all times. Thus, the spreads among them vary, sometimes widely.

- Treasury bill rates represent the safety anchor; the spread between them and other interest rates widens (often dramatically) when confidence in economic and financial stability is shaken; the spread narrows (often dramatically) as steps are taken to restore confidence.

- Prime domestic bank CD rates are heavily influenced by the stance of monetary and bank regulatory policies. The spread between them and T-bills tends to widen (sometimes dramatically) in response to monetary and regulatory stringency and to narrow when those policies are liberalized. Shocks to the stability of the banking system may coincide with changes in monetary or regulatory policies and compound the spread effects.

- LIBOR is closely linked to other bank funding costs, and the spread of LIBOR over alternatives such as CDs is largely a function of banking regulations. Thus, the spreads between LIBOR and other bank funding costs tend to be the smallest of those examined here.

- The prime rate is an administered output price for bank loans. Thus, it tends to have a positive spread over bank input costs such as LIBOR or CD rates. Administrative lags in adjusting prime to fluctuations in funding costs tend to widen the prime-CD or prime-LIBOR spread when interest rates are falling and to narrow it when rates are rising.

CONCLUSION

Understanding the determinants of spreads among interest rates that might be chosen as indexes—whether those spreads examined here or others—contributes to a considered judgment of the most suitable pricing for a floating rate security. The joint choice of an interest-rate index for a floater and the mark-up over that index is an implicit financial, economic, and policy forecast—and should be recognized as such. The choice will affect both the investment performance and the after-the-fact interest cost of a floating rate securities issue.

Choices involved in all financial techniques, however, are implicit forecasts of the future. There is no reason that the floating rate pricing decision should be inherently more difficult than the pricing of a fixed rate security. Indeed, the high correlation among short-term interest rates should make pricing easier, since the rates on floating rate securities are likely to remain closer to current market levels over time than fixed rates. This is the benefit that makes floating rate securities a convenient way for issuers and investors to meet their needs, thus enhancing the efficiency of the capital markets and the capital allocation process. The growing popularity of floating rate securities attests to this.

CHAPTER 12

TRADING STRATEGIES FOR FLOATING RATE NOTES

Tran Q. Hung
Vice President
Merrill Lynch Capital Markets

The market for dollar-denominated floating rate notes has become quite substantial and highly liquid. Moreover, the variety of pricing mechanisms and reference rates has given rise to different price movements among the competing sectors of the floating rate note (FRN) market. Relative price swings will occur in a predictable manner over interest rate cycles and in response to changes in yield spreads.[1] The differentiated price response, in turn, creates ample trading opportunities for actively-managed, fixed-income portfolios. In this chapter, we discuss these trading opportunities.

FRN trading strategies broadly fall into two types: inter-market and intra-market swaps. Opportunities to initiate these swaps can be identified by monitoring the relative movement of FRN prices or some measure of FRN margins over LIBOR. The adjusted total margin (ATM)[2] used in this chapter is one such measure which evaluates a FRN in terms of its ability to provide incremental yield over

---

[1] This is discussed in the next chapter.

[2] See Chapter 9 for how the adjusted total margin is calculated.

233

LIBOR. The ATM incorporates the basic spread over LIBOR, the adjustment of the cost of carry to the purchase price, the straight-line amortization of the discount or premium, and the income earned or foregone by investing the discount or premium in the purchase price over the life of the FRN. The ATM moves inversely with prices.

INTER-MARKET TRADING STRATEGY

This strategy exploits the fact that prices on securities offered by similar or comparable credits, with comparable maturities but issued in different markets (Euro vs. domestic; LIBOR vs. T-Bill) will behave differently due to the internal dynamics of each market as well as varying degrees of efficiency in different markets. The recent spate of new FRN issues has made it possible to identify and monitor the price behavior of several such pairs which form the basis of the inter-market trading strategy. From an investor's point of view, this strategy has the benefit of allowing him to stay within the same credit and maturity confinements, usually important portfolio parameters.

Trading Strategy between Eurodollar Fixed and Floating Rate Markets

Prices on both Eurodollar fixed rate bonds and floating rate notes move inversely with interest rates. However, FRN prices are much more stable because their coupons are refixed periodically at a spread above LIBOR and thus are kept current to market rates. On coupon fixing dates, FRN prices are likely to be close to par; the actual level is dependent on the final maturity and quality of the issuers. Between coupon dates, FRN prices will naturally move if interest rates change with price movements dependent upon the final maturity, current coupon level, time remaining until the next coupon fixing date, and the quality of the issue. Generally, floaters with more frequent coupon fixings (i.e., quarterly instead of semi-annually) will experience even less price volatility. These defensive characteristics suggest that FRNs should be viewed as an alternative to money market instruments.

Exhibit 12–1
Citicorp Overseas Finance: 12% of 1987 versus $\frac{1}{4}$ + 3M LIBOR of 1994

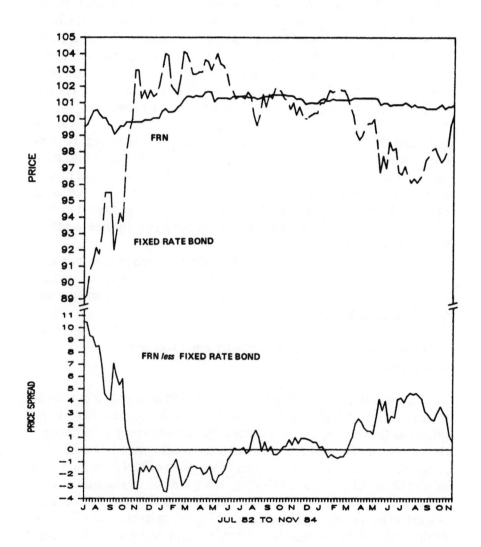

Exhibit 12–1 shows the price behavior of a Eurodollar fixed rate bond issue (12 percent of 1987) versus a floating rate note (1/4 over 3-month LIBOR of 1994), both issued by Citicorp Overseas Finance. It also illustrates the price spread, and the extent of the spread's movement between these two Citicorp issues. During a bond market rally, investors should swap from an FRN to a fixed rate bond issue to reap the maximum benefit of capital gain. During a bear market, or when interest rates are highly uncertain and volatile, investors should swap back into FRNs to preserve capital while getting the highest return among various money market instruments. For example, if this strategy was followed in 1984 (swapping into the Citicorp FRN in the first half of the year, and switching back into the fixed rate issue in early July) investors would have earned a return of 15.3 percent, compared with 11.4 percent return on the FRN and 12.0 percent on the fixed rate bond over the same period. Of course the actual enhancement of return provided by this strategy depends on investors' ability to correctly foresee a major bull or bear market.

Exhibit 12–2 provides a list of Eurodollar fixed-rate bonds and floating rate notes by similar names and of comparable maturities. Their price behavior can be monitored with a view of carrying out such interest rate-anticipation swaps.

Trading Strategy between Eurodollar and Domestic LIBOR-Based FRNs

Taking advantage of the price stability of LIBOR-based debt instruments, U.S. domestic FRNs based on LIBOR recently have been introduced and have become quite popular. However, even though the reference rate and the coupon reset mechanism is similar between this sector and the traditional Eurodollar FRN market, prices on domestic LIBOR-based floaters have tended to fluctuate more than those on Eurodollar floaters. This may result from the fact that while the Eurodollar FRN market is liquid, mature, and efficient, its domestic LIBOR-based counterpart is new and still inefficient as participants are trying to evaluate the market. The result is a thin market which has caused more price volatility.

Exhibit 12–3 shows the ATM of a Eurodollar (1/8 over 6-month LIBOR of 1993) and a domestic LIBOR-based FRN (1/8 over 3-

Exhibit 12-2
Selected Eurodollar Fixed Rate and Floating Rate Bond Issues

Issuer	(Same Issuer, Comparable Maturity) Fixed Rate Bond		FRN
Bank of Montreal	16.25%	1/12/91	$\frac{1}{8}$ + 6M LO, 10/31/91
B.N.P.	13.50%	6/10/89	$\frac{1}{8}$ + 6M LO, 9/05/89
C.N.T.	13.75%	6/20/91	$\frac{1}{4}$ + 6M LO, 6/05/91
Citicorp	12.00%	10/15/87	$\frac{1}{4}$ + 3M LO, 3/12/94
E.E.C.	11.00%	7/15/87	$\frac{1}{8}$ + 6M LO, 7/07/88/90
Genossen, Zentralbank	14.00%	6/30/91	$\frac{1}{4}$ + 3M LM, 10/03/92
L.T.C.B.	11.875%	3/04/89	$\frac{1}{4}$ + 6M LO, 6/11/89
Midland	11.50%	12/01/92	$\frac{1}{4}$ + 6M LO, 6/07/92
National Westminster	11.75%	11/01/92	$\frac{1}{4}$ + 6M LM, 10/25/92
National Bank of Canada	16.50%	5/15/88	$\frac{1}{4}$ + 6M LM, 3/26/88
Nippon Credit Bank	13.875%	7/10/89	$\frac{1}{8}$ + 6M LO, 2/10/90
Quebec Hydro	12.375%	12/15/93	$\frac{1}{8}$ + 6M LO, 1/22/94
Sogen	14.00%	6/29/91	$\frac{1}{4}$ + 6M LO, 1/14/91
Sweden	12.375%	4/26/89	$\frac{1}{4}$ + 6M LO, 2/04/88/93

Note: LO–LIBOR, LM–Mean of London Interbank Bid and Offer Rates, LB–London Interbank Bid Rate, 3M–3 Month, 6M–6 Month, TB–Treasury Bill

month LIBOR of 1996), both issued by Chase Manhattan Bank. The ATM on the domestic issue seems to fluctuate more, even though its coupon is refixed quarterly while that on the Eurodollar FRN is reset semi-annually. Normally, FRNs with more frequent coupon fixing are more stable. Exhibit 12–3 also presents the movement of the differential between the two ATMs. Overall, the domestic floater has traded cheaply compared with the Eurodollar issue, but there is a tendency for the differential to narrow over time as more investors become interested in the domestic market. However, there still seems to be a lot of shorter term fluctuations. Since both floaters are based on LIBOR, it is very unlikely that the ATM on one can deviate very much or very long from that on the other. Consequently, investors should swap between these two FRNs as their ATM differential reaches extreme levels, judged from the historical relationship. According to the present illustration, investors should have stayed with the Eurodollar FRN between April and

Exhibit 12–3
Chase Manhattan Bank: Eurodollar ($\frac{1}{8}$ + 6M LIBOR of 1993) versus Domestic ($\frac{1}{8}$ + 3M LIBOR of 1996) FRNs

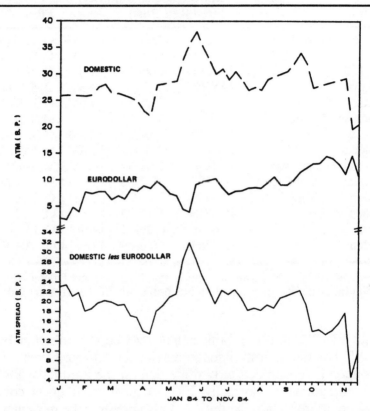

May, then swapped out of the Eurodollar into the domestic floater in May when the ATM differential was at its widest. Then in early November, when the differential had narrowed substantially, that swap should have been reversed. This strategy would have produced a return of 16.8 percent compared with 14.2 percent on the domestic and 15.5 percent on the Eurodollar FRN over the entire period.

Exhibit 12–4 presents a list of selected FRNs issued by the same bank in both the Eurodollar and domestic LIBOR-based FRN markets. Their ATM spreads can be monitored and swaps initiated when the spread reaches extremely wide or narrow levels.

Exhibit 12–4
**Selected Eurodollar and Domestic LIBOR-Based FRNs
(same issuer, comparable maturity)**

Issuer	Eurodollar		Domestic LIBOR-based
Bank of America	$\frac{1}{8}$	+ 3M LO, 9/28/96	$\frac{1}{8}$ + 3M LO, 7/02/96
Chase Manhatten	$\frac{1}{8}$	+ 6M LO, 7/31/93	$\frac{1}{8}$ + 3M LO, 5/03/96
First Chicago	$\frac{1}{4}$	+ 3M LM, 8/21/94	$\frac{1}{8}$ + 3M LO, 4/27/96
Wells Fargo	$\frac{1}{16}$	+ 3M LO, 9/06/94	$\frac{1}{16}$ + 3M LO, 8/01/96

Note: Refer to note in Exhibit 12.2 for terms.

Trading Strategy between LIBOR-Based and T-Bill Based FRNs

Even though U.S. T-Bill based FRNs have their coupons refixed every three or six months, their prices have proven to be quite volatile—much more so compared with Eurodollar floaters. In fact, the price volatility of T-Bill based floaters is more similar to that of a full-coupon, medium-term bond than to any floating rate instrument. The principal reason for the difference in price behavior is that while Eurodollar FRNs are based on LIBOR, structurally the *highest* dollar short-term rate, T-Bill based FRNs are keyed off the T-Bill rate, usually the *lowest* dollar money market rate. Prices on T-Bill based FRNs, as a consequence, have to adjust to changes in the yield spread between T-Bill and other money market instruments (captured in the LIBOR/T-Bill spread) so that T-Bill floaters can remain competitive.

The LIBOR/T-Bill spread, while summarizing the changing relative attractiveness between T-Bills and other money market instruments, is itself made up of several components:

• *The key spread is that between T-Bill and domestic CD rate.* T-Bills usually offer the lowest short-term rate to investors because these paper carry the best possible credit (that of the U.S. government) and because the market in T-Bills is very substantial and liquid. Bank CDs have to offer a yield premium over T-Bills to compensate for the lower credit quality as well as the fact that the CD market is not as liquid. The spread is also affected by the different state and local (in the U.S.) income tax rates applicable on different classes of investors in T-Bills and CDs as well as the relative supply situation in the two markets. The positive yield spread between CD and T-Bill normally widens as the level of interest rates rises because this is usually associated with a tightening monetary policy stance by the U.S. Fed, resulting in a credit scarcity in the banking system which prompts investors' concerns about bank liquidity and induces a preference for quality. Conversely, when interest rates are lower, such concerns diminish and investors want to enhance the return on their portfolios by switching into higher-yielding paper. In recent years, this spread has also moved quite sharply as a result of the funding crisis faced by many U.S. banks: As the crisis approached in the Fall of 1982, the CD/T-Bill spread widened to almost 400 basis points, to be collapsed to a normal level of less than 100 basis points when the crisis was over and confidence in the U.S. banking system was restored (see Exhibit 12–5). It then widened again to about 240 basis points in mid 1984 as the crisis over Continental Illinois flared up.

- *The spread between domestic CD and Eurodollar CD.* This spread used to be 20 to 25 basis points in favor of Eurodollar CD because U.S. banks, through their foreign branches which are major issuers in the Eurodollar CD market, can afford to offer higher rates overseas in competition for funds and end up with all-in costs similar to the domestic CD market. This was due to the fact that Eurodollar liabilities of U.S. banks are subject to lower reserve requirements and no Federal Deposit Insurance Corporation (FDIC) assessments. However, since the passage of the Monetary Control Act of 1980, reserve requirements on domestic and Eurodollar liabilities have been gradually equalized, causing the Eurodollar CD/domestic CD spread to narrow considerably. This spread is now more affected by the relative supply of new paper in each market.

- *The spread between Eurodollar CD and Eurodollar deposit (bid rate).* Eurodollar deposits, being non-marketable, have to offer a higher rate than Eurodollar CDs. The spread is also depen-

Exhibit 12–5
LIBOR and T-Bill Rates
(3-Month Maturities)

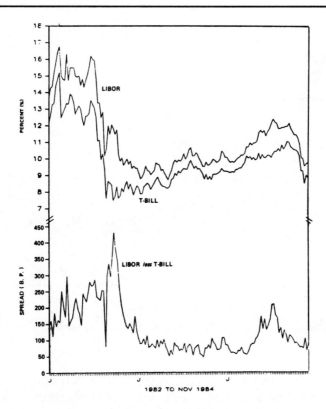

dent on the relative issuing activities in the CD and deposit markets.

- Finally, LIBOR, being the offer side of the London interbank deposit market, usually yields 1/8 more than the Eurodollar deposit bid rate.

Exhibit 12–6 depicts the hierarchical structure of these dollar money market rates and their spreads in recent years.

While each of the above mentioned spreads can move and change

Exhibit 12–6
The Structure of Dollar Money Market Rates
(Yearly Average)

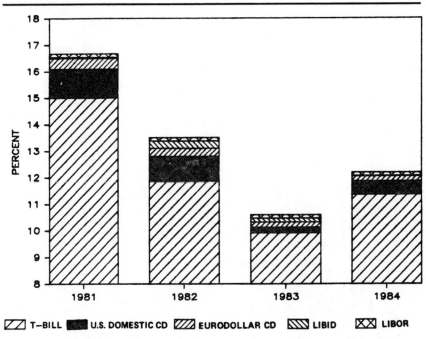

the LIBOR/T-Bill spread, the spread between T-Bill and domestic CD is the most dominant one. As the LIBOR/T-Bill spread widens, the price on a T-Bill based FRN declines to bring the current yield on such paper competitive to other money market rates. Conversely, when the LIBOR/T-Bill spread narrows, the price will rise to prevent the current yield on a T-Bill based FRN from becoming too generous compared with other alternatives. This relationship is illustrated in Exhibit 12–7 which also identifies swap opportunities between a Eurodollar (1/4 over 3-month LIMEAN of 1994) and T-Bill based floater (100 basis points over 6-month T-Bill of 2004) both issued by Chemical Bank. As the LIBOR/T-Bill spread widened sharply from later February 1984 to early June (from 60 basis points to 242 basis points) due to the Continental Illinois crisis

Exhibit 12-7
**Chemical Bank: Eurodollar ($\frac{1}{4}$ + 3M LM of 1994) versus
T-Bill based (100BP + 6M TB of 2004) FRNs**

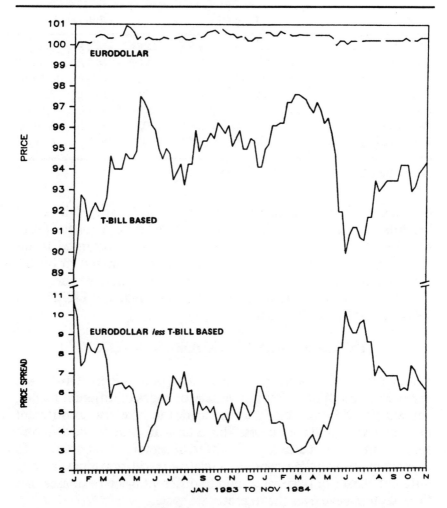

and a general rise in interest rates, investors could swap out of the
domestic T-Bill based floater into its Eurodollar counterpart which
outperformed the T-Bill floater. Then since mid-June, as the U.S.
bond markets rallied strongly and concerns about U.S. banks sub-
sided, the LIBOR/T-Bill spread narrowed to its more normal level

Exhibit 12–8
**Selected Eurodollar and T-Bill Based FRNs
(same issuer)**

Issuer	Eurodollar			T-Bill based		
Chase Manhattan	$\frac{1}{8}$ + 6M LO,	7/31/93		100BP + 3M TB,	6/15/99	
Citicorp	$\frac{1}{4}$ + 3M LO,	3/12/94		100BP + 3M TB,	3/10/92	
Manufacturers Hanover	$\frac{1}{8}$ + 3M LO,	5/30/94		62.5BP + 3M TB,	10/07/90	
Merrill Lynch	$\frac{1}{8}$ + 3M LO,	5/10/87		60BP + 3M TB,	8/23/91	
Chemical	$\frac{1}{4}$ + 3M LM,	6/25/94		100BP + 6M TB,	5/01/04	
Wells Fargo	$\frac{1}{16}$ + 3M LO,	9/06/94		70BP + 3M TB,	12/01/92	
Swedish Export Credit	6M LO, 2/11/87			75BP + 3M TB,	6/30/95	

Note: Refer to note in Exhibit 12–2 for terms.

of around 100 basis points. Investors could have reaped substantial benefits reversing the earlier swap and moved back to the T-Bill based FRN issue. The swap strategy would have returned to investors 12.3 percent, compared with a 1.6 percent return on the T-Bill based floater and 11.3 percent on the Eurodollar issue.

Exhibit 12–8 presents a list of selected Eurodollar and T-Bill based FRNs issued by the same bank.

INTRA-MARKET TRADING STRATEGY

Within each FRN market (i.e., Eurodollar, domestic LIBOR-based, and T-Bill based) there exists a variety of issues of different names, coupon fixing frequencies and maturities to give rise to different price behaviors and anomalies. This is basically due to the different supply and demand situation in different sectors of the market, to changes in investors' perception of relative credit worthiness among different classes of borrowers, and to different price responses that these sectors have over the interest rate cycle.

Trading Strategy between Semi-Annual and Quarterly FRNs

Prices on FRNs with quarterly coupon fixings are less volatile than those on semi-annual floaters as their coupons are more likely to be in line with current market interest rates. Consequently, semi-annual floaters are likely to outperform quarterly issues during bond market rallies and to underperform during bear markets. Thus, investors should swap from a quarterly FRN to a semi-annual issue of the same borrower when they expect interest rates to decline and reverse the swap when they expect rates to rise.

Exhibit 12–9 shows the price behavior of a quarterly (3/8 over 3-month LIMEAN of 2002) and a semi-annual (1/4 over 6-month LIBOR of 1998) Eurodollar FRN, both issued by the Caisse Centrale de Cooperation Economique (C.C.C.E.). When interest rates increased between February and May, investors should have switched into the quarterly issue which clearly outperformed the semi-annual one. During the subsequent period when rates fell, investors should have swapped back to the semi-annual FRN. Between February and

---

Exhibit 12–9
Caisse Centrale de Cooperation Economique C.C.C.E.
Quarterly ($\frac{3}{8}$ + 3M LM of 2002) versus Semiannual
($\frac{1}{4}$ + 6M LO of 1998) FRNs.

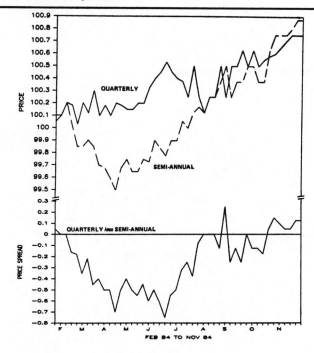

Exhibit 12–10
Citicorp: Quarterly (75BP + 3M TB of 1992) versus Semiannual (70BP + 6M TB of 1995) FRNs

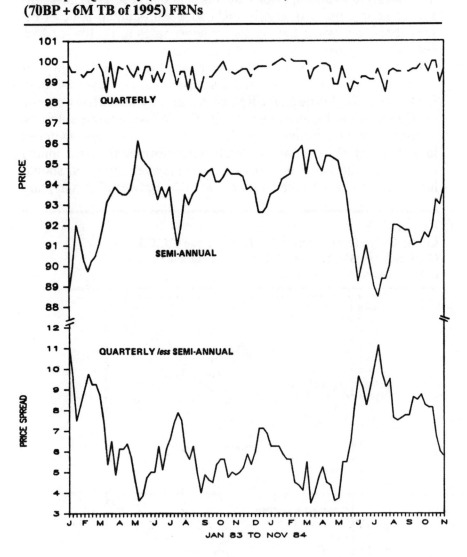

November, investors would have earned a return of 10.8 percent following this strategy, compared with a 9.2 percent return generated by the semi-annual issue and 10.2 percent by the quarterly issue.

Exhibit 12–10 shows that the same principle holds true—with even more price movements—with a quarterly and a semi-annual T-Bill based floater (both by Citicorp). Between January and May of 1984, the quarterly issue outperformed the semi-annual by 4.25 points. In the following period, the semi-annual floater outperformed by 2.50 points.

Exhibit 12–11 presents a list of selected quarterly and semi-annual FRNs in the Eurodollar and T-Bill based market.

Trading Strategy between Short- and Long-Term Maturity FRNs

Even though Eurodollar FRNs closely resemble money market investments, prices on long-maturity floaters tend to be more volatile

Exhibit 12–11
Selected FRNs with Quarterly and Semiannual Coupon Fixings (same issuer)

Eurodollar Market	Quarterly	Semiannual
Bank of Montreal	$\frac{1}{8}$ + 3M LO, 4/26/96	$\frac{1}{8}$ + 6M LO, 10/31/91
Bank of Tokyo	$\frac{1}{8}$ + 3M LO, 10/27/89	$\frac{1}{8}$ + 6M LO, 12/10/88/91
B.N.P.	$\frac{1}{8}$ + 3M LO, 1/31/85/88	$\frac{1}{8}$ + 6M LO, 5/09/89
C.C.C.E.	$\frac{3}{8}$ + 3M LM, 3/14/02	$\frac{1}{4}$ + 6M LO, 8/09/98
CEPME	$\frac{1}{4}$ + 3M LO, 3/06/88	$\frac{1}{4}$ + 6M LO, 6/11/87/92
Mortgage Bank Denmark	$\frac{1}{8}$ + 3M LO, 4/11/96/99	$\frac{1}{4}$ + 6M LO, 9/08/90/93
Chase Manhattan	$\frac{1}{8}$ + 3M LO, 12/05/09	$\frac{1}{8}$ + 6M LO, 7/31/93

T-Bill Based Market		
Citicorp	75BP + 3M TB, 4/10/92	70BP + 6M TB, 5/01/95
Chase Manhattan	53BP + 3M TB, 11/28/92	55BP + 6M TB, 5/01/09

Note: Refer to note in Exhibit 12–2 for terms.

than short-maturity issues. Consequently, long-maturity FRNs will outperform short-maturity issues during a market rally and under-perform when rates rise. Investors should swap from a short- to long-maturity FRN when they expect interest rates to decline and reverse the swap when they expect the opposite.

Exhibit 12–12 shows the ATM behavior and spread on a pair of Kingdom of Sweden FRNs, one maturing in 1989 and the other in 2003. At the peak of short-term interest rates, the long-maturity FRN is more attractive (and should be swapped into on anticipation of the coming rally) whereas at the interest rate trough, the short-maturity issue is relatively cheaper (and the above swap should be reversed). This strategy would have produced a return of 14.5 per-

Exhibit 12–12
Kingdom of Sweden: Short ($\frac{1}{4}$ + 6M LM of 1989) versus Long ($\frac{1}{4}$ + 6M LM of 2003) FRNs

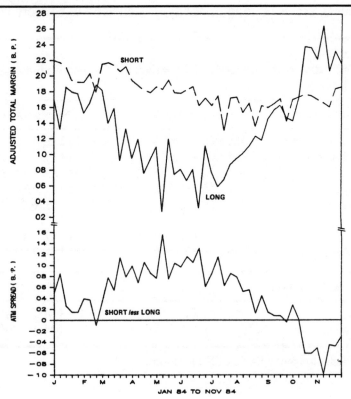

cent compared with 13.5 percent for the short-maturity and 11.1 percent for the long-maturity Sweden FRN over the entire period.

Exhibit 12–13 compiles a list of selected Eurodollar FRNs with short and long maturity.

Trading Strategy with FRNs Having Same Rollover Dates

A variant of the above strategy focuses on swap opportunities between short- and long-maturity FRNs of different issuers but having coupon-fixing dates either exactly similar or within a few days of each other. This guarantees that these issues will have the same or similar coupon for the rest of their lives, if they have the same basic spread over LIBOR. Otherwise, their coupons will be at a constant spread from each other. Their prices, however, still behave differ-

---

Exhibit 12–13
**Selected Eurodollar with Short and Long Maturity
(same issuer)**

Issuer	Short Maturity	Long Maturity
Bank of Montreal	$\frac{1}{4}$ + 6M LM, 12/20/90	$\frac{1}{8}$ + 3M LO, 4/26/96
Bank of Tokyo	$\frac{1}{4}$ + 6M LM, 7/26/87	$\frac{1}{4}$ + 3M LM, 10/24/93
B.F.C.E.	$\frac{1}{4}$ + 6M LM, 1/22/88	$\frac{1}{8}$ + 3M LO, 9/13/99
B.N.P.	$\frac{1}{8}$ + 6M LO, 5/09/89	$\frac{1}{4}$ + 3M LM, 7/19/96
Barclays O/S Inv	$\frac{1}{4}$ + 6M LO, 6/15/90	$\frac{1}{8}$ + 3M LM, 3/04/04
Denmark	$\frac{3}{16}$ + 6M LO, 10/15/88/90	$\frac{3}{16}$ + 3M LO, 2/17/99/04
Genfinance	$\frac{1}{4}$ + 6M LO, 10/31/87	$\frac{1}{8}$ + 3M LO, 1/21/92/94
L.T.C.B.	$\frac{1}{4}$ + 6M LO, 12/17/86	$\frac{1}{8}$ + 3M LO, 5/31/92
Midland	$\frac{1}{4}$ + 6M LO, 12/24/89	$\frac{1}{8}$ + 3M LM, 3/06/99
National Westminster	$\frac{1}{4}$ + 6M LO, 6/25/90	$\frac{1}{4}$ + 3M LM, 4/16/94
Nippon Credit Bank	$\frac{1}{8}$ + 6M LO, 7/16/86	$\frac{1}{8}$ + 3M LO, 2/11/90
Sogen	$\frac{1}{4}$ + 6M LO, 5/09/90	$\frac{1}{4}$ + 3M LO, 3/18/94
Sweden	$\frac{1}{4}$ + 6M LM, 2/28/87/89	$\frac{1}{4}$ + 3M LM, 11/17/93/03

Note: Refer to note in Exhibit 12-2 for terms.

Exhibit 12–14
**Belgium and E.E.C.:   Belgium ($\frac{1}{8}$ + 6M LO of 1/9/2004) versus
E.E.C. ($\frac{1}{8}$ + 6M LO of 7/7/1990) FRNs**

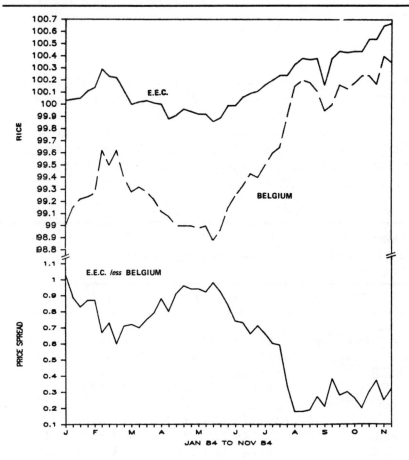

ently over interest rate cycles: Prices on long-maturity floaters are
more volatile than those on shorts. Consequently, the price spread
between shorts and longs is likely to widen when rates rise and narrow
when rates fall. Furthermore, as FRN prices usually return to a certain level close to par on coupon-fixing date, the price spread should
also return to a relatively constant differential on coupon-fixing date.
This enhances the predictability of the price-spread movement, making it safer to use to monitor for swap opportunities.

Exhibit 12–14 shows the price and price-spread behavior of a pair of Eurodollar FRNs with rollover dates within two days of each other. If investors bought the E.E.C. (shorter maturity) in late February 1984 and swapped into the Belgium (longer dated) from mid-May to November, they would have realized a return of 11.1 percent—compared with 10 percent on the E.E.C. and only 8.3 percent on the Belgium issue.

Exhibit 12–15 shows a list of selected Eurodollar FRNs with same or similar rollover dates.

Trading Strategy for FRNs with Different Qualities

Investors' perception of the creditworthiness of different classes of borrowers changes over time in response to market developments. This in turn causes fluctuations in the relative value of different groups of FRNs. In recent years, the unfolding of the U.S. banking crisis has been the single most important factor underlying the changing quality spread between FRNs issued by U.S. banks and those issued by banks in other major countries or by sovereign borrowers. In the domestic LIBOR-based FRN market, similar changes in quality spread is observed between issues by money center banks, which are the most vulnerable to a banking crisis, and by regional banks which are perceived to be on a better financial footing.

Exhibit 12–16 shows the average ATM spread between U.S. bank FRNs and Japanese bank floaters. At the beginning of 1984, U.S. bank names were trading much more expensively than Japanese bank floaters. That ATM relationship reversed abruptly in May and June when the Continental Illinois crisis occurred. Since then, the ATM spread has narrowed somewhat as calm has been restored to the U.S. banking system.

A similar pattern of spread movement is observed in the case of ATM spread between FRNs issued by sovereign borrowers and U.S. banks, as depicted in Exhibit 12–17. However in this case, there was a strong tendency for the ATM spread to collapse over the year. At the time of this writing, FRNs by U.S. banks and sovereign names are trading almost at parity with each other.

Finally, Exhibit 12–18 shows the average ATM spread between domestic LIBOR-based FRNs issued by money center banks and

Exhibit 12–15
Eurodollar FRNs with Similar Roll Over Dates

Issuer	Maturity	Issuer	Maturity
Allied Irish Banks	$\frac{1}{8}$ + 6M LO, 12/10/95	Belgium	$\frac{1}{8}$ + 6M LO, 12/10/99/04
Barclays O/S Inv	$\frac{1}{4}$ + 6M LO, 6/17/95	B.B.L. Int	$\frac{1}{4}$ + 6M LO, 6/17/95
B.N.P.	$\frac{1}{4}$ + 6M LO, 12/27/89	National Westminster	$\frac{1}{4}$ + 6M LO, 6/27/90
RENFE	$\frac{1}{4}$ + 6M LO, 6/14/89	Credit Lyonnais	$\frac{1}{4}$ + 6M LM, 6/14/92/96
E.E.C.	$\frac{1}{8}$ + 6M LO, 7/07/88/90	E.N.E.L.	$\frac{1}{4}$ + 6M LO, 7/07/89
National Bank of Canada	$\frac{1}{4}$ + 6M LM, 1/05/89/91	National Bank of Canada	$\frac{1}{4}$ + 6M LO, 7//07/91
Nippon Credit Bank	$\frac{1}{8}$ + 6M LO, 2/11/90	Sumitomo Trust Fin	$\frac{1}{8}$ + 6M LM, 2/11/92/94
Eldorado Nuclear	6M LO, 2/28/89	Ferrovie Dello Stato	$\frac{1}{4}$ + 6M LO, 2/28/92/99
E.D.F.	$\frac{1}{8}$ + 6M LO, 2/23/99	Spain	$\frac{1}{4}$ + 6M LO, 2/25/97
B.N.P.	$\frac{1}{4}$ + 6M LO, 9/04/99/91	Italy	$\frac{1}{8}$ + 6M LM, 9/04/99
Barclays O/S Inv	$\frac{1}{8}$ + 6M LM, 3/04/04	Mitsui Fin	$\frac{1}{8}$ + 6M LM, 3/04/96
Credit Lyonnais	$\frac{1}{8}$ + 6M LO, 10/11/93/96	Belgium	$\frac{1}{8}$ + 6M LO, 10/11/99/04
C.C.F.	$\frac{1}{4}$ + 6M LO, 4/09/90/95	Credit Foncier	$\frac{1}{4}$ + 6M LO, 10/09/88/93
Bank of Montreal	$\frac{1}{8}$ + 6M LO, 10/31/91	Bank of Nova Scotia	$\frac{1}{8}$ + 6M LO, 10/31/88/93

Note: Refer to note in Exhibit 12–2 for terms.

Exhibit 12–16
ATM of U.S. Bank and Japanese Bank Eurodollar FRNs

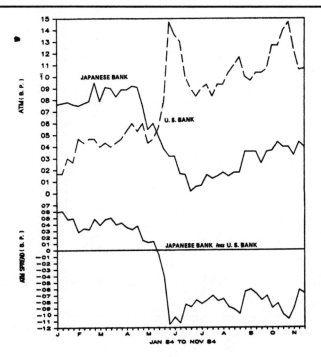

regional banks. Again the same change in quality spread is present.

In all three cases, investors who monitor the market closely can swap out of U.S. money center bank floaters into other alternatives (sovereign names, banks in other countries such as Japan or U.S. regional banks) when a banking crisis starts. Conversely, when investors begin to feel that the storm has blown over, they can swap back to U.S. bank names which at that point would be trading at very cheap levels.

SUMMARY

In recent years, Eurodollar floating rate notes (FRNs) have gained a reputation as a superior investment vehicle, especially in times of rising interest rates or when the outlook for rates is uncertain.

Exhibit 12–17
ATM of U.S. Bank and Sovereign Eurodollar FRNs

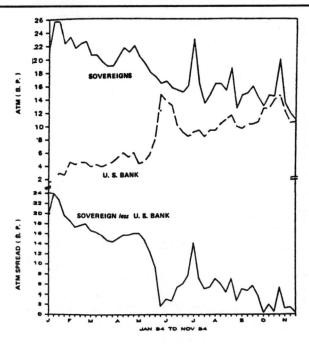

Strong investor demand, in turn, has induced numerous borrowers to tap the FRN market for funds. This has resulted in an explosion of new issues in both the Eurodollar as well as domestic LIBOR-based FRN markets, which not only enhances the liquidity of the market but also creates new trading opportunities through the variety of market sectors and pricing mechanisms. Consequently, FRN investors can now substantially improve the return on their portfolios by carefully monitoring market movements to identify and initiate various forms of inter- and intra-market swaps. This chapter explained these trading opportunities.

Exhibit 12–18
ATM of U.S. Money Center Bank and Regional Bank FRNs

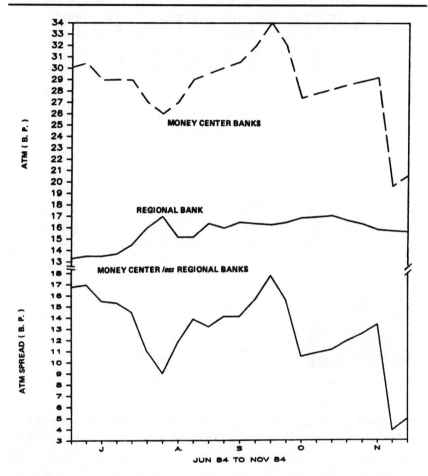

CHAPTER 13

MONITORING SWAP AND TRADING OPPORTUNITIES IN THE FLOATING RATE NOTE MARKET

Michael R. Rosenberg
Vice President
Merrill Lynch Capital Markets

and

Sarah Allen
Fixed Income Analyst
Merrill Lynch Capital Markets

The growing diversity of floating rate note (FRN) instruments in the Eurodollar and U.S. domestic markets has given rise to a variety of profitable trading and swap opportunities. As explained in the previous chapter, these opportunities arise because the price response of different floating rate notes to changes in LIBOR varies depending on the floater's maturity, frequency of coupon refixing, and coupon reset formula. In this chapter, we discuss how a simple moving average trading system can aid investors in identifying underlying trends in LIBOR as well as changes in LIBOR's trend, the necessary ingredients to initiate profitable FRN trading strategies. Also, we illustrate through a variety of simulation studies how a moving average trend-following trading system can be explicitly used to design profitable inter- and intra-market FRN trading strategies. The trading system described in this chapter is intended to supplement and complement (not supplant) other means of forecasting the future direction of LIBOR.

AN OVERVIEW OF FLOATING RATE NOTE TRADING STRATEGIES

Eurodollar floating rate notes have become exceedingly popular to investors for a variety of reasons. First, the yield on LIBOR-based floating rate notes (FRNs) has tended to be higher than competing U.S. money market instruments. This is because LIBOR is structurally the highest interest rate in the U.S. dollar money markets and FRNs generally have their coupons reset at a margin over LIBOR (or more recently, LIBID). Second, total returns on LIBOR-based FRNs have tended to be relatively stable on a month-to-month basis, especially when compared to fixed-rate straight bonds. This is because the variable coupon on FRNs protects investors against major fluctuations in FRN prices. Testimony to the popularity of FRNs was the fact that in 1984 new issue volume in the Eurodollar FRN market exceeded new issue volume in the Eurodollar straight bond market for the first time.

The market in FRNs is highly liquid and diverse. The diversity of FRN instruments gives rise to various trading and swap opportunities because the price response of different FRNs to changes in LIBOR will vary depending on their maturity, coupon reset formula and frequency of coupon refixing. For example, prices on all FRNs tend to move inversely with changes in interest rates, but FRNs with more frequent coupon refixings will not experience as much price volatility as FRNs with less frequent refixings. This is because FRNs with frequent (e.g., quarterly) coupon refixings will likely have their coupons more closely in line with the current yield on LIBOR (and thus their prices will be closer to par) than will FRNs with less frequent (e.g., semi-annual) coupon refixings. If LIBOR is expected to rise an investor would want to swap from FRNs with semi-annual coupon refixings to FRNs with quarterly coupon refixings. In a similar fashion, prices of long maturity FRNs tend to be more volatile (i.e., responsive to changes in LIBOR) than short maturity FRNs. Thus, if LIBOR is expected to rise, an investor would want to switch from long to short maturity FRNs.

Although LIBOR-based FRN prices do vary inversely with changes in LIBOR, the overall price volatility is quite small, especially when compared to fixed rate bonds or T-bill based FRNs. Thus, while the Eurodollar FRN market offers a variety of profitable intra-market trading opportunities, the incremental profit derived from taking advantage of relatively moderate intra-market price swings will not be very large (perhaps an additional 50–100 basis points per year to portfolio return, which is not all that bad for a money market portfolio). This also means that the risk of actively trading a Eurodollar FRN portfolio is small as well.

Greater potential return, and also greater risk, is associated with inter-market swaps between LIBOR-based FRNs and fixed rate bonds, and between LIBOR-based FRNs and T-bill based FRNs. For example, if the general trend in U.S. interest rates is expected to rise an investor would benefit by swapping out of more volatile fixed rate bonds into relatively more stable LIBOR-based FRNs. In the case of trading strategies that involve LIBOR and T-bill based FRNs, it is the expected change in the LIBOR/T-bill yield spread rather than the general trend in LIBOR which initiates profitable swap opportunities. However, the general trend in LIBOR indirectly affects the LIBOR/T-bill yield spread because changes in the interest rate environment exert a strong influence on market perceptions of banking risk and the quality of competing financial instruments.

Changes in the LIBOR/T-bill yield spread give rise to profitable swap opportunities because prices of FRNs referenced to T-bills are highly sensitive to change in this yield spread relationship. While LIBOR is structurally the highest short-term dollar money market rate, T-bill rates are structurally the lowest. Thus, if the LIBOR/T-bill yield spread should widen or narrow, the prices of LIBOR-based FRNs would be largely unaffected but the prices of T-bill based FRNs would have to fall or rise so that the yield on T-bill based FRNs would remain competitive with yields on LIBOR-based FRNs. As a consequence, if it is expected that the LIBOR/T-bill yield spread will widen, an investor should swap from T-bill based FRNs to LIBOR-based FRNs.

PROJECTING THE TREND IN LIBOR USING A SIMPLE MOVING AVERAGE TRADING SYSTEM

Since the price response of different FRN instruments to changes in LIBOR occur in a systematic manner, the ability to enhance return by engaging in inter- and intra-market FRN swaps depends on an investor's ability to project the future trend in LIBOR. In this section we investigate how a simple moving average trading system can aid in projecting the future trend in LIBOR and how an investor can use such a system to design profitable FRN trading strategies.

A simple system based on the crossover of short and long run moving averages provides an investor with a means of identifying underlying market trends as well as changes in market trend. We choose this simple approach because we want to focus attention on the fact that U.S. short-term interest rates tend to move in very discernible systematic trends, both upward and downward, and the trends tend to persist for months at a time. This is evident in Exhibit 13–1 which shows the trend in three-month LIBOR since October 1979. The amplitude of the swings in LIBOR have diminished somewhat from the turbulent 1980-82 period, but the trends are nonetheless apparent. There is a fundamental reason why U.S. short-term interest rates have behaved in such a manner and this is discussed in the following section. The point that we wish to make here is that in the case of projecting the future trend in LIBOR, the "trend is your friend."

Exhibit 13–2 (left) shows how a simple moving average trading system works. The solid line is a short-run moving average (SRMA) of the three-month LIBOR rate and the dashed line is a long-run moving average (LRMA) of the three-month LIBOR rate. We use moving averages to smooth out the often erratic daily and even weekly interest rate movements to get a clearer picture of the direction that interest rates are taking. Since the SRMA weighs the impact of recent LIBOR movements more heavily than the LRMA, the SRMA will tend to lie above the LRMA when LIBOR is rising and below it when LIBOR is falling. Thus, the tendency of the SRMA to move about (at point U) or below (at point D) the LRMA can be used to indicate when an uptrend or downtrend in LIBOR is beginning to develop. An investor following a moving average crossover

Exhibit 13-1
Three-Month LIBOR Rate One and Fifteen-Week Moving Averages

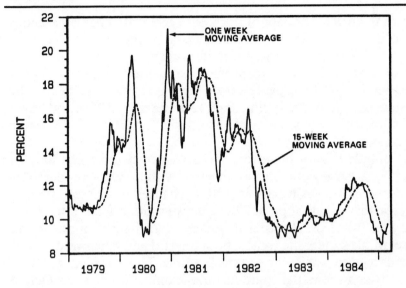

Exhibit 13-2
How a Moving Average Crossover Trading System Works

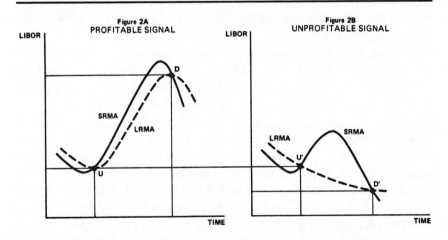

trading system would swap out of more volatile FRN instruments into more stable ones when the trading system signals that LIBOR is likely to rise (U) and would reverse such trades when the trading system signals that LIBOR will fall (D). The spread between U and D would represent the profit margin per dollar invested if an investor rigidly followed this moving average crossover trading system.

However, it should be made clear that such a trading system is by no means infallible. Since we are using moving averages to identify changes in trend, the crossover signals will tend to lag the actual shift in market trend. In addition, as one engages in active trading of FRN portfolios, greater transaction costs are incurred. Furthermore, on a number of occasions, the crossover of the moving averages may give rise to false signals (see Exhibit 13–2B). In order for a moving average system to work, the duration and extent of interest rate movements must be sustained and pronounced, to permit an investor time to recognize and profit from each interest rate swing. If the interest rate swings are not pronounced or if interest rate trends quickly reverse, losses may be incurred. For example, an uptrend is falsely signaled when the SRMA crosses the LRMA at U′ in Exhibit 13–2B. The uptrend signal is false because the uptrend is quickly reversed and a downtrend signal is not issued until the SRMA crosses the LRMA at D′. An investor following this moving average crossover system would have incurred a loss, the spread between U′ and D′ representing the margin of loss per dollar invested.

Evidence from past interest rate cycles suggests that investors will probably face both profitable and unprofitable trading signals if they follow a moving average trading system. The trick is to ride for profit those interest rate swings that are correctly predicted, and to quickly close positions that turn against an investor. Thus, it is not necessary that interest rates always move in large swings for a simple moving average system to prove remunerative, but that such swings should occur frequently enough to overcome those periods when interest rate movements are not highly trended.

Why a Moving Average Trading System Is Appropriate for Projecting The Future Trend in LIBOR

There is always a fundamental reason why markets behave in the manner that they do. In the case of U.S. interest rates, the tendency of LIBOR and other short-term dollar rates to move in discernible, systematic intermediate-term trends can be traced to the way that the Federal Reserve (Fed) conducts policy. The Federal Reserve's approach to interest rate and monetary control is based on the principle of gradualism. Policy is exercised judiciously and cautiously to meet the Fed's ultimate objectives, great care being taken not to unduly disrupt the U.S. financial markets and economic conditions. In the process, the Fed has adjusted interest rates gradually, (although the moves have been quite pronounced at times) instead of rapidly in response to changes in monetary growth and economic activity, and it has been this gradual adjustment process which has made it possible for moving average trading systems to project underlying trends in U.S. interest rates.

The Federal Reserve's Gradual Approach to Monetary Control. Each year the Federal Reserve sets annual growth targets for the monetary aggregates and non-financial credit. These targets are set so that they are consistent with the Fed's ultimate objectives on economic growth and inflation. The Federal Reserve does not feel that it has to keep money growth exactly within its target band on a week-to-week or even on a month-to-month basis. Instead, it is willing to tolerate an overshoot or undershoot in money growth from its long-run target path in one period as long as it can be corrected in subsequent periods. At each Federal Open Market Committee (FOMC) meeting the Fed sets short-run objectives for the monetary aggregates, usually for the next three months, to correct any deviation of the aggregates from their annual target path. Depending on the extent of the deviation from the long-run target path, the Fed's shorter-run objectives will be set to return money supply growth back to its desired trajectory in a way that will be least disruptive to the financial markets and economic activity. For example, efforts to correct a large overshoot or undershoot in money growth over a relatively short time span might entail extremely large and very rapid changes in U.S. interest rates. Since the Fed wishes to avoid large and rapid interest rate swings, it would favor attaining control over money supply growth gradually rather than rapidly to give the markets and the economy time to adjust to rising or declining interest rates. By doing so, interest rates will tend to adjust gradually to the level the Fed desires and this gradual adjustment process could be captured with a moving average, trend-following trading system.

The reason that the Fed does not feel it has to keep money growth exactly within its target band during all points in time is that over or undershooting for brief periods, according to most studies, exerts no lasting discernible impact on real economic activity. In addition, the Fed chooses not to respond to transitory changes in the money supply in the belief or hope that extremely large changes in the money supply will wash out over time. Since there is a large amount of noise in the weekly and even monthly money data, the Fed waits to see if changes in money growth are temporary or permanent. This point was made emphatically by Federal Reserve Chairman Paul Volcker: "The Federal Reserve should not be expected to respond, and does not plan to respond, strongly to various 'bulges' or for that matter 'valleys' in money growth that seem likely to be temporary."

By taking a gradual approach to monetary control, the Fed reduces the odds that it will overreact to temporary changes in money growth and trigger needless and excessive volatility in U.S. interest rates. Stephen Axilrod, Chief Economist of the Federal Reserve Board in Washington, describes the timetable the Fed has set for itself to achieve monetary control:

> The Fed has studied how fast one can get back on the path for the aggregates, while minimizing as it were, interest rate disturbances. It looked like three months would be a good time at getting back. You would still have considerable interest rate volatility, but there would be much more if you tried to get back faster . . .

Looking ahead, there is little reason to expect that the Federal Reserve will deviate from its gradualist approach to interest rate and monetary control. As a consequence, a trend following trading system based on the crossover of short and long run moving averages of LIBOR should continue to serve as a reliable guide in identifying underlying trends in dollar money market rates and in indicating what FRN trading strategies appear attractive.

SIMULATED TOTAL RETURNS FROM ACTIVELY TRADING A FLOATING RATE NOTE PORTFOLIO

No one can guarantee that a trading system that worked well in the past will continue to do so in the future. However, it may still prove instructive to see precisely how a particular trading system identi-fied profitable FRN trading strategies in the past. One may gain valuable insights into the way investors may capitalize on FRN swap and trading opportunities in the future. In this section we provide evidence on simulated total returns that investors could have earned by swapping among different FRN instruments had they followed a moving average crossover system to initiate trades in the 1983–84 period. The results are quite favorable in that the simulated returns from actively trading an FRN portfolio signifi-cantly exceeded the returns available from a passive strategy of buy and hold.

Simulations of three different trading strategies are illustrated below. The trading strategies include:

• swaps between semi-annual and quarterly floating rate notes

• swaps between long and short maturity floating rate notes

• swaps between LIBOR and T-bill based floating rate notes

In each case, we show graphically how a moving average crossover system would have identified profitable FRN trading opportunities. The moving averages that were used in the simulation exercise were the one- and fifteen-week moving averages of LIBOR, except in the case involving swaps between LIBOR and T-bill based FRNs where we used the six- and twenty-week moving averages of the LIBOR/T-bill yield spread. We used longer moving averages in the latter case because the LIBOR/T-bill yield spread is subject to greater short-run variability than LIBOR itself, and thus greater smoothing was required to prevent needless whipsaws.

Simulated returns from actively swapping among different FRNs according to the recommendations of the moving average crossover trading system are shown in Exhibits 13–4, 13–6, and 13–8. These exhibits compare the simulated returns from active trading with the returns that could have been earned on the individual FRN instru-ments themselves if investors chose a passive strategy of buying and holding the underlying securities over the entire investment time horizon. The exhibits detail the recommended transactions, the transaction dates, the price plus accrued interest that must be paid if the security is purchased or received if the security is sold, the nominal amount that is actually purchased or sold, the dollar value of the actively traded portfolio at each transaction date and the comparable value of the individual securities if bought and held, i.e., not actively traded.

Monitoring Swap Opportunities between Semi-Annual and Quarterly Floating Rate Notes

If an investor had swapped from a semi-annual refix FRN (the Bank of Tokyo, 10/29/89) to a quarterly refix FRN (the Bank of Tokyo, 12/12/91) when the one-week moving average of LIBOR moved above the fifteen-week moving average of LIBOR (U), and then swapped back into the semi-annual refix FRN when the one-week moving average moved below the fifteen-week average (D), he could have earned a compounded annualized return of 12.11 percent over the March 1983–January 1985 period. (See Exhibits 13–3 and 13–4.) This return compares with an 11.64 percent annualized return on the semi-annual floater and an 11.14 percent annualized return on the quarterly floater if the investor simply purchased these securities and held them over the March 1983–January 1985 period. Seven out of the eight signals proved profitable.

Monitoring Swap Opportunities between Long and Short Maturity Floating Rate Notes

If an investor had swapped from a long maturity FRN (the Barclay's Bank, 7/31/95) to a short maturity FRN (the Midland Bank 12/14/89) when the one week moving average of LIBOR moved above the fifteen week moving average of LIBOR (U), and then swapped back into the long maturity FRN when the one week average moved below the fifteen week average (D), he could have earned a compounded annualized return of 12.71 percent over the March 1973–January 1985 period. (See Exhibits 13–5 and 13–6.) This return compares with an 11.49 percent annualized return on the long maturity floater and an 11.27 percent annualized return on the short maturity floater if the investor simply purchased these securities and held them over the March 1983–January 1985 period. Six out of the eight signals proved profitable.

Exhibit 13–3
Price Ratio: Quarterly FRN/Semiannual FRN

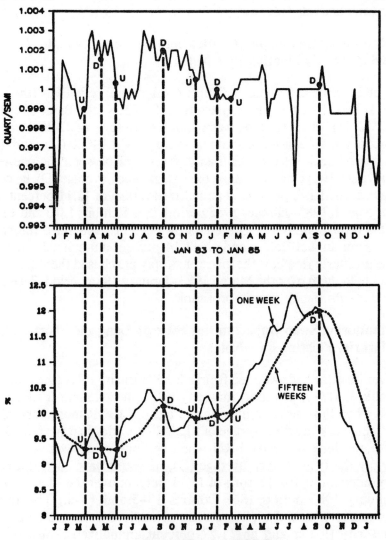

JAN 83 TO JAN 85

Three-Month LIBOR Rate
Crossover of 1 and 15 Week
Moving Averages

Exhibit 13–4
Total Return Analysis
Simulated Returns from Swapping between Semiannual (Bank of Tokyo 10/29/89) and Quarterly (Bank of Tokyo 12/12/91) Refix Eurodollar Floating Rate Notes* Compared with Buy and Hold Strategy

Transaction Date	Transaction	Price + Account Interest	Amount Purchased/ Sold**	Dollar Value of Trading Portfolio	Dollar Value: Buy & Hold Semiannual	Quarterly
Week 4, March '83	Buy Quar	101.58	.9845	$100.00	$100.00	$100.00
Week 4, April '83	Sell Quar	100.37	1.0081	101.18	100.90	101.18
	Buy Semi	103.94	.9735			
Week 5, May '83	Sell Semi	104.68	.9735	101.91	101.63	101.67
	Buy Quar	100.84	1.0105			
Week 3, Sept '83	Sell Quar	101.99	1.0339	105.45	104.99	105.21
	Buy Semi	103.13	1.0226			
Week 1, Dec '83	Sell Semi	105.34	1.0226	107.71	107.24	107.25
	Buy Quar	101.35	1.0628			
Week 3, Jan '84	Sell Quar	102.59	1.0628	109.03	108.50	108.56
	Buy Semi	101.44	1.0758			
Week 3, Feb '84	Sell Semi	102.35	1.0758	109.99	109.57	109.43
	Buy Quar	100.92	1.0910			
Week 3, Sept '84	Sell Quar	102.29	1.1493	117.42	116.91	116.84
	Buy Semi	103.76	1.1328			
Value, End Jan '85				123.33	122.38	121.37
Annualized Returns March 1983–Jan 1985				12.11%	11.64%	11.14%

*Buy and sell signals issued by the crossover of one and fifteen-week moving averages of LIBOR
**It is assumed that coupon income is reinvested in underlying security

Exhibit 13–5
Price Ratio: Short Maturity FRN/Long Maturity FRN

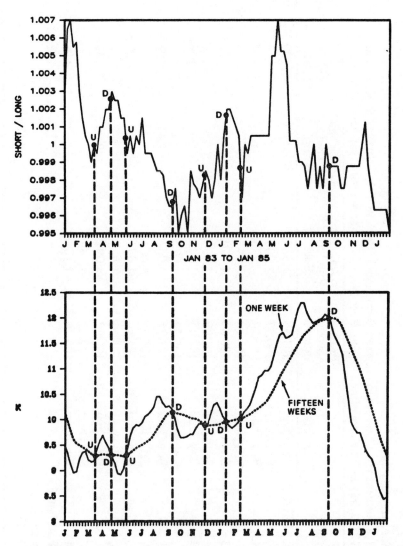

Three-Month LIBOR Rate Crossover of 1- and 15-Week Moving
Averages

Exhibit 13-6
Total Return Analysis
Simulated Returns from Swapping Between Long (Barclay's 7/31/95) and Short (Midland 12/14/89) Maturity Eurodollar Floating rate Notes* Compared with Buy and Hold Strategy

Transaction Date	Transaction	Price + Account Interest	Amount Purchased/Sold**	Dollar Value of Trading Portfolio	Dollar Value: Buy & Hold	
					Long	Short
Week 4, March '83	Buy Short	103.51	.9661	$100.00	$100.00	$100.00
Week 4, April '83	Sell Short	105.00	.9661	101.44	100.10	101.44
	Buy Long	102.48	.9899			
Week 5, May '83	Sell Long	104.19	.9899	103.13	101.78	101.81
	Buy Short	105.39	.9786			
Week 3, Sept '83	Sell Short	103.54	1.0285	106.49	105.32	105.12
	Buy Long	102.76	1.0363			
Week 1, Dec '83	Sell Long	104.80	1.0363	108.50	107.40	107.10
	Buy Short	105.49	1.0295			
Week 3, Jan '84	Sell Short	101.98	1.0823	110.36	108.82	108.84
	Buy Long	106.17	1.0395			
Week 3, Feb '84	Sell Long	101.53	1.0959	111.26	109.70	109.36
	Buy Short	102.46	1.0859			
Week 3, Sept '84	Sell Short	103.69	1.1444	118.66	116.32	116.63
	Buy Long	102.44	1.1584			
Value, End Jan '85				124.53	122.07	121.63
Annualized Returns March 1983–Jan 1985				12.71%	11.49%	11.27%

*Buy and sell signals issued by the crossover of one and fifteen week moving averages of LIBOR

**It is assumed that coupon income is reinvested in underlying security

Exhibit 13–7
Price Ratio: Eurodollar FRN/T-Bill FRN

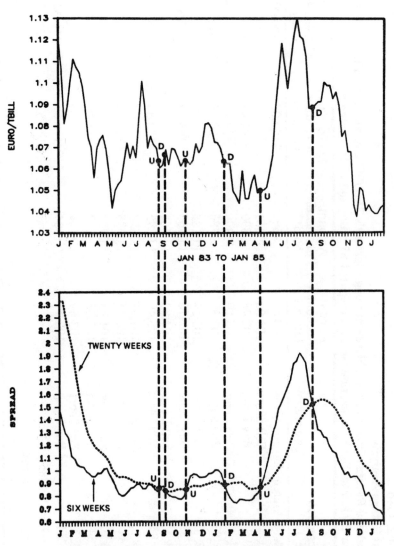

Three-Month LIBOR—Treasury Bill Yield Spread
Crossover of 6- and 20- Week Moving Averages

Exhibit 13–8
Total Return Analysis
Simulated Returns from Swapping between LIBOR (Chase 7/31/93) and T-bill (Citicorp 5/1/04) Floating Rate Notes* Compared with Buy and Hold Strategy

Transaction Date	Transaction	Price + Account Interest**	Amount Purchased/ Sold	Dollar Value of Trading Portfolio	Dollar Value: Buy & Hold LIBOR	T-Bill
Week 4, Aug '83	Buy LIBOR	101.18	.9884	$100.00	$100.00	$100.00
Week 2, Sept '83	Sell LIBOR	102.30	.9884			
	Buy T-bill	97.81	1.0337	100.11	101.11	101.03
Week 2, Nov '83	Sell T-bill	94.85	1.0844			
	Buy LIBOR	103.62	.9962	102.85	102.41	102.77
Week 1, Feb '84	Sell LIBOR	100.48	1.0461			
	Buy T-bill	97.04	1.0832	105.11	104.66	105.14
Week 3, April '84	Sell T-bill	99.91	1.0832			
	Buy LIBOR	102.31	1.0579	108.22	106.57	108.26
Week 4, Aug '84	Sell LIBOR	101.09	1.1114			
	Buy T-bill	95.39	1.1777	112.34	110.62	108.63
Value End Jan '85				123.03	116.61	118.96
Annualized Returns Aug 1983–Jan 1985				15.76%	11.45%	13.04%

*Buy and sell signals issued by the crossover of six and twenty week moving averages of the LIBOR/T-bill yield spread
**It is assumed that coupon income is reinvested in underlying security

Monitoring Swap Opportunities between LIBOR and T-Bill-Based Floating Rate Notes

If an investor had swapped from a domestic T-bill based FRN (the Citicorp, 5/1/04) to a Eurodollar LIBOR-based FRN (the Chase, 7/31/93) when the six-week moving average of the LIBOR/T-bill yield spread moved above the twenty-week moving average of the LIBOR/T-bill yield spread (U), and then swapped back into the T-bill based FRN when the six-week average moved below the twenty week average (D), he could have earned a compounded annualized return of 15.76 percent over the August 1983–January 1985 period. (See Exhibits 13–7 and 13–8.) This return compares with an 11.45 percent annualized return on the LIBOR-based FRN and a 13.04 percent annualized return on the T-Bill based FRN if the investor simply purchased these securities and held them over the August 1983–January 1985 period. Five out of the six signals proved profitable.

CHAPTER 14

RETURN ENHANCEMENT BY USING FLOATERS IN SWAP TRADES

Ronald J. Ryan, C.F.A.
Managing Director
Ryan Financial Strategy Group

The track record of floaters indicates that they are better performers than cash equivalents (i.e., Treasury bills, Certificates of Deposit, etc.). They therefore represent an ideal alternative for cash in strategies that involve a cash vehicle. The present chapter illustrates how, under certain conditions, floaters can be used instead of cash in a GNMA time swap so as to enhance the return of the swap.

GNMA TIME SWAP

The time swap concept has historically been a savings and loan (S&L) investment strategy to enhance the yield on S&L portfolios without a loss. According to this strategy, a S&L will sell and buy back the same coupon GNMA at some specified price at some specified settlement date in the future (the forward market). It is assumed that the S&L will invest in some cash equivalent between the sale date and repurchase date. Because S&L accounting considers this transaction a "no sale," there is no accounting of a loss or gain on the transaction. This accounting quirk has allowed S&Ls to sell low book yielding assets and to buy higher yielding assets with absolutely no change to the portfolio structure.

Usually, S&Ls will consummate such a transaction—frequently called a "dollar roll"—only when they can pick up yield. This occurs when they can buy back the same GNMA at a lower price in the forward market. The forward market price is determined by two factors: financing costs (the carry) and supply and demand.

Financing costs (or the costs of carry) are determined by calculating the difference in yields of holding (warehousing) the GNMA position until the settlement date versus the money market rate attainable over the same period. This yield difference could be positive or negative. Since a Wall Street investment dealer typically acts as the principal on the trade, the forward market prices will be set accordingly. If it is favorable (that is, positive carry) for them to warehouse this GNMA trade instead of being in a cash equivalent, they will discount (lower) the forward market price, and vice versa.

Supply and demand are always major considerations. The traders' perception of the market, as well as new pass-throughs being created for forward market settlement, are based on available supply, and will dictate pricing trends.

Both aggressive S&Ls and pension fund managers have gone well beyond the traditional yield objective of a time swap (dollar roll) to enhance their portfolios. They have found that time swaps have many valuable characteristics sought by money managers. These include:

- **Liquidity:** Transactions can be quite sizable.

- **Selection:** Time swaps are available on many coupons and many types of mortgage pass-throughs.

- **Leverage:** Time swaps require no transfer of funds until settlement date, which could be several months away.

- **Quality:** Time swaps on mortgage pass-throughs deal with only the highest rated securities.

- **Timing:** Based on interest rate forecasting and/or anticipated flow of funds, investors can time or speculate more efficiently.

- **Performance:** Because a time swap is an overinvested situation involving ownership of two securities until settlement date, returns can be greatly enhanced. A time swap actually allows investment in two different markets at the same time.

With the track record of floaters being better than cash equivalents, the return on a swap may be enhanced by using floaters instead of a cash vehicle in a swap. In the mortgage pass-through market, for example, purchases of most coupons can be made with a delayed settlement of one to three months and occasionally six months out.[1] The delay of settlement can be accomplished by using the forward market. The forward market is a market in which the parties agree to trade "something" at a fixed price for future delivery.[2] When using the forward market, no funds must be put up until settlement. A Government National Mortgage Association (GNMA) issued pass-through is one example of a mortgage pass-through security.[3]

ILLUSTRATION

Let us now take a closer look at the mathematics that supports the risk/reward merits of a GNMA time swap. Suppose that an investor can sell or give up the opportunity to own a GNMA 13 percent for immediate settlement in August (cash market) and buy it back or purchase it in November at some specified price (forward market). The basic information for this GNMA time swap and the framework for evaluating it are presented in Table 14–1. Here it is assumed that the investor is in a cash equivalent in the three-month interval (August–November) at the yield shown on line G. To understand the risk/reward of this swap, the investor simply compares the give-up to the pick-up. The difference is the reward or value

---

[1] A mortgage pass-through security is a security that derives its cash flow from an underlying pool of mortgages. Each month, the issuer passes through to the holder of the security the principal and interest payments.

[2] Unlike the futures market, the forward market is a nonregulated market in which nonstandardized contracts for future delivery are traded. There is no daily "mark to market" requirement in the forward market.

[3] The Government National Mortgage Association is a government-owned corporation established under the Housing and Development Act of 1968. GNMA guarantees pass-through securities for timely payment of principal and interest.

TABLE 14–1
GNMA Time Swap

A.	GNMA Coupon	13%	
B.	Settlement-Sale	August	
C.	Market Price	$96-12.	
D.	FORWAD Market	3	
E.	Settlement-Buy	November	
F.	Market Price	$94-20.	
G.	Cash Equivalent Yield (CYE)	10%	
	Sale Giveup		
H.	Income from GNMA Sold	$32,139	
I.	Prepayment from GNMA	$0	
J.	Total (H + I)		$32,139
	Purchase Pickup		
K.	Takeout (C-F)	$17,500	
L.	Income from CYE	$24,361	
M.	Total (K + L)		$41,861
N.	Increased Return (M-J)	$ 9,722	
O.	Nonannualized % Return	1.01%	
P.	Annualized % Return		4.09%

Note: A $1 million position on sale is assumed.
Source: Ryan Financial Strategy Group.

added, shown on lines N, O, and P of Table 14–1. As the time swap analysis indicates, a 1.01 percent enhanced return (4.09 percent annualized) can be expected by delaying settlement for three months on this trade. This is an example of an actual trade and strategy that existed on August 3, 1983. Later in this chapter, the actual performance over the three-month investment horizon is presented.

At the time of this GNMA time swap, the floater market looked attractive in light of a key issue: Citicorp (FNC) due 5/1/04, whose coupon changed semiannually on May 1 and November 1. Citicorp's coupon was based on a formula that basically took the average interest yield equivalent[4] of the six-month Treasury bill

[4] The interest yield equivalent is the yield of a security based on the actual proceeds (without a reinvestment assumption). It is computed as follows:

$$\frac{\text{Discount per } \$1,000}{\$1,000} \times \frac{360}{\text{No. of days}}$$

for a two-week period in April and October and added 105 basis points to this average.[5] On August 13, 1983 the coupon was set at 11.15 percent and due for a change on November 1, which was near the delivery date of the GNMA 13 percent (third week in November).

The next step, therefore, was to compare the floater as an alternative to cash for the three-month investment horizon.

FLOATER VERSUS CASH

Since interest rates at the end of the investment horizon can be either higher, lower, or the same as when the investment began, it is important to appraise potential strategies under each interest rate scenario to assess the impact on total return. The analysis of whether to use a floater or cash under three possible interest rate scenarios at the end of the investment horizon is shown in Table 14–2.

The analysis in Table 14–2 indicates that whether rates go up or down, the floater returns are higher. Consequently, replacing cash with floaters in the GNMA time swap should enhance expected return even more.

FLOATER PLUS GNMA TIME SWAP

Adding the risk/reward of floaters to an attractive GNMA forward market results in quite a "dynamic duo." Once again, this synergistic investment should be evaluated under the three alternative interest rate scenarios.

For the three-month forward market period, the investor will not receive any income from the GNMA position, since the investor does not settle until November. However, the investor is exposed to price return risk since the November price will change with rates. If interest rates are unchanged at the end of the investment horizon, the November price of 94 20/32 will become the August price of 96

---

[5] Specifically, the coupon formula for the Citicorp (FNC) due 5/1/04 is the interest yield equivalent of the arithmetic average of the weekly market rate for the 181-day U.S. Treasury bill as published by the Federal Reserve during the 14 calendar days immediately prior to the last 10 calendar days of April and October.

TABLE 14–2
Analysis of Floaters versus Cash

Levels	Unchanged	+ 50 B.P.	– 50 B.P.
6-Month T-Bill	10.10%	10.60%	9.60%
6-Month CD	10.50%	11.10%	10.10%
FNC Coupon	11.15%	11.65%	10.65%
FNC Present Price	$93.38	$93.38	$93.38
FNC Current Yield	11.94%	12.48%	11.40%
FNC Yield vs. CD (at 1.25% over CD)	1.44%	1.38%	1.30%
New FNC Yield	11.75%	12.35%	11.35%
New FNC Price (3 month returns)	$94.99	$94.33	$93.83
Income Return	2.45%	2.45%	2.45%
Price Return	1.63%	1.02%	0.49%
Total Return	4.08%	3.47%	2.94%
3-Month Cash Return	2.50%	2.50%	2.50%
FNC Return – Cash Return	1.58%	0.97%	0.44%

Note: The assumptions are: (1) T-bill to CD spread widens to ± 50 B.P., (2) CD to FNC spread changes to + 125 B.P., and (3) 3-month CD rate of 10% for cash return used.

12/32 in November. The price will appreciate 1.85 percent as a result. The reason for this is that the forward market becomes, or gets marked to, the cash market through time. If the August price represents the cash market, and the market is unchanged, the cash market by definition is unchanged.

As noted earlier, when an investor makes a purchase in the forward market, no funds must be put up until settlement. As a result, the investor owns a floater position in the meantime and will use this floater position as funds to pay for the GNMA 13s in November. This creates a temporarily overweighted investment position, allowing the investor to add the returns of the GNMA and floater position instead of averaging the two. This extra positioning power allows the dynamic duo strategy to gain a considerable head start or extra yield over other investment alternatives. This can be seen in

TABLE 14–3
**Performance of "Dynamic Duo" under Three
Interest Rate Scenarios (8/3/83)**

	Unchanged	+ 50	– 50
GNMA:			
Value of Time Swap	1.85	1.85	1.85
Price Return	0	– 2.90	3.05
Total Return	1.85%	– 1.05%	4.90%
Floater (FNC 04):			
Income Return	2.45	2.45	2.45
Price Return	1.63	1.02	0.49
Total Return	4.08%	3.47%	2.94%
Total Return (Dynamic Duo)	5.93%	2.42%	7.84%
Investment Alternatives:			
3-Month CD	2.50%	2.50%	2.50%
Treasury 2-Year	2.75	1.97	3.53
Treasury 30-Year	2.97	– 0.99	7.28

Note: There is a three-month horizon.

Table 14–3. The analysis indicates that the dynamic duo strategy has the risk of a three-month CD but offers the reward of a 30-year Treasury.

THE ACTUAL RESULTS

Three months later, on November 3, 1983—the end of the investment horizon—the dynamic duo strategy was reviewed and the performance evaluated. The results are shown in Table 14–4.

The total return on the GNMA time swap was 8.42 percent (nonannualized) with the GNMA contributing 4.62 percent (nonannualized) and the floater 3.80 percent (nonannualized). The lower panel of Table 14–4 shows the actual return for alternative investments. As can be seen, the dynamic duo clearly outperformed these alternative investments by a wide margin.

TABLE 14–4
"Dynamic Duo" Performance
(8/3/83–11/3/83)

GNMA:

Value of Time Swap	1.85%
Price Return	2.77
Total Return	4.62%

Floater:

Income Return	2.45%
Price Return	1.35
Total Return	3.80%
Total Return (Dynamic Duo)	8.42% (Nonannualized)
	38.18% (Annualized)

Investment Alternatives:
Treasury 2-Year = 3.77%
Treasury 10-Year = 4.29%
Treasury 30-Year = 3.24%

CONCLUSION

Any time a GNMA swap analysis signals a positive return by extending settlement, the floater market should be reviewed to see if returns can be further enhanced. In fact, floaters should be considered an investment alternative to cash whenever a cash equivalent strategy is selected for other than liquidity reasons. A cash strategy is usually a bearish position suggesting a higher interest rate forecast, an environment from which floaters would benefit. Accordingly, floaters would enjoy a higher new coupon plus potential price appreciation if present pricing were not too high or higher rates were not fully discounted.

Unfortunately, few investors understand floaters or feel sufficiently comfortable to regard them as an ordinary investment selection. Now that the mortgage market is creating adjustable rate securities, we may finally create a floating rate sector that has the quality, liquidity, and features that will eliminate all present biases against using floaters as a major investment vehicle.

CHAPTER 15

THE ROLE OF COUPON SWAPS IN FLOATING RATE MARKETS

Carl R. Beidleman, Ph.D.

Allen C. DuBois
Professor of Finance
Lehigh University

Dollar-based floating rate markets have shown remarkable growth in recent years. Eurodollar issues of floating rate notes based on LIBOR (London Interbank Offer Rate) have grown from $11,160 million in 1982 to $28,749 million in 1984. Domestic floaters have shown an even more outstanding growth rate, with annual issuance growing from $800 million in 1982 to $4 billion in 1984. Treasury bill-based floater issuance grew from $1 billion to $2 billion over the same period, with approximately three quarters of the volume in the domestic market.

In 1984 domestic floating rate note issues began to appear with a dual basis or index (LIBOR/Treasury bill) or other floating rate indices such as certificates of deposit (CD), commercial paper (CP), prime, or some combination of these. These hybrid-basis instruments grew from nil to $4.8 billion in 1984. In addition, floating rate note issuance facilities grew from $2.7 billion in 1982 to $20 billion in 1984. This represents a total issuance level of nearly $60 billion in 1984. Issuance in the first quarter of 1985 reached $27.7 billion, nearly half of that issued in all of 1984, assuring the continued growth of floating rate markets.

FINANCIAL FLEXIBILITY

The huge volume of floating rate instruments that has been issued reflects the preferences of issuers and investors for paying or receiving the current level of interest rates, that is, a preference for floating rates over a long period of time as opposed to a predetermined fixed rate over the life of a term instrument. While such a preference for floating rates may have been reasonable at the time the notes were placed, conditions may change through time causing alternative coupon configurations to appear more desirable. For instance, the floating rate basis incorporated in an instrument may lose its appeal, the reset frequency may become undesirable, or the overall level or term structure of interest rates may change, making the contractual interest payments less desirable than alternative configurations currently available.

In addition, certain anomalies in markets make it possible to utilize a particular type of financing or investment to obtain a lower cost or higher yield than would otherwise be available. These situations occur when certain markets are not equally accessible by all players or when regulatory, cultural, or market convention differences influence market availability.[1] For example, a player might find it advantageous to use the floating rate markets together with swaps or swaplike instruments to assemble a financial package that reduced its all-in cost or improved its all-in return. Such simulated financing or investment strategies have become quite popular in recent years. In general, the key to their implementation has been the application of asset/liability management techniques using a recently developed set of instruments called interest rate swaps or coupon swaps.

---

[1] For a fuller discussion of market inefficiencies and their impact on financial costs and returns, see Carl R. Beidleman, *Financial Swaps,* Chapter 4, Homewood, IL: Dow Jones-Irwin, 1985.

ASSET/LIABILITY MANAGEMENT

Informed portfolio managers have always been ready to shift assets and asset categories to fit the current objectives of their portfolio, based on the set of market opportunities available at a given time. In the process, they have developed complex managerial techniques to identify changes in actual or proposed portfolio content.

These concepts of modern portfolio management were primarily confined to asset portfolios until the early 1960s. Professionally astute banks and other financial intermediaries then became aware that their liquidity needs and their risk-return preferences could be more effectively managed by actively managing their liabilities. As a result, sourcing and trading liabilities became an active practice among the funds managers of progressive financial institutions. If an institution was well-managed and had a good name, fluctuations in funding needs could be handled simply by purchasing or selling liabilities. In terms of its impact on the risk-return calculus of the institutions, liability management was conceptually quite similar to asset portfolio management. Despite this similarity, liability management did not catch on as quickly as portfolio management. This may have been due to the lack of understanding or the lack of acceptance of these techniques as suitable to the liability side of the balance sheet.

Modern liability management, as it is now practiced by banks and financial institutions, can be employed by other types of players to reduce their cost of funds. Certain debt markets are more accessible to some borrowers than to others but have undesirable debt service or coupon characteristics. Natural fixed rate payers may be best advised to attach floating rate funds in order to obtain finance, and natural floating rate payers may find it beneficial to tap fixed rate markets in which they have an advantage. The aim is for each type of payer to swap its interest obligations with the other in order that each obtains the preferred market access and interest configuration. The instruments needed to accomplish this exchange are called interest rate or coupon swaps.

The use of coupon swaps to obtain a lower all-in cost of funds through access to financial markets in which one has a relative advantage enables financial managers to tailor the interest configuration on their liabilities to a different pattern from the initial one.

Similarly, portfolio managers can employ coupon swaps to alter the coupon characteristics of their portfolio and, in the process, simulate investments that have higher all-in returns than the equivalent directly accessible risk assets. The key link is the use of a coupon swap. In the next section, we examine the essential characteristics of coupon swaps. A brief description of the standardization of instruments and the growth in the swap market follows. Finally, we present a comprehensive section covering representative applications of coupon swaps to floating rate instruments.

COUPON SWAPS

A coupon or interest rate swap provides a convenient means of altering the coupon cash flows on a debt instrument. Its primary objective is to exchange fixed rate interest payments for floating rate payments or vice versa. Prior to the advent of long-term floating rate instruments, contractual coupon payments were fixed over the life of a debt security. However, as we have seen, debt issues that call for coupon payments that float or are reset each three or six months have abounded in recent years. The basis for these revisions is some well-documented market rate such as LIBOR, a short-term Treasury bill rate, commercial paper or certificate of deposit composite rate, or other index of rates.

The quality or certainty of the level of coupon cash payments or receipts on floating rate instruments is lower or more uncertain than it is on fixed rate instruments. This uncertainty may provide attraction or aversion for various types of market participants. That is, some players prefer to receive floating rate payments over fixed rate payments or vice versa. On the financing side, certain borrowers prefer to pay a fixed rate of interest, while others, because of their asset structures, are more inclined to pay floating rates.[2] Despite these preferences, players frequently find it less onerous and costly to access debt markets that require coupon flows that conflict with their preferences. A natural solution to this financial dilemma rests in the use of a coupon swap.

[2] For an extended discussion of the preferences of coupon payers and receivers, see Beidleman, op. cit. pp. 203–209.

A coupon swap may be defined as the exchange of a coupon or interest payment stream of one configuration for that of a different configuration, on the same notional principal amount. Coupon swaps in which payments are based on one floating rate index or basis in exchange for a different floating rate index or basis are also available, i.e., a floating rate versus floating rate swap in which LIBOR flows were exchanged for prime flows less some negotiated percentage. These swaps would be made in order to alter the quality or configuration of the coupon cash flows and to make them more compatible with the preferences of investors or issuers of debt instruments.

It is important to note that, in a coupon swap, the principal is only notional to the transaction. While the principal determines the size of the coupon flows, it is not swapped; hence, it is not at risk. This point significantly reduces the risk to the parties and to the market intermediaries. All that is at risk is the interest differential between the fixed and floating rate coupon determinants. Because of the financial characteristics of the parties, however, this difference generally acts to satisfy their underlying preferences.

MARKET DEVELOPMENT OF COUPON SWAPS

As we have seen, the risk involved in coupon swaps excludes the principal and is limited to the interest differential between the fixed and floating rate basis of the coupon payments. This basis risk can be readily managed within reasonable limits, providing market makers with a means of limiting their exposure. As a result, the market in coupon swaps has developed rapidly, becoming nearly standardized and fully productized by early 1985.

The coupon swap product was originally introduced in the Euromarket in early 1982 as a modification of the currency or foreign exchange swap. These instruments had been in rather common use since 1976, but their annual volume had reached only $4 to $5 billion by 1982. Because of a large volume of ready applications and reduced risk to the parties, coupon swaps took off quickly after their introduction. It has been estimated that approximately $5 billion of coupon swap transactions were done in 1982, followed by $25 billion in 1983 and $50 billion in 1984.

The initial rapid growth of the coupon swap market was given a major impetus by the existence of a rather deep-seated difference between the fixed and floating rate markets. This market anomaly or imperfection is reflected in the differential premium for risk demanded by each market. For example, in 1982, a BBB rated industrial company faced a 1.5 percent risk premium over an AAA bank in the fixed rate market and only a 0.5 percent premium in the floating rate Eurodollar market. The difference of 1 percent represented a credit arbitrage opportunity. That is, given these differential spreads, the AAA bank might borrow fixed-rate funds at approximately 11 percent and pass this rate on to the BBB firm. The latter might borrow at LIBOR plus 50 basis points and swap this floating rate obligation with the bank. In this example, the coupon swap would provide for the bank to receive 11 percent from the BBB with which to service its fixed rate debt, and the BBB would receive LIBOR less 0.25 percent with which to service its floating rate debt. The bank would save 0.25 percent under its cost to access floating rate funds directly (LIBOR) and the BBB firm would see a fixed rate cost difference of 1.5 percent under its directly accessible cost of fixed rate funds, 12.5 percent. This saving is reduced by the 0.75 percent difference between what the BBB pays and receives for floating rate funds. It is further reduced by the fact the the BBB is required to pay the transactions costs of the swap and related credit intermediation fees. The net result is that the bank would obtain a net saving of 0.25 percent and the BBB would realize an all-in saving of 0.43 percent. It is important to note that, in addition to the saving, each party obtained the financing configuration that it preferred.

CHARACTERISTICS OF THE COUPON SWAP MARKET

The development of the coupon swap market took place rapidly because the product could be standardized with relative ease and risk could be managed within relatively narrow limits by market makers. Standardized documentation was available from an early date, drawing on the concepts used in currency swaps. Pricing was based on a dual threshold: the fixed rate quotation at some spread over term Treasuries of the same maturity as the coupon swap, versus the floating rate index flat. An example of this pricing is presented in Table 15–1.

Figure 15–1 presents a record of coupon swap pricing for various maturities against the six-month LIBOR floating rate index over a period of a year. This data reflects the degree of sophistication that the coupon swap market has achieved in a remarkably short period of time.

A principal reason for this rapid development of the coupon swap market was that the exposure to the market makers could be readily managed. There is very little risk on the floating rate side. Price risk is limited to the short period until repricing occurs. Any basis risk due to funding assets with liabilities that float on a different basis or funding cost would not be excessive and could be controlled by careful management. The exposure on the fixed rate side is similar to being long (short) in term bonds. This can be managed by selling (buying) sufficient Treasury note or bond futures to obtain the needed offset protection.

Complete productization of coupon swaps also depends on the way in which credit risk can be managed. From the outset, credit risk to each of the parties could be handled by bringing a bank intermediary into the transaction to provide a letter of credit-like assurance that each of the parties would perform on its obligation. When a bank is one of the parties to the coupon swap it naturally fills this function. Other means of providing for the credit risk inherent in coupon swaps include the use of collateral or margin and a periodic mark-to-market to determine the level of margin requirements.

TABLE 15–1
Interest Rate Swap Spreads (May 2, 1985)
(Quoted for Generic Swaps as a Basis Point Spread to the Treasury
Yield Curve versus the Floating Index Flat)

	2 Years	5 Years	7 Years	10 Years
3-Month LIBOR	62	52	40	43
3-Month Bill	– 20	– 48	– 70	– 70

Source: Salomon Brothers Inc., *Bond Market Roundup*, May 3, 1985.

Figure 15-1
The Interest Rate Swap Market: Six-Month LIBOR (Floating) versus U.S. Treasuries (Fixed)

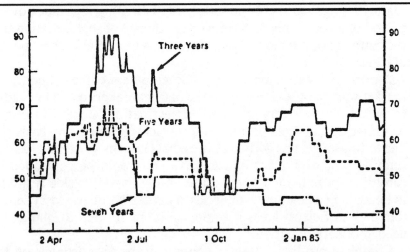

Note: Chart displays the fixed spread over U.S. Treasuries (for the indicated maturities) one would receive (or pay) in an interest rate swap arrangement in return for paying (or receiving) six-month LIBOR.

Source: Salomon Brothers Inc., *Floating-Rate Financing Quarterly*, March 1985, April 22, 1985.

Improved ability to manage credit risk has also contributed to the ability to trade or transfer coupon swaps. If the credit risk of an assignee or its guarantor is acceptable to a principal market maker, it is now possible to assign a coupon swap as required in a trading process. Thus, market sophistication has proceeded to the point where coupon swaps have become trading vehicles and gains or losses may be taken as the players seek to redress their balance sheets and/or income statements.

APPLICATIONS TO FLOATING-RATE INSTRUMENTS

The growth in annual volume of coupon swaps affirms the validity of the concept and its demand by both floating rate and fixed rate payers and receivers. A few actual case studies will be helpful in providing a clearer understanding of how coupon swaps can be used to reduce costs, increase yields, or revise the basis of coupon flows to suit the preferences of the parties.

Liability Management

The first case study actually took place in November, 1984. A rather small, regional commercial bank which faced a large increase in its money market deposit accounts sought to improve its interest sensitivity by buying a $5 million floating rate note indexed to six-month Treasury bills and reset each six months. This floating rate note (FRN) was acquired in 1983. Although it improved the gap management and interest sensitivity of the bank over investment in longer term assets, it became clear after the FRN was acquired that two significant shortcomings still remained. First, every major credit crisis in the U.S. resulted in a flight to quality instruments, which, in turn, caused a decline in short-term Treasury interest rates. Thus the income from the FRN was depressed from time to time with a resultant adverse affect on the net interest margin of the bank. Second, the bank had some asset sensitivity at six months which it wanted to shorten.

The solution was a floating versus floating rate coupon swap in which the bank received six-month LIBOR with a six-month reset, and paid the bond equivalent rate on six-month Treasury bills plus 90 basis points (0.90 percent) with a weekly reset based on the weekly Treasury auction. The notional size of the swap was $5 million. In this way the bank eliminated its six-month asset sensitivity by effectively refunding its six-month asset with weekly reset payments. In addition it converted its Treasury bill based FRN to a six-month LIBOR based FRN and no longer needed to fear the effects on net interest income from a domestic flight to quality.

Although its objective was to balance its interest sensitivity and exposure to the effects of a domestic financial crisis, the bank earned an average of $4,000 a month on the swap during the first reset period. This occurred due to movements in the rates such that its Treasury bill funding costs plus the 90 basis point spread fell below the six-month LIBOR that the bank was receiving. The counterparty to this swap may have been one with bill based liabilities, such as a number of large U.S. banks and financial intermediaries, or the World Bank, which have been significant issuers of bill based FRNs. Others could be issuers of variable rate certificates of deposit or commercial paper whose rates tend to parallel Treasury rates.

Asset Swap

The second case study involves an asset or portfolio swap. This example can be used to highlight the limited risk features of a coupon swap. In this case a U.S. life insurance company purchased a five-year floating rate CD in mid-1983 at six-month LIBOR plus 0.25 percent. The life insurance firm preferred term fixed-rate assets with cash flows more nearly coincident with its expected disbursements, and fixed-rate returns that could be relied upon to produce required returns for policyholders. Therefore the life insurance firm sought to swap its floating rate CD interest income with a weak (BBB) corporate credit. Other logical counterparties might have been thrift institutions or small banks. The BBB-rated firm in this case utilized existing floating rate or short-term debt. It could also have sourced its funds from a bank, relying on the floating rate interest payments from the life insurance firm to service its floating rate debt.

The BBB firm was interested in fixed rate debt and was willing to pay a spread of 300 basis points over five-year Treasuries. Five-year Treasuries were yielding 10.5 percent, making the fixed rate payment to the life insurance firm 13.5 percent. In exchange, the life insurance firm paid over to the BBB firm its floating rate interest receipts of 0.25 percent over a six-month LIBOR (10 percent at the time) or 10.25 percent in the first interest period. Of course, the six-month LIBOR rate was reset each six months.

The advantage to the life insurance firm was that it received fixed rate income at a yield reflecting a BBB-rated credit, as if it had lent the funds to a BBB-rated firm rather than investing them in a bank-issued floating rate CD. The BBB firm enjoyed the benefits of obtaining fixed rate finance at a time when fixed rate funds were not otherwise available and at a cost which reflected no increase in its cost of debt capital.

The risk profile faced by the life insurance firm in this example is interesting. First, the risk of principal was limited to that of the issuer of the CD, a bank in this case, since principal is not swapped in a coupon swap. Thus, the only risk to which the insurance company was exposed was the uncertainty that the BBB firm might not remit the required fixed rate interest flows. Even then the level of exposure was only the difference between the 13.5 percent fixed rate and the 10.25 percent and subsequent floating rate payments. Moreover, this risk is really an opportunity type of risk, i.e., a risk that the insurance firm may have to reinvest its principal at a lower fixed rate.

Thus there was no principal risk and only a small coupon risk based on possible reinvestment at lower rates. Moreover the reinvestment rate risk was symmetric and tended to operate in the favor of the life insurance firm. That is, if interest rates were to go down and the reinvestment rates of return decline, this would probably coincide with a period of economic expansion and would probably be at a time least likely for the BBB-rated firm to fail or default. Similarly, if rates moved higher following an economic recovery, any likely loss due to reinvestment risk would become nil, at the same time that the probability of failure of the lower credit party became greater. Nevertheless, this prospect would cause little concern or detriment to the life insurance firm because reinvestment of the principal would produce higher yields under such conditions. Hence, this asset or portfolio coupon swap permits both parties to obtain the interest characteristics that they prefer, at rates that are mutually attractive and without undue risk to the swapping investor.

Capital Market Swap

A third example in which the coupon swap market provided an attractive financing alternative in the first quarter of 1985 is shown in Figure 15–2. Here we see that substantial spreads below LIBOR could have been obtained over a nine-month period by using the coupon swap market to transform a fixed rate obligation to a floating rate obligation. The strategy would entail an AAA borrower tapping the five-year Eurodollar bond market at a fixed interest rate lower than the borrower would receive on the fixed rate side of a fixed for floating rate coupon swap against six-month LIBOR. The positive spread that the borrower received could be used to reduce

Figure 15-2
**The Interest Rate Swap Market: Effective Costs versus
Six-Months LIBOR**

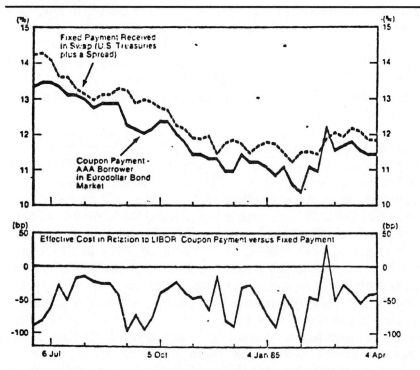

Note: The borrower in this example enters into a swap agreement where he agrees as a "floating-rate payer" to pay six-month LIBOR and receive a fixed-rate which is five-year U.S. Treasuries plus a spread. At the same time, he issues a fixed-rate Eurodollar bond. To the extent that what he receives (U.S. Treasuries plus a spread) exceeds his coupon obligations on this bond, the borrower has achieved an effective cost below LIBOR.

Source: Salomon Brothers Inc., *Floating-Rate Financing Quarterly*, March 1985, April 22, 1985.

the effective floating rate cost that must be borne for the financing. It can be seen from Figure 15-2 that, at times, this cost savings has exceeded 100 basis points and has averaged about 50 basis points over the period. Figure 15-3 provides approximate cash flows for a swap made on March 22, 1985. From this it can be seen that the use of a coupon swap enabled the borrower to obtain floating rate finance at 50 basis points under the rate that first-name Eurobanks charged one another for six-month funds.

Figure 15–3
Capital Market Swap
Illustrative Cash Flows

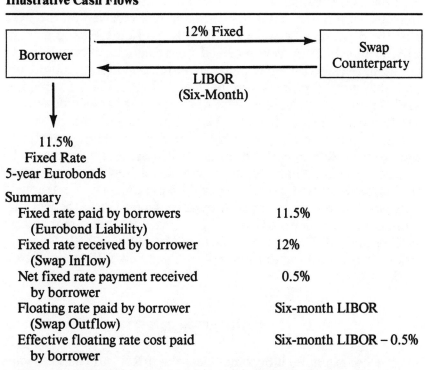

Summary

Fixed rate paid by borrowers (Eurobond Liability)	11.5%
Fixed rate received by borrower (Swap Inflow)	12%
Net fixed rate payment received by borrower	0.5%
Floating rate paid by borrower (Swap Outflow)	Six-month LIBOR
Effective floating rate cost paid by borrower	Six-month LIBOR – 0.5%

Simulated Investment

A final example illustrates how a coupon swap can be utilized to construct a synthetic investment opportunity capable of producing a more attractive yield than alternative investments with similar risk. On December 19, 1984 a commercial bank was offered a $5 million FRN issued by Republic Bank of New York at 98.55. The FRN matures on December 19, 2009 and reset quarterly at 0.125 percent over three-month LIBOR. The current rate had just been set at 9.1875 percent. On the same day the bank was offered a two-year coupon swap to pay three-month LIBOR and receive the two-year Treasury note yield plus 62 basis points. On that day, the two-year Treasury rate was 10.01 percent and three-month LIBOR was 9.0625 percent.

The combined opportunity of the swap and the Republic of New York FRN enabled the bank investor effectively to earn 10.76 percent on its investment for the next two years. This was obtained from the sum of the 10.63 percent fixed rate received on the swap plus the difference between the LIBOR paid on the swap and the LIBOR plus 0.125 percent received from Republic of New York. In addition, because the FRN could be purchased at a discount from par, the current yield would be higher by 0.1352 percent, i.e., 9.3227 percent instead of 9.1875. Moreover, the bank could accrete the 1.45 point discount and further increase its yield for book purposes. In sum, the yield obtainable on this simulated investment exceeded 10.90 percent, more than 0.40 percent above the 10.50 percent available on an alternate Republic of New York shelf registration bond at the time and a full 89 basis points above the yield curve on two-year Treasuries. A negative factor lies in the fact that there is more credit exposure on the 25-year FRN because it doesn't mature until 2009, but the bank may already have had the credit risk or may be willing to assume it in a name like Republic of New York.

CONCLUSION

From these examples it becomes clear that FRN and coupon swaps were made for each other. Together they enable investors to improve their all-in rate of return under appropriate conditions. Applied in alternative combinations, they enable issuers to obtain a lower all-in cost of capital, and in that configuration in which they wish ultimately to service it. They enable portfolio managers to restructure their assets without incurring asset transactions with their concomitant tax and cash flow implications. They allow liability managers to adjust their liability and asset structures in order to improve interest sensitivity and strengthen gap management processes. Finally, they facilitate the breaching of market anomalies in order to extract arbitrage opportunities where market inefficiencies exist. It is evident that the need for these types of transactions will continue to increase with the growth of floating rate markets. Coupon swaps can be expected to play a dominant role in their execution for the foreseeable future.

CHAPTER 16

IMMUNIZATION OF FLOATING RATE NOTES

Don M. Chance, Ph.D.
Associate Professor of Finance
Virginia Polytechnic Institute and State University

and

George E. Morgan, Ph.D.
Associate Professor of Finance
Virginia Polytechnic Institute and State University

Due to the growing popularity of immunization strategies for fixed income portfolios, the issue of whether floating rate notes can be immunized in a similar fashion or even whether they need to be immunized at all deserves some attention. Floating rate notes have relatively stable prices, creating the temptation to assume that interest rate effects can be ignored. Indeed, the impact of interest rate changes on the price of the security is generally small, because the price is largely hedged by the changing coupon. Interest rate risk, however, can be great in the form of reinvestment risk, the uncertainty associated with the returns earned from reinvesting the coupons.[1]

As a consequence, holders of floating rate notes as well as holders

[1] For a discussion of reinvestment rate risk see S. Homer and M. L. Leibowitz, *Inside the Yield Book*. New York: Prentice-Hall and the New York Institute of Finance, 1972, chapters 10 and 15.

of fixed rate securities can either gain or lose from interest rate changes, with the outcome dependent on the balance they select between the relatively small price volatility and the relatively large reinvestment risk on a floating rate security.

BALANCING RISK—THE ROLE OF DURATION

Achieving the proper balance of these two opposing forces—price volatility and reinvestment risk—is the essence of immunization with duration. Traditionally, the weighted average time to each cash flow date has been considered equivalent to the duration for certain characterizations of interest rate shifts.[2] Immunization is achieved, under those characterizations, if duration is equal to the length of the investor's holding period. If duration exceeds holding period and the shift in interest rates is small, price volatility more than offsets reinvestment risk; the bondholder gains if interest rates fall by a small amount and loses if interest rates rise by a small amount. This is because a longer duration bond is more price sensitive. The holding period is not long enough for the additional compounding effects of reinvesting coupons, at only a slightly higher interest rate, to offset the price volatility. The converse is true if holding period exceeds duration, in which case the investor benefits from a slight rise in interest rates and is hurt by a slight fall in interest rates.[3]

For fixed rate bonds and for the traditionally assumed parallel shift in the structure of yields on zero coupon bonds, duration is easily calculated as the weighted average of the time to each payment date. The weight used for a particular payment is the present value of the payment divided by the price of the bond. For floating rate notes the computation of duration is not so simple.

---

[2] For an excellent explication of duration see F. K. Reilly and R. S Sidhu, "Duration and Its Properties," *Handbook of Fixed Income Securities,* ed. F. Fabozzi and I. Pollack. Homewood, IL: Dow Jones-Irwin, 1983.

[3] A demonstration of the immunization technique is found in P. E. Christensen, S. G. Feldstein, and F. Fabozzi, "Bond Portfolio Immunization," in Fabozzi and Pollack, *op. cit.*

DURATION OF FLOATING RATE NOTES

Since interest rates change continuously, floating rate notes with coupon rates which do not adjust immediately must eventually catch up. For an ideal floating rate note with coupon payments made and adjusted continuously, the coupons would immediately reflect current market rates. The duration would be zero for this type of security.[4] As a practical matter, however, coupon payments cannot adjust immediately. Moreover, some floating rate note indentures stipulate that the coupon change only to a current rate which may not necessarily reflect the accumulation of interest since the last coupon payment date. Alternatively, the indenture may specify that the rate for the entire period between payment dates be determined by the rate level at the beginning of the period, regardless of whether rates have risen rapidly over the interim. Thus a change in interest rates can affect the value of the security even though the rates float over the life of the asset. In short, a continuously adjusting floating rate note will have a zero duration. A periodically adjusting floating rate note will have a slightly longer duration because the rate paid will not always reflect the ups and downs of interest rates over the period between coupons. Even so, however, the duration of such a security is likely to be far shorter than that of a similar fixed rate note.

The technique for computing the duration of a floating rate note is similar to that for a fixed rate security except that there is the need to incorporate a term reflecting the effect of a change in interest rates on the coupon payments. In either case the price of the security is given by the sum of the present values of each of the cash flows. For the purpose of examining a floating rate note, we require a set of forecasts of one-period interest rates over the life of the

---

[4] See D. M. Chance, "Floating Rate Notes and Immunization," *Journal of Financial and Quantitative Analysis,* September, 1983, pp. 365–380, and G. E. Morgan, "Floating Rate Securities and Immunization: Some Further Results," *Journal of Financial and Quantitative Analysis,* forthcoming. Under certain schemes for calculating the new coupon payments, a continuously and freely floating rate security can have a non-zero duration. In this paper we consider only securities whose rate is calculated by adding a fixed markup to a base rate (the markup may be zero); therefore a continuously floating rate note will have a zero duration.

security, so that we may construct forecasts of the coupon payments. The measure of duration which we will consider here is based on the belief that actual one-period rates can shift by some amount from our original forecast. For example, we may forecast the future path of rates to be 3 percent, 4 percent, 5 percent, and 6 percent (annualized), while they may turn out to be 4 percent, 5 percent, 6 percent, and 7 percent or 2 percent, 3 percent, 4 percent, and 5 percent over the next four periods.[5]

For the sake of a concrete argument, we use the example of a floating rate note having quarterly payments based on the level of interest rates at the beginning of each month in the quarter. That is, the coupon is paid quarterly but the rate is adjusted monthly. While there are many possible contractual arrangements for the adjustment scheme, we chose a relatively common and simple arrangement. The concepts may apply equally well to other schemes not explicitly considered here. The security we examine computes the amount of the coupon payment by taking the prevailing interest rate at the beginning of each month in the quarter and multiplying that monthly rate by the face value of the security. The dollar amount of interest is computed for each month, the cumulative sum for the three months in the quarter being the amount paid at the beginning of the following quarter. In addition, the rate for the first month in the life of the note is determined and fixed at the date of the issuance of the note. Therefore, any shifts in interest rates which occur after the issuance of the note cannot affect the first month's interest even though all other coupon payments may be affected by such shifts.

Given the forecast of interest rates for each month over the life of the note and given the above description of the payment scheme, the price of the note can be calculated as can the note's duration. The duration is calculated as the weighted average time of coupon payments *minus* an additional term which reflects the effect of a shift in the time path of monthly interest rates. Because a $1 increase in every coupon payment will increase the security's price by the sum of the present value factors used to obtain the price, the additional

[5] This approach assumes an additive shift in the forward rates rather than in the term structure rates. Although this is a rather non-traditional framework, it facilitates the illustration. As a consequence, the formulas which are used here differ slightly from the standard formulas.

term in the duration calculation is related to the sum of the present value factors, or what is also called a present value annuity factor.

Specifically, let D be the duration of a security which would pay the forecasted payments whether or not interest rates differed from the forecasted rates. In that sense the coupons are fixed, although they are not the same at every payment date. Let D_f be the duration of the floating rate note described above and let K be the total number of coupon payments promised. Thus the securities have a maturity of K/4 years. Then the relationship between the durations of the two notes is given by

$$D_f = D - (F/P)[2PV(1) + 3 \sum_{t=2}^{K} PV(t)]$$

where PV(t) is the present value factor for discounting a cash flow t quarters from the issue date, F is the face value of the note, and P is the price of the note. The sum of present value interest factors is an annuity factor as discussed above. The factor is multiplied by three because of a 1 percent shift in *monthly* rates will have a threefold effect on the quarterly coupon. Each quarterly payment is the accumulation of the interest for the three months in the quarter. The first quarter's coupon, however, only experiences a twofold effect because, as described earlier, the first month's interest is fixed before the shift in interest rates occurs. The term 2PV(1) in the above formula reflects this twofold effect.

A NUMERICAL EXAMPLE

Consider an example of a floating rate note and its duration. Table 16–1 presents the calculations for a two-year $1,000,000 floating rate note with quarterly coupons. These monthly rates could, of course, be interpreted as Treasury bill rates plus a premium as specified in the indenture. The projected monthly rates can be considered the forward rates under the unbiased expectations theory of the term structure of interest rates.[6]

The resulting duration is a very short 1.26 months. The duration is slightly longer than one month because of the fixed nature of the

---

[6] For a discussion of the unbiased expectations theory see R. W. McEnally, "The Term Structure of Interest Rates," in Fabozzi and Pollack, *op. cit.*

TABLE 16-1
Computation of Duration of Two-Year, $1,000,000 Floating Rate Note

Month	Interest Rate	Coupon Payment	Principal	Discount Factor	Present Value	Duration
1	.078			1.0065		
2	.0782			1.0131		
3	.0784	$19,550		1.0197	$19,173	.057202
4	.0786			1.0264		
5	.0788			1.0331		
6	.079	19,700		1.0399	18,944	.113038
7	.0792			1.0468		
8	.0794			1.0537		
9	.0796	19,850		1.0607	18,715	.167496
10	.0798			1.0677		
11	.08			1.0748		
12	.0802	20,000		1.0820	18,484	.220570
13	.0804			1.0893		
14	.0806			1.0966		
15	.0808	20,150		1.1040	18,252	.272250
16	.0810			1.1114		
17	.0812			1.1190		
18	.0814	20,300		1.1265	18,020	.322532
19	.0816			1.1342		
20	.0818			1.1419		
21	.082	20,450		1.1497	17,787	.371412
22	.0822			1.1576		
23	.0824			1.1656		
24	.0826	20,600	1,000,000	1.1736	869,642	20.753124
Totals					$999,017	22.2776
Minus Adjustment Factor for Duration						21.0139
Duration						1.26

Notes: • Each coupon payment is three times the mean of the three previous months' rates. For example, the first coupon is (.078/12 + .0782/12 + .0784/12) ÷ 3 × 3 = .019555 or simply the sum of the three monthly rates.

• Each discount factor reflects the present value of one dollar discounted back using the rates in column 2. For example, the discount factor for month 3 is (1 + .078/12)(1 + .0782/12)(1 + .0784/12) = 1.0197.

• The Duration column is found by multiplying the time factor for each payment date by the coupon and dividing by the discount factor. Then that figure is divided by the price.

interest for the first month and is, therefore, longer than the length of time between the adjustment of the coupons. Furthermore, for an otherwise equivalent note with coupons that did not differ from the expected coupons, the duration would have been about 22 months. This illustrates the substantial difference between the durations of these two types of instruments. The consequences of not recognizing this difference when combining fixed and floating rate securities can be quite severe. For example, suppose the portfolio manager computed duration of the floating rate note using just the weighted average maturity formula to compute the duration of the fixed rate note. Then a portfolio containing 50 percent of the funds in the fixed rate note and the remaining 50 percent in the floating rate note would have a duration of about 11 months and not 22 months as the manager believed.

The short duration of the floating rate note is important in terms of immunizing against interest rate risk. The investor would be immunized only if the note were held for 1.26 months or approximately 39 days. Any holding period different from 39 days would subject the holder of the floating rate note to interest rate risk. Such a short holding period is unlikely to be applicable to most investors, but if an investor combined a floating rate security with a fixed rate security, the floating rate security could be used to shorten the holding period for a bond portfolio. In the following section we provide a numerical example of the immunization procedure for a portfolio which is a combination of fixed and floating rate notes.

AN IMMUNIZATION EXAMPLE

Consider the floating rate note previously described. Suppose we combine this security with a fixed rate note having a two-year maturity and 8 percent coupon, paid semiannually. Given the forecasted time path of rates in the previous example, the price of this bond will be 99.7 and the duration is about 22.5 months.

Let us assume that the investor has a desired holding period of 10 months and that the total amount of funds available for investment is $1,000,000. To keep things simple, assume that any dollar amount of either security is obtainable; that is, fractional purchases can be made. The investor wants to allocate his wealth between each of the two securities so that the duration of the portfolio is approximately 10 months. Accordingly, the percentage of wealth invested in the floating rate note should be 59.2 percent while the remaining 40.8 percent should be invested in the fixed rate note. This produces a portfolio duration of 9.9. The market value of the portfolio is $1 million because that is the assumed amount of wealth which our investor has to place in the bond markets.[7]

It is important to note that the duration of the portfolio is the weighted average of the durations of the individual bonds in the portfolio no matter whether the bonds have fixed or floating coupons. No additional adjustments to the portfolio duration are necessary as long as the adjustment has already been made in the calculation of the duration of the floating rate security.

In order to examine the immunization problem, let us assume that immediately after the portfolio is established, the series of forecasted monthly rates shifts by 100 basis points (annualized). Although a shift of that size is not common in the very short run, we felt it necessary to exaggerate the interest rate change. The total return might not be especially sensitive to a small interest rate change, particularly for the short maturities used here.

Table 16–2 illustrates the immunization process. At the beginning of each quarter, interest is collected and reinvested at the new interest rate. Each month the accumulated wealth from reinvesting coupons is rolled over at the newly prevailing interest rate for that month. The column labeled "Wealth" indicates the sum total of reinvested coupons and the market value of the portfolio of the original bonds. The column labeled "Promised Wealth" is found by taking the $1,000,000 initially invested and compounding it forward at the forecasted interest rates. The promised wealth at a given month is the total dollar return that would have been received if interest rates had not changed and, therefore, is the standard of

---

[7] The duration is not set to exactly 10 months because of our assumption about how interest rates shift. Because all the forward rates are assumed to shift by an identical amount, the "term structure" rates shift by more than that amount due to compounding. The larger increase in those rates means that the price volatility effect is larger than under the traditional assumption of a parallel shift in the term structure. Thus a portfolio with a duration of 9.9 months is immunized for a holding period of ten months.

comparison for the portfolio's performance. The final column indicates the difference between actual wealth and promised wealth. A negative difference implies that the portfolio falls short of achieving its goal. This is what we find for the first nine months. Since duration is approximately 10 months, holding the portfolio for nine months or less means that duration exceeds holding period and, therefore, that the portfolio is dominated by price volatility. Since interest rates increased, the value of the portfolio declined by more than the increase in reinvestment income resulting from higher reinvestment rates and the upward adjustment of the floating rate note's coupon.

For holding periods of 10 months or longer, the increase in interest rates resulted in an increase in reinvestment income which more than covered the loss in market value. At 10 months, the portfolio is immunized. For the upward shift in rates shown in the table, the portfolio is worth $35 more than the promised level of wealth using the original forecast of rates. By the same token, a downward shift in rates will produce $36 more than the promised wealth. For holding periods greater than 10 months, a downward shift in rates will produce actual wealth less than the promised wealth. For holding periods of nine or fewer months, a downward shift in rates will result in the portfolio being worth more than the promised wealth.

Thus, no matter the direction in which interest rates shift, the investor who holds this portfolio for exactly 10 months will never do worse than the promised wealth and will usually do better. In contrast, an investor who holds the portfolio for a length of time other than 10 months (whether shorter or longer) will sometimes do worse and sometimes do better than the promised wealth. This clearly illustrates the advantages of duration immunization which remain valid for purchasers of floating rate securities.

Finally we should note that if the portfolio manager computed the duration of the floating rate note as he would compute the duration of the fixed rate note (i.e., without the adjustment term) the overall portfolio duration would have been perceived to be about 22 months. As a result, the portfolio which the manager thought was "immunized" for 22 months would have shown a gain of $11,590 over the promised wealth. The manager would have been pleased with that result especially given that it occurred in a bear market.

TABLE 16-2
Immunization of a Portfolio Combination of a Fixed and Floating Rate Note
($1,000,000 initial portfolio value. Increase of 100 basis points in forward interest rates)

Month	Portfolio Cash Flow	Value of Portfolio	Reinvested Coupons	Realized Wealth	Promised Wealth	Difference
1		$999,065	-0-	$999,065	$1,006,500	$ - 7,435
2		1,006,408	-0-	1,006,408	1,013,059	- 6,651
3	$12,565	1,001,257	$12,565	1,013,822	1,019,678	- 5,856
4		1,008,650	12,657	1,021,307	1,026,357	- 5,050
5		1,016,114	12,751	1,028,865	1,033,096	- 4,231
6	29,529	994,121	42,375	1,036,496	1,039,898	- 3,402
7		1,001,510	42,690	1,044,200	1,046,761	- 2,561
8		1,008,971	43,008	1,051,979	1,053,687	- 1,708
9	13,236	1,003,269	56,565	1,059,834	1,060,676	- 842
10		1,010,777	56,988	1,067,765	1,067,730	35
11		1,018,358	57,416	1,075,774	1,074,848	926
12	29,707	996,306	87,554	1,083,860	1,082,032	1,828
13		1,003,811	88,214	1,092,025	1,089,281	2,744

14		1,011,390	88,880	1,100,270	1,096,598	3,672
15	13,414	1,005,629	102,966	1,108,595	1,103,981	4,614
16		1,013,255	103,747	1,117,002	1,111,433	5,569
17		1,020,956	104,535	1,125,491	1,118,954	6,537
18	29,885	998,848	135,216	1,134,064	1,126,544	7,520
19		1,006,472	136,248	1,142,720	1,134,205	8,515
20		1,014,172	137,291	1,151,463	1,141,936	9,527
21	13,591	1,008,356	151,934	1,160,290	1,149,739	10,551
22		1,016,103	153,102	1,169,205	1,157,615	11,590
23		1,023,927	154,281	1,178,208	1,165,564	12,644
24	1,030,062	-0-	1,187,300	1,187,300	1,173,587	13,713

Notes:

- "Portfolio Cash Flow" is based on percentage of funds invested in each of the two securities and reflects the revised coupon rates on the floating rate note.

- "Value of the Portfolio" is the total future market value of each security weighted by the percentage of funds invested. The computed market value of each security accounts for the effects of the passage of time on the value of the securities.

- "Reinvested Coupons" is the accumulation of the portfolio cash flow times the one-period interest rate, reinvested at the beginning of each month at the new one-period interest rate.

- "Realized Wealth" is the sum of portfolio value and reinvested coupons.

- "Promised Wealth" is based on compound growth of $1,000,000 invested at the original interest rates.

Had rates decreased, however, the manager would have found that the portfolio had fallen short of its target by $11,408. The portfolio would actually have been substantially riskier than the immunized portfolio which the manager had thought he was holding.

CONCLUSION

The increased use of floating rate notes makes it necessary to consider their implications for immunized portfolios. We have shown here that the duration of a floating rate note equals the duration of an otherwise equivalent fixed rate note minus an adjustment factor. The adjustment factor will vary directly with the frequency of the coupon adjustment. The more the floating rate note's coupon fails to keep up with current market rates, the longer will be the duration. For most floating rate notes, however, the duration will still be very short, quite close to zero. Consequently, they can be used to shorten the duration of the portfolio. It is also important to note that immunization of portfolios containing floating rate notes is still very much a valid and useful procedure.

Some caveats are in order. The computation of duration for the floating rate note is specific to the type of coupon adjustment procedure stipulated in the indenture. The illustration we have given is not generic. Duration of a floating rate note can vary depending on the frequency and procedure for coupon adjustments and will also be influenced by assumptions about the manner in which interest rates shift. We have chosen a fairly typical example. Actual problems faced by portfolio managers may call for slightly different measures of duration. Nevertheless, the general concept of duration and immunization remains a legitimate and practical tool for bond portfolio managers.

Index